The War Film

Rutgers Depth of Field Series

Charles Affron, Mirella Jona Affron, Robert Lyons, Series Editors

———————

Richard Abel, ed., Silent Film

John Belton, ed., Movies and Mass Culture

Matthew Bernstein, ed., Controlling Hollywood: Censorship and Regulation in the Studio Era

John Thornton Caldwell, ed., Electronic Media and Technoculture

Angela Dalle Vacche, ed., The Visual Turn: Classical Film Theory and Art History

Robert Eberwein, ed., The War Film

Peter X Feng, ed., Screening Asian Americans

Marcia Landy, ed., The Historical Film: History and Memory in Media

Peter Lehman, ed., Defining Cinema

James Naremore, ed., Film Adaptation

Stephen Prince, ed., The Horror Film

Stephen Prince, ed., Screening Violence

Ella Shohat and Robert Stam, eds. Multiculturalism, Postcoloniality, and Transnational Media

Valerie Smith, ed., Representing Blackness: Issues in Film and Video

Janet Staiger, ed., The Studio System

Virginia Wright Wexman, ed., Film and Authorship

Alan Williams, ed., Film and Nationalism

Linda Williams, ed., Viewing Positions: Ways of Seeing Film

Barbie Zelizer, ed., Visual Culture and the Holocaust

Edited and with an Introduction by
Robert Eberwein

The War Film

Rutgers
University
Press
New Brunswick,
New Jersey and
London

Second paperback printing, 2006

Library of Congress Cataloging-in-Publication Data

The war film / edited and with an introduction by Robert Eberwein.
     p. cm. — (Rutgers depth of field series)
   Includes bibliographical references and index.
   ISBN 0-8135-3496-8 (alk. paper) — ISBN 0-8135-3497-6 (pbk. : alk. paper)
  1. War films—History and criticism. I. Eberwein, Robert T., 1940–. II. Series.
   PN1995.9.W3W36 2004
   791.43'658—dc22

                                       2004003820

A British Cataloging-in-Publication record for this book is available from the British Library.
Manufactured in the United States of America

In memory of
Ruth Y. Reed and Edward J. Recchia

Contents

GENDER

HISTORY

Acknowledgments

I am grateful to Mirella Jona Affron, Charles Affron, and Robert Lyons for the invitation to contribute to their Depth of Field Series and for their thoughtful suggestions. As always, Leslie Mitchner, Associate Director and Editor in Chief of Rutgers University Press, has been immensely helpful and supportive. Thanks to Alison Hack, the Production Coordinator, for her cooperation. I received welcome assistance from Bruce Mann, chair of the English Department at Oakland University, and Rosemary Aiello and Dana Pierce, our tireless secretaries. Dana in particular used her impressive knowledge of computers in preparing the manuscript. Krin Gabbard, Peter Lehman, and William Luhr provided their typically generous counsel. Jane continued to offer her sustaining wisdom and encouragement.

The War Film

Robert Eberwein

Introduction

The essays in this anthology explore films about the Civil War, World Wars I and II, the Korean War, the Vietnam War, and the Persian Gulf War. The one significant war not represented is, in fact, the first one ever to be photographed with the motion picture camera: the Spanish-American War of 1898. Prior to 1898, photographic records of war had been limited to the still camera. Speaking of the Mexican-American War of 1847–1848, the first war ever to be photographed, Beaumont Newhall explains that the daguerrotypes "show[ed] officers and men, but there is no evidence that they were taken during combat." When the war photographer Roger Fenton went to the Crimea, in 1855, his photographs were produced "using the wet collodion process." These showed "landscapes and portraits—battlefields and fortifications, officers and men. There were no scenes of action; to record them was beyond the power of the camera." Newhall quotes a commentator from the *London Times* reviewing Fenton's photographs who observed: "The photographer who follows in the wake of modern armies must be content with the conditions of repose and with the still life which remains when the fighting is over."[1] Matthew Brady, who documented the battlefields and carnage of the Civil War in his *Photographic Sketch Book of the War,* left a vast array of photographs, but they too were of stillness: photographic portraits, shots of battlefields, and (literally) still lifes of the dead.

By the time of the Spanish-American War, the motion picture camera was available to record such historical events. James Castonguay, Robert Sklar, and Charles Musser have all commented on the use of the new medium at this time. Castonguay in particular remarks on the "giddy anticipation of the new medium's novel ability to project motion pictures of real battles for the viewing pleasure of American consumers across the country."[2] An article in the *New York Journal and Advertiser* on 16 April 1898 promised its readers forthcoming motion pictures about the recently declared war, including sights of Key West and the funeral of the victims who had died on the battleship *Maine.* These films would provide "the vivid impression that an eye witness gets in viewing an unusual or striking situation."[3]

Such a comment confirms Tom Gunning's description of early silent film as a "cinema of attractions," one "that directly solicits spectator attention, inciting visual curiosity, and supplying pleasure through an exciting spectacle—a unique event, whether fictional or documentary, that is of interest in itself."[4] The early spectacles had been separate and unrelated records of events, such as the arrival of a train, a baby's meal, or the destruction of a wall. Beginning with the conflict with Spain over Cuba and the Philippines, though, the spectacles were inevitably related since they were all about the war. For the first time the motion picture camera was being used extensively to record and represent an ongoing historical event.

But no "real battles" were filmed; none appear in the 107 titles documented in the *Library of Congress Paper Print Collection*. *The American Memory Website of the Library of Congress* contains sixty-seven titles about the Spanish-American War, divided into categories such as "Films at the Beginning of the War," "Films of Military Preparation," "Actualities of the War in Cuba," "Reenactments of Events in Cuba," and "Reenactments of Events in the Philippines." In the latter two categories one can see depictions of "real battles."[5]

In "A Semantic/Syntactic Approach to Film Genre," Rick Altman distinguishes between semantic and syntactic elements in genres. The former includes "a list of common traits, attitudes, characters, shots locations, sets," while the latter refers to the way these elements are put together, "the constitutive relationships . . . the genre's fundamental syntax."[6] It is possible to look at these films about the Spanish-American War as presenting the earliest display of a number of semantic elements that will appear in later war films.

These elements appear in three kinds of films. First, some films document events pertaining to the war. For example, *Burial of the "Maine" Victims* (Edison Manufacturing Co., 1898) records the ceremony, which occurred in Key West on 27 March 1898. The film, shot with a fixed camera, lasts 1:50 minutes and shows servicemen followed by the hearses and mourners. This is the first recorded American funeral for victims of war, a scene that becomes an ongoing feature of all kinds of war films, whether in newsreels, combat films at the front such as *Wake Island* (John Farrow, 1942) and *Guadalcanal Diary* (Lewis Seiler, 1943), or at home such as *Gardens of Stone* (Francis Ford Coppola, 1987). Other records of war-related activities also prefigure elements in later films. *Troops Making Military Road in Front of Santiago* (Edison Manufacturing Co., 1898) displays soldiers engaged in preparing a road for equipment and vehicles. *Wounded Soldiers Embarking in Row Boats* (American Mutascope & Biograph Co., 1898) shows an evacuation of casualties after a battle as soldiers leave in a decidedly unstable-looking rowboat.

Blanket-Tossing of a New Recruit (Edison Manufacturing Co., 22 June 1898) shows the initiation of a new man in the First Ohio Volunteers division. We see a group of men having a good time bouncing the recruit up and down on a blanket. This kind of high jinks during basic training is a staple of the war films to follow. Similarly, the film of *Soldiers Washing Dishes* (Edison Manufacturing Co., 22 June 1898) anticipates K.P. scenes that occur in both comic and serious films.

A different kind of semantic element, not exactly covered by Altman's taxonomy but relevant nonetheless, appears in *Colored Troops Disembarking* (Edison Manufacturing Co., 1898). Here ten African Americans descend a gangplank. Some walk gingerly and unsteadily and look apprehensively at the water below them. This film can be seen as the first document to record the contribution of a racial minority to war and also to demonstrate the segregation of the troops. Both issues will figure in war films to follow.

In contrast to such works, which document events that are being recorded as they occur, are reenactments, such as *U.S. Infantry Supported by Rough Riders at El Caney* (James H. White, 1899). The film opens on a road in a forest clearing. Soon foot soldiers carrying the American flag appear, fire their guns, and move on, backed by two cavalry soldiers. In what seems to be the same space, the scene is repeated, this time with more cavalry support. Then horsemen impersonating the Rough Riders ride in boisterously. In *Raising Old Glory Over Morro Castle* (J. Stuart Blackton, 1898), we see a quite unconvincing painted background of the castle (according to Castonguay, presumably painted by Blackton himself). In front on a flagpole, the Spanish flag is lowered and the American flag is raised over the fortress at the entrance to Havana harbor. Although not the first film to concentrate exclusively on the American flag, this scene anticipates other works in which the primacy of the flag is central, from the Little Colonel's charge in *Birth of a Nation* (D. W. Griffith, 1915) to the climactic event in *Sands of Iwo Jima* (Allan Dwan, 1949).[7]

The third kind of film, and one of particular interest, is *Love and War* (James H. White, 1899), as far as I know the earliest surviving narrative film about the war. Lasting a little over three minutes, it includes six scenes. It begins as a youth leaves his anxious family to go to war. Next we see his mother reading newspapers for accounts of him. His father comes in with a dismal report: he has been killed or wounded and the family is distraught. We then see the youth engaging in a battle that has already occurred; wounded, he is rescued by his courageous comrade. He is taken to a small tent that is part of a field hospital. In the last scene he returns home and is reunited with his family and embraces his girlfriend.[8]

This short film contains a number of semantic elements (the home front, departure, battle, wounding, hospitalization, grieving, return) that will appear in later war films. But for the first time, these are combined into what Altman would call a syntactical relationship. In fact, the unified narrative suggests a move beyond a mere cinema of attractions. Certainly the individual elements of spectacle (gunfire, battle) are here, but in the larger service of a sustained narrative about what happens before and after battles.[9]

The war films examined in this anthology are, of course, fully developed narrative works in which various semantic elements are combined in constitutive syntactic relationships. In a variety of essays employing different critical approaches, the authors examine the way films present the effects of war on combatants and their loved ones; consider war films' narrative elements and generic conventions; analyze their depictions of race and gender; and demonstrate their ideological implications. I have organized the essays into four sections: genre, race, gender, and history. Although a chronological pattern of organization would have been possible (e.g., Civil War, World War I, World War II, Korea War, Vietnam War, Persian Gulf War), I believe that would do a disservice to the wide-ranging comprehensiveness that characterizes the essays collected here.

Genre

The first section includes essays focused on generic aspects of the war film. Andrew Kelly identifies primary conventions of the antiwar film. Jeanine Basinger examines basic elements of the World War II combat film and offers a formula for its characteristic makeup. Dana Polan explains what has happened to genre conventions in recent war films.

Kelly's essay, the conclusion to his study of the production and reception history of *All Quiet on the Western Front* (Lewis Milestone, 1930), identifies several generic elements in that work about World War I common to most antiwar films: the demonstration of war's brutality, the extent of suffering, and the betrayal by incompetent commanders. Historians consider two films he mentions here to be classics of the antiwar genre: *La Grande Illusion* (Jean Renoir, 1937) and *Paths of Glory* (Stanley Kubrick, 1957). Other films about World War I in this antiwar category include silent works such as *Civilization* (Thomas Ince, 1916) and *The Big Parade* (King Vidor, 1925) and sound films made before World War II such as *The Dawn Patrol* (Howard Hawks, 1930) and *Hell's Angels* (Howard Hughes, 1930).

Many later films about World War I continue the antiwar tradition, such as those about Australian and British soldiers: *Gallipoli* (Peter Weir, 1981), *Regeneration* (Gillies MacKinnon, 1998 [also known as *Behind the Lines*]), and *The Trench* (William Boyd, 2002).[10] *Johnny Got His Gun* (Dalton Trumbo, 1971, adapted from his novel), about an American casualty in a near-vegetative physical state, is a stridently antiwar film readable in light of the Vietnam War in which America was then mired. As will be clear from other essays in the anthology, particularly in the last section on "History," war films can be particularly effective vehicles for commenting on the periods in which they were made as well as the period they depict.

An antiwar theme is less pervasive in *What Price Glory?* (Raoul Walsh, 1926) and *Wings* (William Wellman, 1927). The first, based on a popular play by Maxwell Anderson and Laurence Stallings, offers scenes of battle as well as broadly comic elements. The second, with well-photographed aerial combats, focuses on friends competing for the same woman.

In fact, some films have been made to support American involvement in war. One of the earliest combat films about World War I, *Hearts of the World* (D. W. Griffith, 1917), originated as a propaganda device sponsored by the British hoping to enlist American support for entering into the war in support of the European Allies.

A much better known example of a film made in support of war is *Sergeant York* (Howard Hawks, 1941), ostensibly about the gradual change of heart in the pacifist Alvin York (Gary Cooper), who became the most highly decorated soldier in World War I. Michael Birdwell suggests that the film played an important part in the Warner Bros. campaign to enlist American support for the Allies against fascism prior to World War II. According to Birdwell, "it was York's conversion to . . . interventionalism, that Americans in 1940–41 needed to see in order to be convinced that the war in Europe was indeed their concern."[11] Cooper won the Oscar for Best Actor in 1941 for *Sergeant York,* eleven years after the overtly antiwar film *All Quiet on the Western Front* had won the Oscar for Best Picture.

Anyone studying the war film quickly discovers how useful Basinger's *The World War II Combat Film: Anatomy of a Genre* has been in elucidating the conventions of this genre. Earlier in that work she explains how the combat film's features evoke various kinds of war-related films in the 1930s such as service comedies and musicals. Elements in *The Fighting 69th* (William Keighley, 1940), a film about World War I starring James Cagney as a cowardly soldier who becomes a hero, strongly anticipate many of the generic features she identifies in World War II films: "the tough drill sergeant," "the equally tough major," "the understanding chaplain," "the cynic who must be taught by danger to understand the nobility of the cause and group," and "the war correspondent figure, or man who keeps a diary."[12] Her thorough survey of the conventions' appearance in combat films actually made during World War II, such as *Bataan* (Tay Garnett, 1943) and *Guadalcanal Diary,* leads to her proposal of a template for an as yet-unproduced combat film, a suggestion that should be considered in relation to Thomas Doherty's projection in this anthology of what conventions will appear in films about 9/11.

Later in her book, Basinger reflects on "Problems of Genre," acknowledging that many of the conventions she identifies in the combat film also appear in *Brute Force* (Jules Dassin, 1947), a prison film. But this does not invalidate her taxonomy or conception: "in genre, there is an inner story (a group of men undergoing duress in an attempt to remain free) and an outer story (the actual setting which identifies the genre as prison or combat.)."[13]

Whatever the generic roots of the films Basinger describes, or the extent that they may be seen to complement other genres, her categories provide useful ways of organizing our thinking about essential elements of the combat film made by directors such as Raoul Walsh and Howard Hawks. Polan's point in "Auteurism and War-teurism" is that we need to recognize a different kind of generic consciousness at work in contemporary filmmakers. Following the argument of Marita Sturken, Polan suggests that the generic conventions we observe are not anchored to a unified framework of the genre itself as they were during earlier periods: "the organic unity of the genre is no longer to be had." The discrete generic elements now gain coherence in relation to the filmmaker's personal interests and filmmaking practices rather than to the stable corpus of a genre.

In his commentary on *The Thin Red Line* (Terrence Malick, 1998), rather than promoting an auteurist aesthetic of the kind seen earlier in association with Walsh and Hawks, Polan is explaining the displacement of coherence from the genre to the artist as a phenomenon symptomatic of American life since the Vietnam War. This focus by auteurs on war films is not a negation of "the social and political conditions of the nation, but . . . a force generated by those conditions, personal creativity becoming one of the ways in the '70s and after to live out issues of constraint and conformity." *The Thin Red Line* and other auteurs' Vietnam War films—Francis Ford Coppola's *Apocalypse Now* (1979), Oliver Stone's *Platoon* (1986), Stanley Kubrick's *Full Metal Jacket* (1987), and Brian DePalma's *Casualties of War* (1989)—do not display the full array of integrated generic elements such as appear in a war film like John Ford's *They Were Expendable* (1945). Following the theoretical position of Gilles Deleuze, Polan says we have instead "the glimpsing of experientiality itself, a pure immersion in temporality, in a duration that only vaguely adds up to either meaningfulness or anything resembling realism." When viewing, we see particular moments such as Sergeant Hartman's barracks tirades in *Full Metal Jacket* and the endless progress through the tall grass in *The Thin Red Line* as "non-cumulative explosions of violence that lead nowhere and mean nothing."[14]

Race

Essays collected in this section approach race in war films from three different directions. Robert Burgoyne examines the Civil War film *Glory* (Edward Zwick, 1989) in relation to concepts of nationhood. Michael Rogin considers *Home of the Brave* (Mark Robson, 1949) in the context of American social history after World War II. And Brian J. Woodman examines the way African Americans have been depicted in films about the Vietnam War.

Burgoyne's *Film Nation: Hollywood Looks at U.S. History,* in which the essay in this volume appeared, is informed by recent theoretical work on the concept of nationhood. Benedict Anderson in particular has exerted immense influence on analysts of culture trying to explain how individual groups of people conceive of themselves in relation to what they understand of their nation. Anderson defines a nation as "an imagined social community. . . . It is imagined because the members of even the smallest nation will never know most of their fellow-members, meet them, or hear of them, yet in the minds of each lives the image of their communion."[15]

Burgoyne thinks that *Glory* bears an uncanny connection to the first important film ever made about the Civil War, D. W. Griffith's *The Birth of a*

Nation, since both concern "the struggle between competing ideals of nation, ethnic and civil, and their equally potent claims to recognition and belonging."[16] In the earlier film, whose racism prompted passionate protests and calls for banning by various groups, African American characters are portrayed by white actors in blackface. The characters and their supporters are uniformly obnoxious and/or dangerous, a threat to the nation. In contrast, *Glory's* treatment of Robert Gould Shaw's black regiment that fought in the Civil War seems to present a very different conception since the African Americans are integrated into the white fighting unit, dying along with their comrades and being buried in the same communal grave. But Burgoyne sees problematic elements in the film. Even though the "collective martyrdom" at the end suggests a bond of nationhood, the film manages to qualify or counter this sense of unity. He points to the tension at work in the film between a conception of an emerging black individual nation within and one whose identity is inflected by the white nation that authorizes it from without.

Glory, which won three Oscars, including Best Supporting Actor for Denzel Washington, was followed by a number of works about the Civil War: Ken Burns' *The Civil War* (1990), an eleven-hour PBS documentary; Ronald Maxwell's *Gettysburg* (1993) and *Gods and Generals* (2003); and Anthony Minghella's *Cold Mountain* (2003). Ang Lee's *Ride with the Devil* (1999) is of particular interest in terms of Burgoyne's concern with nationhood, since Daniel Holt, the character played by Jeffrey Wright, is an isolated African American associating with the Bushwackers, a white Southern group not formally connected to the Confederate Army. In the course of the narrative, although not well educated like Thomas Searle (Andre Braugher) in *Glory,* Holt is partially absorbed into the white community in a way that invites commentary from the perspective offered by Burgoyne.

Rogin contextualizes *Home of the Brave* in relation to important cultural issues of anti-Semitism and racism in postwar America. He explores the rationale of the filmmakers who changed the mentally ill hero of the original play from a Jew to an African American, Peter Moss (Jame Edwards). In terms of actual military history, Moss's presence in this military division would not have been possible. As Rogin notes, African Americans served separately from whites in the U.S. Armed Forces until President Harry Truman formally integrated them in 1948. Thus the appearance of African American combatants in *Bataan* and *Guadalcanal Diary* is inaccurate. Only the black soldier in *Sahara* (Zoltan Korda, 1943) is narratively probable because he is a Sudanese, not an American.[17]

The separation of servicemen was particularly evident in the documentary Rogin mentions: *The Negro Soldier* (Stuart Heisler, 1943; Frank Capra, producer). According to Thomas Cripps, the film was a response to African American concerns about racism and the Office of War Information's desire to stress that the United States was "a melting pot."[18] The film demonstrates quite matter-of-factly how the troops were separated. It opens in a church, as a mother reads a letter from her son describing his experiences in the Army, which are then shown. First, we see both African Americans and whites together in the initial stages of the induction process. However, once the preliminary stages of basic training have concluded, the film shows that African Americans continue their training in total racial isolation from whites—thus setting the pattern for their actual combat experiences.[19]

In the book from which this essay is drawn, Rogin is particularly interested in the way the concept and practice of "blackface" have dominated American culture and entertainment. Specifically, he explores not only "the literal meaning of blackface—blacking up to play the African American role" but even more the way "African Americans who whether or not literally under burnt cork, perform against themselves for white eyes." For example, he thinks the way that Peter Moss is treated and cured dissipates the narrative issue of segregation by absorbing it in the larger (and racially neutral) concern for war-related psychoses. That is, what begins as a film about segregation ends up as a study of a healing that ignores race. This is similar to Burgoyne's argument that the concept of black nationhood in *Glory* is defused by being absorbed into a larger concern for the nation, at the expense of African American autonomy.[20]

In some ways *Bright Victory* (Mark Robson, 1951) offers a significant complement and, perhaps, a corrective to the kinds of problems Rogin identifies in *Home of the Brave. Bright Victory* depicts life in an Army rehabilitation hospital for soldiers blinded during World War II. The hospital itself is integrated, a historically accurate depiction. Larry Nivens, a white veteran played by Arthur Kennedy, whose performance received an Oscar nomination for Best Actor, befriends Joe Morgan, an African American veteran, played by James Edwards (Moss in *Home of the Brave*). Because of his blindness, Larry doesn't realize his friend is black until he makes a racial slur that exposes his ignorance. Eventually the two are reunited. Although significant narrative attention is paid to the love story that involves Larry and Judy (Peggy Dow), the film's conclusion focuses on the reunion of the black and white soldiers.

While Rogin points out the historical inaccuracy in the depiction of the African American soldier in *Home of the Brave*, Woodman addresses the issue of authenticity from a different direction. He argues that some of the films about the Vietnam War fail to represent the actual contributions of African Americans fairly, most tellingly in regard to the number of combatants. Drawing on the work of Loren Baritz, Thomas Johnson, and Wallace Terry, he points out that African Americans "were more likely to be drafted, faced discrimination both home and abroad, and made up a disproportionate amount of casualties." *The Green Berets* (John Wayne and Ray Kellogg, 1968) is probably the most despised American war movie ever made because of its pro-war stance at a time when protests against the war had become increasingly intense in the United States. Besides its reprehensible stance on the war, Woodman criticizes its treatment of Doc McGee (Raymond St. Jacques), and connects his character to a tradition of presenting "safe" African

Americans, the "ebony saint" figure identified by Ed Guerrero. Woodman's discussion of other Vietnam War films, particularly the sadly neglected *Boys in Company C* (Sidney Furie, 1978), provides a helpful assessment of what seems to be a positive trajectory, culminating in *Hamburger Hill* (John Irvin, 1987). Like Burgoyne and Rogin, he is interested in exploring the extent to which the voices of the African American soldiers and their own history are muted.[21]

Gender

The four essays in this section focus on gender in complementary ways. Guerric DeBona explains the treatment of masculinity in the Civil War film *The Red Badge of Courage* (John Huston, 1951) in terms of pressures exerted by MGM on the filmmaker because of the political climate in 1951. Looking at the *Rambo* films, Susan Jeffords demonstrates how the representation of Rambo's masculinity is inflected by the political power and influence of President Ronald Reagan on the American public. Tania Modleski explores how elements of melodrama and women's films affect the generic integrity of the traditionally "masculine" genre of the war film, and pays particular attention to *Dogfight* (Nancy Savoca, 1991). Examining the female officer in the Persian Gulf War film *Courage Under Fire* (Edward Zwick, 1996), and the female Navy SEAL in *G.I. Jane* (Ridley Scott, 1997), Yvonne Tasker asks whether we should reject a binary concept of gender roles in favor of a view that sees "masculinity" and "femininity" as elements spread over the characters and narratives and linked to other discourses.

DeBona's explanation of how MGM changed *The Red Badge of Courage* addresses several issues. He sees a pattern of "demythologizing" of "traditional modes of masculinity and male behavior" throughout Huston's films, including documentaries, such as *The Battle of San Pietro* (1945) and *Let There Be Light* (1946), and narrative films, beginning with *The Maltese Falcon* (1941). Although anyone familiar with the history of the Hollywood studio system knows that negative audience responses to test screenings can result in changes to a film, the underlying context for the changes made to Huston's film is of special interest. Since the film emerged at time when the United States was engaged in the Korean War, there was pressure from MGM to downplay any antiheroic elements. Moreover, its production and release were connected to the studio politics at MGM at a time when liberal and conservative ideologies were in contention. Certainly *The Red Badge of Courage* is not "about" the Korean War or studio politics, but our perception of it today in its socio-cultural context is inevitably over-determined by this knowledge.[22]

DeBona shows how the studio's rewriting of Huston's text constructs its original creator, the novelist Stephen Crane, as a visible "author" in the credits, and eliminates problematic material in a way that strengthens the character of the hero, played by Audie Murphy, who was the most highly decorated soldier in World War II. Both the rewriting and the revisions in plot defuse suggestions of masculinity in crisis, thus defeating Huston's project of challenging patriarchy.

Jeffords also explores the connection between the United States and the kind of character whose masculinity is related to the collective national mood in films about the Vietnam veteran John J. Rambo (Sylvester Stallone): *First Blood* (Ted Kotcheff, 1982); *Rambo: First Blood, Part 2* (George Cosmatos, 1985); and *Rambo III* (Peter MacDonald, 1986). In *The Remasculinization of America*, she uses the term *masculinity* "to refer to the set of images, values, interests, and activities held important to a successful achievement of male adulthood in American cultures."[23] Her treatment of the three films suggests that Rambo's exploits tap into several powerful veins. In the first, as the neglected and abused veteran who must defend himself against the bullying Sheriff Teasle, Rambo serves as a point of reference for Americans tired of being pushed around, as had occurred during the Iranian hostage crisis. Even more, though, the power embodied in Rambo literally (his powerful body) and figuratively (his moral stance) proves that the crisis in masculinity that had previously gripped the country was capable of amelioration. That is, the presidency of Jimmy Carter was over, and Ronald Reagan was now at the helm.

Rambo: First Blood Part 2 was the immensely extremely successful film (domestic box office of $150,415,432) that prompted Reagan's oft-quoted response after seeing it that he would know what to do "the next" time the United States faced a military challenge as it had just experienced in Lebanon. Like the injured president, who survived his gunshot wound during an assassination attempt, Rambo shows himself to be invulnerable and capable of withstanding physical assault and torture from the Russians. Thus in the 1980s Americans watch two bodies, two Hollywood stars who were subject to physical attack but remained invulnerable, and two reclaimers getting to win this time: Rambo by getting the prisoners of war back, Reagan by getting the country running again. The larger reclamation is of masculinity itself. In *The Remasculinization of America*, in keeping with her definition of masculinity that connects it to "images, values, interests, and values," Jefford sees "a regenerated masculinity . . . not simply an aspect but the primary project of regenerating American culture as a whole."[24]

Jeffords cites Steve Neale's well-known observation about the unsettling effects that attend representation of the wounded male body. In *The Remasculinization of America* she discusses representation from another direction by citing Klaus Theweleit's *Male Fantasies* (1987, 1989). That work examines the psychosexual makeup of the Freikorps, a group of males in post–World War I Germany who became a powerful force within Hitler's regime. Records of various fantasies and commentaries by these fascists convey a disturbing and frightening picture that helps one understand more fully how the men's warped, antagonistic views of violence and gender account for the presence of a ready-made force prepared to be led to an inevitable war. Theweleit explores the psychic power over men of the mother and women who constitute an all-powerful, consuming force. Jefford uses Theweleit to explain how Rambo's response to Co Bao before she is killed relates to the various scenes in Rambo in which he emerges triumphantly from water after having been submerged:

> Theweleit traces the release of waters prominent in Fascist literature—floods, streams, rivers, burst dams—to its function as sublimated "release" of sexual energies. In an uncontrolled state, it is a release to be feared, possibly over-running the soldier male and drowning him. What is preferred are controlled streams of water in which the soldier male can immerse himself to be reborn. . . . Intimately connected to these fears are women, especially women of the lower class, for women are reminders of that sexuality from which the purifying water has rescued the soldier male. . . . The taint of impure sexuality is identified with "dirty" women . . . who must be rejected in order for the soldier male to maintain his purity and energy.[25]

Obviously, Rambo's question to Trautman in *Rambo: First Blood Part II*, "Do we get to win this time?" informs the title of Modleski's essay, "Do We Get to Lose This Time?" In "A Father Is Being Beaten," her earlier discussion of war films, mentioned above, Modleski argues that war films such as *Platoon* and *Full Metal Jacket* all privilege masculine values. Like Jeffords, she sees 1980s films illustrating a "desire to rewrite the history of Vietnam to prove that we were not cowardly losers but merely unacknowledged winners." In language that recalls DeBona, Modleski sees this being accomplished by a "rewriting that frequently expresses a yearning for a strong paternal figure who will enable young men to go off and . . . become heroic soliders in the new wars to come."[26]

Here she suggests that films about the Vietnam era such as *Coming Home* (Hal Ashby, 1978), *In Country* (Norman Jewison, 1989), *Jacknife* (David Jones, 1989), and *Dogfight* privilege feminine values. Rejecting male critics who dismiss elements of "feminine discourse" in the war film, she demonstrates how such elements as the love story and sexual awakening of Sally (Jane Fonda) in *Coming Home* provide an important and necessary perspective on women, who have been neglected by the masculine genre. The ability of Luke (Jon Voight) to affect Sally, and the film's emphasis on her response, contrast with the treatment of another disabled veteran, Ron Kovic (Tom Cruise) in *Born on the Fourth of July* (Oliver Stone, 1989) and the woman with whom he has sex.

Using *Dogfight* as her prime example of a film that displays "feminine discourses," Modleski argues that Savoca's film actually surpasses other films' anti-war messages by letting us observe the "warrior mentality" through the eyes of Rose (Lily Taylor). Moreover, in subtle ways, particularly through the use of folk music, Savoca gives her heroine a commanding presence hitherto denied women in war films. Because she is a person with a system of values articulated within the film, Rose's interactions with Eddie (River Phoenix) put her in a position of moral authority. Unlike war films that depict male misogyny without adequate attention to its effects on women, *Dogfight* uses the presence of an articulate woman in a way that foregrounds such viciousness even more glaringly.

Modleski's argument that a feminine perspective in the war film provides a needed window for understanding masculinity is complemented by Tasker's challenge to the binary feminine/masculine dichotomy as a way of differentiating characters' behavior in the genre. Both *Courage Under Fire* and *G.I. Jane* have military women as heroines engaged in traditionally male combat roles. Acknowledging the importance of psychoanalytic semiotics in past analysis of gender roles, Tasker offers a cautionary restraint here.[27] Tasker sees an impasse created by the way that critics have discussed women in films like *Alien* (Ridley Scott, 1979), *Thelma and Louise* (Ridley Scott, 1991), and *Terminator 2* (James Cameron, 1991). Clearly aware of feminists' concerns about "essentialism" that limits women biologically to constrained social roles, Tasker argues that a quality associated with masculinity, such as "a muscular physique," can be a "signifier of strength" for both sexes, not just males. She resists restricting the concept of "masculinity" strictly to men since that guarantees that females and femininity will necessarily be understood in terms of an opposition.

The treatment of the heroines in these films leads to her suggestion that "gender is best understood as a set of discourses that are contested, accepted, and resisted within networks, rather than binaries." Her call to avoid thinking of masculinity strictly in terms of men and femininity only in terms of women thus authorizes us to look at "these qualities operating across characters, scenarios, and narratives as well as interacting with other discourses."

The logic of her argument is important not only for consideration of the female characters and narrative situations presented in her analysis of these films. It can be applied to male characters as well. For example, when Antony Easthope speaks of "male femininity," he is accounting for a negative quality of behavior in men during war as a result of the pressures of battle. Discussing *The Deer Hunter* (Michael Cimino, 1978), he observes that "the pain of war is the price paid for the way it expresses the male bond. War's suffering is a kind of punishment for the release of homosexual desire and male femininity that only war allows."[28] Were Tasker's suggestion to be applied to males in war films, the qualities of feeling and emotion implied by "male femininity" would not be coded in a gender-specific way that implies lack (e.g., weak men acting temporarily like women).

History

All the essays in this section display a concern with the relationship between war films and history, especially how a real or narrativized past becomes a way of commenting on the present. Mimi White discusses how the treatment of female factory workers during World War II in the documentary *The Life and Times of Rosie the Riveter* (Connie Field, 1980) and the narrative film *Swing Shift* (Jonathan Demme, 1984) speaks to the present concerns of feminists. Albert Auster explores how *Saving Private Ryan* (Steven Spielberg, 1998) offers its contemporary audience a positive alternative to the negative residual of recent inconclusive U.S. military actions. Thomas Doherty examines the significance for contemporary audiences of *Black Hawk Down* (Ridley Scott, 2002), about a disastrous rescue attempt in Somalia, and *We Were Soldiers* (Randall Wallace, 2002), about the first major battle of the Vietnam War, in order to demonstrate how much their reception has been affected by 9/11.

White's examination of *The Life and Times of Rosie the Riveter* and *Swing Shift* suggests that the films idealize the past in different ways. White points to the complexities that attend presenting "a contemporary version of the past's self-representation" in the archival footage because of the inevitable gap between past and present. Since the contemporary interviews are "retrospective accounts," they can only give us "a present truth about the past." Paradoxically, such accounts give us a history that "emerges and is defined on the basis of a past which is simultaneously excluded and preserved."

Swing Shift presents even more of an interpretive challenge from a historical perspective. While its black-and-white opening credits and newsreel footage evoke the sense of a "real" past used to contextualize the fictional narrative that takes place during World War II, its depiction of Kay (Goldie Hawn) and other working women actually collapses past and present time in a "temporal-historical sleight of hand" that serves simultaneously to idealize a past moment of women's achievements while establishing it as a historical moment that has been surpassed. *Swing Shift* may actually be seen to display a contemporary sense of dissatisfaction, and we should not think of it as presenting a historical problem that has been solved in contemporary society. Instead, the film displays "the effect of unresolved issues and contradictions in women's current status."

White's essay invites consideration in relation to theoretical work by Fredric Jameson and Linda Hutcheon on how audiences use and respond to history as it is represented in film. Jameson discusses what he calls the presence of pastiche or "blank parody" in period films such as *Chinatown* (Roman Polanski, 1974), which conveys a sense of the 1930s, or films that evoke the experience of period films, such as *Star Wars* (George Lucas, 1977), which revives audience's experiences with serials. He thinks that the implications of such films and their reception are negative, for it seems to him "symptomatic to find the very style of nostalgia films invading and colonizing even those movies today which have contemporary settings; as though, for some reason, we were unable today to focus on our own present, as though we have become incapable of achieving aesthetic representations of our own current experience." These constitute "a terrible indictment of consumer capitalism" by suggesting "an alarming and pathological symptom of a society that has become incapable of dealing with time and memory."[29]

Hutcheon's approach to nostalgia and films about the past is even more relevant to the consideration of the war films that appear in this section. She thinks that

> nostalgia . . . may depend precisely on the irrecoverable nature of the past for its emotional impact and appeal. It is the very pastness of the past, its inaccessibility, that likely accounts for a large part of nostalgia's power. . . . This is rarely the past as actually experienced . . . ; it is the past as imagined, as idealized through memory and desire. . . . [N]ostalgia exiles us from the present as it brings the imagined past near. . . . The aesthetics of nostalgia might . . . be less a matter of simple memory than of complex projection; the invocation of a partial, idealized history merges with a dissatisfaction for the present.[30]

Just as the unresolved issues in women's status suggest dissatisfaction with the present in *Swing Shift*, so too does the eroding of American hegemony figure in Auster's commentary on *Saving Private Ryan*. He thinks the film addresses a present lack by invoking the past. The uneasy victories in the Persian Gulf War and in the Balkans provided no sense of "real resolution." While David O. Russell's *Three Kings* (1999) presents heroic figures who are "good guys," the film itself does not offer "any real sense of triumph" in that war. *Saving Private Ryan* permits a displacement from the temporal period of actual and inconclusive wars in the 1990s to the triumphal epoch of World War II, a move he compares to what occurred in 1970 with *M*A*S*H* (Robert Altman, 1970). Although that film, made at the height of the Vietnam War, is overtly about Korea, its irreverence can be read both as a commentary on our experiences in Vietnam and a nod back to a much less controversial war. Essentially *Saving Private Ryan* offers a way to deal with the present by appropriating a viable and "indispensable symbol of American patriotic virtue and triumph" from the past.

Doherty's essay provides a particularly appropriate way to conclude the anthology since he ends his commentary by anticipating how films as yet unmade will deal with 9/11. In the absence of films directly "about" 9/11, audiences' responses to the war films *Black Hawk Down* and *We Were Soldiers* are inflected by their memory of that disaster. Doherty talks about films in terms of the generic conventions, such as the characters in *Black Hawk Down* who seem diminished representations of the usual variety, and the more effective "star-dependent and character-driven" hero played by Mel Gibson in *We Were Soldiers*, and that film's treatment of women on the home front. The latter work departs from traditional war film conventions in its treatment of the North Vietnamese, who are "neither demonized nor glamorized."

Auster's analysis of *Saving Private Ryan* explains the positive treatment of the military in terms of the current sense of lack. Doherty's commentary shows how a post-9/11 sensibility logically accounts for "war-minded films [that] embrace a set of suddenly au courant values—a respect for public servants in uniform, a sympathy for military codes of conduct, and a celebration of the virtues forged in the crucible of combat."

The essays thus cover a variety of wars and issues. Even though their methodological emphases may differ, together all constitute an essential model for thinking about the ways the war film genre has become an essential part of our cinematic history. Even more, they provide a perspective for thinking about war films as yet unmade. Why do certain wars continue to engage our historical and cultural imaginations and serve as the subjects of films? Is it because a current international crisis is replaying an earlier one? Is it a chance to withdraw from contemporary malaise and revive past glory? Is it a chance to correct or reverse a past wrong?

The Persian Gulf War of 1991 has not prompted many films, although some writers have suggested that the televisual treatment of that war was, as J. Hoberman suggests, "a highly successful made-for-television movie even as it was happening."[31] The Vietnam War evoked only one film while it was being fought, although it was accessible as what Michael J. Arlen refers to as the "living-room war," given its coverage on television.[32] In contrast World War II and the Korean War occasioned the production of many war films. In fact, the films from the Spanish-American War that I discussed in the beginning of this essay anticipate these two wars in that films about the conflicts were made while the fighting continued. Certainly the newness of the technology and the economic riches to be gained by showing audiences what was happening during the war played an important part in accounting for the production of those films in 1898. But during World War II and the Korean War, there were very real fears about what impact the wars would have on the United States. As we know, genres gain and lose popularity for a number of reasons. It remains to be seen what role the war film will continue to play in the future and to what extent the war with Iraq will become a subject for narrative films.[33]

NOTES

1. *The History of Photography* (New York: Museum of Modern Art, 1964), 67. He identifies his source of the quotation from the *Times* as a reprint in the *American Journal of Photography* 1 (October 1862): 145. See Martha A. Sandweiss, "Photography and the Mexican-American War," in *Print the Legend: Photography and the American West* (New Haven: Yale University Press, 2002), 16–45.

2. James Castonguay, "The Spanish-American War in United States Media Culture," *Hypertext Scholarship in American Studies* <http://chnm.gmu.edu/aq/> (accessed 4 November 2003), section on "Media Culture in the 1890s"; Robert Sklar, *Movie-Made America: A Cultural History of American Movies* (New York: Vintage, 1976), 22; Charles Musser, *The Emergence of Cinema: The American Screen to 1907* (New York: Charles Scribner's Sons, 1990), 240–261.

3. "The Journal's Vivid Moving War Pictures," *New York Journal and Advertiser*, 16 April

1898, qtd. in Charles Musser, *Edison Motion Pictures, 1890–1900, An Annotated Filmography* (n.p., [printed in Italy]; Smithsonian Institution Press, 1997), 420.

4. "The Cinema of Attractions: Early Film, Its Spectator and the Avant-Garde" [1986], in *Early Cinema: Space Frame Narrative*, ed. Thomas Elsaesser (London: BFI, 1990), 58.

5. Kemp R. Niver, *Early Motion Pictures: The Paper Print Collection of the Library of Congress*, ed. Bebe Bergsten (Washington: Library of Congress, 1985), 495; http://memory.loc.gov/ammem/sawhtml.satitles.htm.

6. "A Semantic/Syntactic Approach to Film Genre," in *Film Genre Reader II*, ed. Barry Keith Grant (Austin: University of Texas Press, 1995), 30.

7. The first film made about the flag seems to be *The United States Flag* (American Mutascope Co., 1896). The Biograph summary states: "A special colored film of the Stars and Stripes fluttering in the breeze." *The American Film Institute Catalog of Motion Pictures Produced in the United States. Film Beginnings, 1893–1910, A Work in Progress*, comp. Elias Savada (Lanham, Md.: Scarecrow, 1995), I:1129. The *AFI Catalog* lists other titles. For flag films made during the war, see also Musser, *Edison Motion Pictures, 1890–1900*, 409–410. Castonguay says that the first fictionalized reenactment of any event of the war was *Tearing Down the Spanish Flag* (J. Stuart Blackton, 1898; lost): "The Spanish-American War in American Culture," section on "Early Cinema and the Spanish-American War."

8. The description of the film in Musser, *Edison Motion Pictures, 1890–1900* (526–527) and the *AFI Catalog* (I:621–622) differs from the film available online at the Library of Congress Web site. The former was accompanied by songs. The soldier's love interest is a nurse he meets on the battlefield. Professor Musser kindly responded to my inquiry about the differences in the viewable and described films: "As I recall, it appears that the paperprint film is incomplete. A couple of scenes are missing. This could have happened for any number of reasons. So, if this is the case, I think you should consider the LOC material incomplete and the catalog description something like what people might have seen" (e-mail, 5 December 2003).

9. In *The Anarchy of Empire in the Making of U.S. Culture* (Cambridge, Mass.: Harvard University Press, 2002), 153, Amy Kaplan draws attention to Charles Musser's suggestion about the relation of the practice of programmers at the time to the development of narrative. When the war began, various films about it might be interspersed with unrelated films such as the *Annebelle Butterfly Dance* or *Storm at Sea*. But gradually more focus on the war figured in the total program: "war images were always separated from one another by vastly different subjects from the repertoire of comedy, travel, dance, melodrama, boxing, and the like. . . . By 1898, however, programs that offered a much higher degree of continuity were very common." *The Emergence of Cinema*, 258–259.

10. For studies of World War I films and commentary on generic features as well as reception, see Leslie Midkiff DeBauche, *Reel Patriotism: The Movies and World War I* (Madison: University of Wisconsin Press, 1997); Michael T. Isenberg, *War on Film: The American Cinema and World War I, 1914–41* (East Brunswick, N.J.: Fairleigh Dickinson University Press, 1981); Michael Paris, ed., *The First World War and Popular Cinema* (New Brunswick: Rutgers University Press, 2000): and Peter C. Rollins and John E. O'Connor, eds., *Hollywood's World War I: Motion Picture Images* (Bowling Green: Bowling Green State University Popular Press, 1997). See also Paul Fussell's masterful and essential *The Great War and Modern Memory* (New York: Oxford University Press, 1975; 2000).

11. Michael Birdwell, *Celluloid Soldiers: Warner Bros.'s Campaign Against Nazism* (New York: New York University Press, 1999), 128.

12. *The World War II Combat Film: Anatomy of a Genre* (Middletown: Wesleyan University Press, 2003), 93. Although not all are directed at film, the following are important works about World War II: Michael C. C. Adams, *The Best War Ever: America and World War II* (Baltimore: Johns Hopkins University Press, 1994); Philip D. Beidler, *The Good War's Greatest Hits: World War II and American Remembering* (Athens: University of Georgia Press, 1998); John Whiteclay Chambers II and David Culbert, eds., *World War II and Modern Memory* (New York: Oxford University Press, 1996); Bernard F. Dick, *The Star-Spangled Screen: The American World War II Film* (Lexington: University of Kentucky Press, 1997); Thomas Doherty, *Projections of War*, rev. ed. (New York: Columbia University Press, 1999); Paul Fussell, *Wartime: Understanding and Behavior in the Second World War* (New York: Oxford University Press, 1989); Clayton R. Koppes and Gregory Black, *Hollywood Goes to War: How Politics, Profits and Pro-*

paganda Shaped World War II Movies (Berkeley: University of California Press, 1990); Studs Terkel, *The "Good War": An Oral History of World War Two* (New York: Pantheon, 1984).

13. Basinger, *World War II Combat Film*, 237. For more commentary on the genre, see Steve Neale, "War Films," in *Genre and Hollywood* (London: BFI, 2000), 125–133. Thomas Schatz draws an interesting connection between "two seemingly disparate war films, *Air Force* [Howard Hawks, 1943] and *Since You Went Away* [John Cromwell, 1944]. The most basic similarity between this combat film and home-front melodrama is their mutual celebration of distinctive American 'fortresses'—one a Boeing B-17 bomber and the other a two-story brick colonial home—while valorizing the occupants and the special wartime rites of each domain. . . . Both are conversion narratives that trace the adjustment and sacrifices that American men and women had to make for the war effort to succeed." "World War II and the Hollywood 'War Film,'" in *Refiguring American Film Genres*, ed. Nick Browne (Berkeley: University of California Press, 1998), 116. Allen W. Woll explores another interesting generic phenomenon in his study, *The Hollywood Musical Goes to War* (Chicago: Nelson-Hall, 1983): "Between 1941 and 1945, the film musical achieved its greatest popularity and its greatest relevance. . . . After Pearl Harbor, winning the war became the number one priority of the musical film, as escapism swiftly became an impossibility" (xi).

14. Deleuze observes: "This is the first aspect of the new cinema: the break in the sensory-link (action-image), and more profoundly, in the link between man and world (great organic composition). The second aspect is the abandoning of figures, metonymy as much as metaphor, and at a deeper level the dislocation of the internal monologue as descriptive material of the cinema." *Cinema 2: The Time Image*, trans. Hugh Tomlinson and Robert Galeta (Minneapolis: University of Minnesota Press, 1989), 173. See Marcia Landy on the influence of Deleuze: "Deleuze gives us a new conception of the uses of past and present. . . . [I]nstead of the unifying dimensions of action and effect, there is a new kind of narration, one that is discontinuous and fragmenting, rather than connected and unified." "Introduction," in *The Historical Film: History and Memory in Media*, ed. Marcia Landy (New Brunswick: Rutgers University Press, 2001), 6.

15. Benedict Anderson, *Imagined Communities: Reflections on the Origin and Spread of Nationalism* (London: Verso, 1991), 6.

16. Earlier silent films about the Civil War include works by Thomas Ince: *Drummer of the Eighth* and *Grand-Dad* (both 1913). See Michael Rogin, "'The Sword Became a Flashing Vision': D.W. Griffith's *The Birth of a Nation*," in *Ronald Reagan, the Movie and Other Episodes in American Demonology* (Berkeley: University of California Press, 1987), 190–235. Included in this essay is commentary connecting Griffith's work in *Hearts of the World* with *Birth of a Nation*.

17. See Lawrence Suid on Dore Schary's knowledge that having a black soldier in *Bataan* was inappropriate: *Guts and Glory*, rev. and exp. ed. (Lexington: University of Kentucky Press, 2002), 69. See also Thomas Cripps, *Making Movies Black: The Hollywood Message Movie from World War II to the Civil Rights Era* (New York: Oxford University Press, 1993), 72–76. Commentary on the Center for the Study of Racial Minorities in the Military Web site indicates there were isolated instances during World War II when African American troops were joined with whites. See Section IV, World War II at: http://www.gaymilitary.ucsb.ed/Publications/evans_Minority200306_2.htm#4

18. Thomas Cripps, *Slow Fade to Black: The Negro in American Film*, 1900–1942 (New York: Oxford University Press, 1977), 380.

19. For a modern reconstruction of how such camps looked, see *A Soldier's Story* (Norman Jewison, 1984), a film about a murder investigation of an African American sergeant at an Army camp in 1944. The chief officers are white. The HBO film *The Tuskegee Airmen* (Robert Markowitz, 1995) presents the story of one of the most famous African American divisions in World War II.

20. Rogin, *Blackface, White Noise* (Berkeley: University of California Press, 1996), 18. See David Van Leer's argument in "Visible Silence: Spectatorship in Black Gay and Lesbian Film," in *Representing Blackness: Issues in Film and Video*, ed. Valerie Smith (New Brunswick: Rutgers University Press, 1997), 159. "Some works treat sexuality and race as interchangeable. In *Home of the Brave* (1949), gay playwright Arthur Laurents rewrites his stage drama about an anti-Semitic slur within the military as a racial incident. Denying the black character a separate identity, Laurents' plot merely substitutes racism for anti-Semitisim, which itself symbolizes

the more important but unmentionable problem of homophobia." E. Ann Kaplan suggests that Moss be considered in relation to other analysands in 1940s films: "Perhaps because the successful role of analysand is inherently a 'feminized' one, most Hollywood narratives about psychoanalysis have female—that is *white* female—protagonists. When the patient is male and *black,* he too is feminized, as in a film like *Home of the Brave.*" "Darkness Within: Or, The Dark Continent of Film Noir," in *Looking for the Other: Feminism, Film, and the Imperial Gaze* (New York: Routledge, 1997), 106.

21. See the following for useful commentaries on the Vietnam War film: Michael Anderegg, ed., *Inventing Vietam: The War in Film and Television* (Philadelphia: Temple University Press, 1991); Jeremy M. Devine, *Vietnam at 24 Frames a Second* (Austin: University of Texas Press, 1999); Linda Dittmar and Gene Michaud, eds., *From Hanoi to Hollywood: The Vietnam War in American Film* (New Brunswick: Rutgers University Press, 1990); and John Carlos Rowe and Rick Berg, eds., *The Vietnam War and American Culture* (New York: Columbia University Press, 1991).

22. *The Red Badge of Courage* appeared in October 1951, ten months after the release in January 1951 of *The Steel Helmet* (Sam Fuller, 1951), the first film about the Korean War. Fuller's second Korean War film, *Fixed Bayonets,* was released the following month, in November. For more on the production of these films, see Fuller's autobiography, *A Third Face: My Tale of Writing, Fighting, and Filmmaking* (New York: Knopf, 2002).

23. *The Remasculinization of America: Gender and the Vietnam War* (New Brunswick: Rutgers University Press, 1989), xii.

24. Ibid., 135. Rambo's reclaiming of the captive prisoners of war also relates to a deeply embedded pattern of rescue in American history described by Tom Engelhardt in *The End of Victory Culture: Cold War America and the Disillusioning of a Generation* (Amherst: University of Massachusetts Press, 1995), 278. Engelhardt demonstrates the reasons for the prevalence of captivity narratives in American cultural texts and, in a later section of the work, comments on Rambo: "the 'good wars' of screen history could not be brought back without a form of overexplanation that verged on the grotesque. Traditionally brute physique had been the least of the qualities of the western hero needed to enter 'Indian country.' His strengths were, if anything, visually understated, not a spectacle in their own right. Even John Wayne was no giant. Rambo's gargantuan musculature, however, was a form of explanation. He bulged with visible strength, while the camera repeatedly took roller coaster rides over his mountainous muscles, reiterating that he was such a hero." See also Peter Lehman, *Running Scared: Masculinity and the Representation of the Male Body* (Philadelphia: Temple University Press, 1993*). First Blood* belongs to the subgenre identified in the last essay in this anthology by Thomas Doherty as the "extraction film." It was preceded by *Uncommon Valor* (Ted Kotcheff, 1982) and *Missing in Action* (Joseph Zito, 1984).

25. Jeffords, *Remasculinization of America,* 132. Jeffords cites from volume I of Klaus Theweleit, *Male Fantasies,* trans. Stephen Conway (Minneapolis: University of Minnesota Press, 1987). Tania Modleski also makes use of Theweleit in her commentary on *Full Metal Jacket:* "The ending of the film thus corroborates Theweleit's finding that the war fantasies he studied invariably build to a climax in which the woman/enemy is rendered a bloody mass." "A Father Is Being Beaten: Male Feminism and the War Film," in *Feminism Without Women: Culture and Criticism in a "Postfeminist" Age* (New York: Routledge, 1991), 62. See also Michael Selig: "The language of bodily contamination that Theweleit describes as a threat to the male also emerges in the Vietnam films. Theweleit finds a strong connection in the Freikorps writing between the symbolic female body and 'dirt . . . slime . . . pulp . . . shit . . . [and] rain.'" "Genre, Gender, and the Discourse of War: The a/Historical and Vietnam Films," *Screen* 34, no. 1 (Spring 1993): 8.

26. "A Father Is Being Beaten," 71.

27. The criticism on this subject is vast. Many of the following anthologies offer important essays employing this methodology: E. Ann Kaplan, ed., *Psychoanalysis and Film* (New York: Routledge, 1990); Steven Cohen and Ina Rae Hark, eds., *Screening the Male: Exploring Masculinities in Hollywood Cinema* (New York: Routledge, 1993); and Diane Carson, Linda Dittmar, and Janice R. Welsch, eds., *Multiple Voices in Feminist Criticism* (Minneapolis: University of Minnesota Press, 1994). Laura Mulvey's essay, "Visual Pleasure and Narrative Cinema," is standard reading: *Visual and Other Pleasures* (Bloomington: Indiana University Press,

1989), 14–26. See two particularly interesting essays about *The Best Years in Our Lives* (William Wyler, 1946) in which psychoanalytic and gender issues are explored fruitfully: Kaja Silverman, "Historical Trauma and Male Subjectivity," in *Male Subjectivity at the Margins* (New York: Routledge, 1992), 52–121; and Sonya Michel, "Danger on the Home Front: Motherhood, Sexuality, and Disabled Veterans in American Postwar Films," *Journal of the History of Sexuality* 3, no. 1 (July 1992): 109–128.

28. Antony Easthope, *What a Man's Gotta Do: The Masculine Myth in Popular Culture* (New York: Routledge, 1992), 66. Robin Wood's examination of *The Deer Hunter* focuses on the "male love story" and the complexities in the narrative created by the "boundaries in gender construction"(291). "Two Films by Michael Cimino," in *Hollywood from Vietnam to Reagan* (New York: Columbia University Press, 1986), 270–317.

29. Fredric Jameson, "Postmodernism and Consumer Society," in *The Anti-Aesthetic: Essays on Postmodern Culture*, ed. Hal Foster (Port Townsend, Wash.: Bay, 1987), 117.

30. "Irony, Nostalgia, and the Postmodern" [1998]: http://www.library.utoronto.ca/utel/criticism/hutchinp.html.

31. J. Hoberman, "Burn, Blast, Bomb." *Sight and Sound* 18 (March 2000): 18–20. See also Tom Engelhardt, "The Gulf War as Total Television," in *Seeing Through the Media: The Persian Gulf War*, ed. Susan Jeffords and Lauren Rabinovitz (New Brunswick: Rutgers University Press, 1994), 81–95.

32. Michael J. Arlen, *The Living-Room War* (New York: Viking, 1949).

33. As of November 2003, the war had already resulted in *Uncovered: The Whole Truth about the Iraq War*, an antiwar DVD produced and directed by Robert Greenwald. According to Jonathan Bing, 30,000 DVDs had been "sold through the Web sites of left-wing political outlets like Moveon.org, Alternet and the National Institute." "Antiwar Doc Spins Up on Direct-sale DVD," *Variety*, 17–23 November 2003, 7.

Genre

Andrew Kelly

The Greatness and Continuing Significance of *All Quiet on the Western Front*

There are many reasons why *All Quiet on the Western Front* (Lewis Milestone, 1930) retains its power and has continued to capture the imagination, despite the fact that few have seen a full version and that over half a century of cinema has passed since its first release. It brings together—indeed, helped establish—the classic themes of the antiwar film, book, play and poem: the enemy as comrade; the brutality of militarism; the slaughter of trench warfare; the betrayal of a nation's youth by old men revelling in glory; the incompetence of the High Command; the suffering at home, in particular by women; the dead; and the forgotten men who survived. And it did so in style, without recourse to the romanticism and glorification that marred such war films as *The Big Parade* (King Vidor, 1925).

All Quiet on the Western Front was a leap forward for cinema in critically addressing war and peace issues. Here the Great War is seen as it was: a brutal waste. No film up to then had shown this—indeed, had been able to show this as the time was not right and the camera was incapable, in the early sound era, of recreating the reality of trench combat. Only *Paths of Glory* (Stanley Kubrick, 1957) has since been able to capture the terror of war, the waiting for the attack, the inevitability of death.

In its attack on militarism, *All Quiet on the Western Front* was telling millions what the Great War poets had stated so eloquently, and with its own eloquence. A. P. Herbert, in his poem about Gallipoli, spoke for all the dead of the war (*All Quiet on the Western Front* was not about Gallipoli, but the sentiments are the same):

> This is the Fourth of June
> Think not I never dream
> The noise of that infernal noon,
> The stretchers' endless stream,
> The tales of triumph won,
> The night that found them lies,

The wounded wailing in the sun,
The dead, the dust, the flies.

The flies! oh God, the flies,
That soiled the sacred dead.
To see them swarm from dead men's eyes
And share the soldiers' bread!
Nor think I now forget
The filth and stench of war,
The corpses on the parapet,
The maggots in the floor.

Apart from what these poets told them, few, even the relatives of those who had fought and survived, would have been aware of the *totality* of the suffering of the soldiers in the trenches. Those who had returned did not—sometimes, owing to disability, could not—talk about the deaths and injuries they had seen, the smell of war, the fouling of trousers, the lack of sleep.

All Quiet on the Western Front showed the brutality of war, but it went further. By saying that the ordinary soldier on one side was equal to those on the other it provided a message of hope. Lew Ayres said: "[it] showed the Germans as having the same values that you and I have . . . just people caught in this thing that's bigger than all of us. . . . *All Quiet on the Western Front* became one of the first voices for universality. . . . [it said] that unity was possible within the world."[1]

This was a point Carl Laemmle wished to stress, because he believed in it and because he felt that it might help offset German concerns about the film. In his cable to Berlin newspapers during the political crisis over the film in late 1930, he said that *All Quiet on the Western Front* "indicts no nation, no individuals, but . . . records an international human experience."[2] In the film, Milestone shows this through the death of Duval and Bäumer's promise, never fulfilled, to apologize.

Few soldiers on the battlefield were close enough to the enemy, except in hand-to-hand combat or as prisoners of war, to see this. Fraternization, where it occurred, was condemned: the rapid ending of the Christmas truce in 1914, when German and British soldiers met in no-man's-land to talk, shake hands, and play football, showed how the High Command of both countries were terrified of their men discovering that the enemy wanted peace. Cinema has shown well what can result from an encounter with a representative of the enemy: in *Paths of Glory*, the tired and bitter soldiers recover their humanity when listening to the German girl sing, even though her song is in German; in *La Grande Illusion* (1937), Jean Renoir showed that it was class and not nationality that bound people together, and that ordinary people in different countries had more in common than they at first thought. But it was the meeting between Bäumer and Duval, where they are forced to stay in no-man's-land for days, the Frenchman fatally wounded and Bäumer pleading for forgiveness, that showed how unnecessary the war was.

Betrayal is another key antiwar theme in the film: the boys are betrayed by their teacher, by their fathers, and by the High Command. These are the old

The horror of war: Paul (Lew Ayres) watches Duval (Raymond Griffith), the man he stabbed, die before his eyes. All Quiet on the Western Front. Courtesy: Photofest

men of the war—those who forced their boys to fight. Bäumer and his friends are sent away by their teacher (their mentor) and by Himmelstoss. Kantorek is too old to fight, but revenge is sweet for the boys when Himmelstoss arrives at the front. Here he is a coward; his brave words and the military songs of the parade ground are irrelevant. Like the others, he is simply there to die, and for him death comes quickly. The boys also get their own back on Kantorek in the book, when he becomes a member of the reserve army and is forced by one of his ex-pupils to do parade duty. In the film the condemnation is more direct when Bäumer returns to the classroom and condemns Kantorek.

The incompetence of the High Command, in a war where military inep-titude was a daily event, was another common theme in the best antiwar cinema. The culmination of this point of view in cinema can be seen in *Paths of Glory*, the true story of three men executed by firing squad to hide the mistakes and arro-gance of senior officers. This point is not so evident in *All Quiet on the Western Front*, though those behind the lines are criticized. Himmelstoss, the mild post-man, is transformed into a sadistic drill sergeant and then found to be a coward at the front; Ginger, the cook, fails to deliver food when the going is rough. Kubrick's film is more direct; perhaps another twenty-five years needed to pass before such bitter thoughts could be put on the screen.

The men endure severe treatment during basic training. All Quiet on the Western Front. Courtesy: Photofest

The only social group absent from the film are the politicians, probably the greatest of all liars, who betrayed the troops the most. *Paths of Glory* illustrated this betrayal graphically (Stanley Kubrick has always been interested in power and the abuse of authority, as he has shown in all his films).[3] *All Quiet on the Western Front* did not show this—the focus of condemnation was elsewhere— although the book did include a visit by the Kaiser to the front, where the soldiers benefit from new uniforms.

Unlike many other war films, there is no romanticism of combat in *All Quiet on the Western Front*. Howard Barnes, in his perceptive review of the film in 1930 in the *New York Herald Tribune*, wrote: "With all preceding war stories brought to the stage or screen . . . there has always been an inevitable glamour attaching to fighting, no matter how carefully avoided. . . . In *All Quiet* there is no glamour. It is courageously bitter."[4] Apart from the start, when the teacher sends them away to fight, little is said about the glory of the fatherland. There are also few women (though, ironically, they were placed center stage in some publicity—even for such a film, Universal saw the value of attractive women). Those who do appear are there to make a telling point: a brief interlude, tastefully done— though not according to censors at the time—of lovemaking in the midst of horror; and Paul's tortured visit back home to see his dying mother. The scene with the French women is particularly important in stressing the point about the futility of international differences. These were classified as enemies, but there is no animosity between them and the men.

Women rarely had opportunities to appear in antiwar films. It was different in the pro-war film in Hollywood. Here, in such films as *Arms and the Girl* (Joseph Kaufman, 1917), *The Little American* (Cecil B. DeMille and Joseph Levering, 1917), *War and the Woman* (Ernest C. Wade, 1917), and *Little Miss Hoover* (John S. Robertson, 1918), women played the daring sister, the exposer of the slacker (particularly if it was a cowardly boyfriend), the brutalized victim, the spy (at home and overseas), and the dutiful wife. The women at home in *All Quiet on the Western Front* are not like this. From the little seen of her, Mrs. Bäumer is worried, sick, and dying. While she might come across as simple, and a little naive, she is clearly concerned, as she knows that death is near for her son. And those at the front—the French women—reject national hostility by sleeping with the soldiers.

The coverage of the themes outlined above—and, just as important, the way in which they were covered—were all important reasons for the film's success. Another reason is more straightforward: the film was good; it was well made, superbly acted, fast moving, dramatic, emotional. In a collaborative effort, all those involved in *All Quiet on the Western Front* made it the great film that it is: Remarque, for the book without which the film would not exist; the Laemmles with their vision; Edeson with his cinematography; the whole screenwriting team for probably the best script of the early sound period; the technical team for choreographing the battlefields of the war; and the actors and actresses, each of whom plays a memorable role, however small. Few films have been as fortunate as *All Quiet on the Western Front* in having such an excellent team.

It was the first film to meet the demands of the sound era, as it succeeded in overcoming the difficulties posed by early sound technology and re-creating the mobility of the silent film camera. The director D. W Griffith said in June 1930: "*All Quiet on the Western Front* is the greatest talkie because it is the most adept combination of the techniques of the old silent films with the new medium of sound and dialogue."[5] More recently, the film historian David Robinson has praised Milestone's work: "He brought all the fluidity of silent films to the camera—which freely tracked and panned and soared over the battlefields of the little German town from which the hero and his schoolboy friends march out to war—and to the editing. At the same time Milestone imaginatively explored the possibilities of sound, from the beginning where the bellicose harangues of the schoolteacher are drowned by the noise of a band outside, to the haunting echoes of the battlefield as the cry of 'Mind the wire' goes down the line."[6]

At the end of *All Quiet on the Western Front* most of the boys are dead; as their ghostly figures march away they look directly at the audience, accusing us of sending them to their death, challenging us not to let this happen again. "To this end you have doomed us," as one reviewer described their thoughts.[7]

The dead, inevitably, featured in many an antiwar film. In *The Road Back* (James Whale, 1937) there is an outstanding shot where the company lines up and the few remaining soldiers are joined by the specters of their comrades. And in Abel Gance's *J'accuse* (1919) the dead actually rise up, pleading for justification for their deaths. If the dead could rise they would constitute an army of the betrayed and brutalized carrying an indictment so strong that none could question it. Those who survived were forgotten—for a time. There were no homes fit for heroes, and jobs were scarce for veterans in the Great Depression. Antiwar cinema covered the forgotten man creatively: in the musical (the song "My Forgotten Man" from *Gold Diggers of 1933* [Mervyn LeRoy, 1933]) and the gangster movie—*I Am a Fugitive from a Chain Gang* (Mervyn LeRoy, 1932), *They Gave Him a Gun* (W. S. Van Dyke, 1937), and *The Roaring Twenties* (Raoul Walsh, 1939)—which took the antiwar message to new audiences. Remarque's books *The Road Back* and *Three Comrades* covered postwar Germany, where the returning soldiers were, in many ways, forgotten men.

The world has remembered, though—and in many ways: the annual Armistice Day commemoration; the creation of war memorials that dot villages, towns, and cities in most combatant countries; and the creation of the tomb of the Unknown Soldier. This is an issue covered wonderfully in Bertrand Tavernier's *La Vie et Rien d'Autre* (Life and Nothing But) (1989), when the lead is told to find a corpse for burial in the Arc de Triomphe. He has to make sure that the corpse is French, and not British or a Hun. The real memorials for most, though, lie in unmarked graves in the trenches and in no-man's-land, where soldiers died.

In the end it comes down to the fact that the outcome of World War I was not victory or glory: it was slaughter and waste. This is the view of the war today, for which *All Quiet on the Western Front* is partly responsible. Did it work? Jean Renoir said that ultimately all the antiwar films about the Great War failed, as a second World War followed (he said it cynically—World War II was a very different war).[8] But they were important then and they remain important today. At a time when warfare and genocide have reemerged, at the end of this most violent of centuries, there is a continuing need to remember and to warn. In the absence of the personal witness, as most veterans are now dead, the arts provide this service. And as the most popular of the arts, the cinema reaches the widest audience. Out of the thousands of films made about the war, only a few can be described as classics. *All Quiet on the Western Front* is the most important of them all. It comes down through the years with an ever-timely message: where cinema exists, this most disastrous of wars, this appalling waste of a nation's youth, will never be forgotten. It is a memorial—and an ever-present warning—as fitting and honorable as any that grace a village, town, or city.

NOTES

1. J. L. Yeck, "An Interview with Lew Ayres," in *Magills Cinema Annual 1986* (Pasadena: Salem, 1986), 13.

2. C. Laemmle quoted in *Exhibitors' World Herald*, 13 December 1930, 25, and cited in J. Simmons, "Film and International Politics: The Banning of *All Quiet on the Western Front* in Germany and Austria 1930–1931," *Historian* 52 (1989): 47.

3. See J. Baxter, *Stanley Kubrick: A Biography* (London: HarperCollins, 1997).

4. See H. Barnes in *Herald Tribune,* quoted in "War Without Glamour on the Film," *Literary Digest,* 105, 17 May 1930, 20.

5. D. W. Griffith, *Los Angeles Evening Herald,* 3 June 1930.

6. D. Robinson, in *Movies of the Thirties,* ed. A. Lloyd (London: Orbis, 1985).

7. Anonymous reviewer in "War Without Glamour on the Film," 20.

8. See Renoir's comments in R. Hughes, *Film: Book 2—Films of Peace and War* (New York: Grove, 1962), 183: "In 1936 I made a picture named *La Grande Illusion* in which I tried to express all my deep feelings for the cause of peace. This film was very successful. Three years later the war broke out. That is the only answer I can find to your very interesting enquiry."

Jeanine Basinger

The World War II Combat Film: Definition

Critics of the day, who almost unanimously gave *Bataan* (Tay Garnett, 1943) favorable reviews, referred to the film's "gritty realism." It is interesting to see a film like this, filmed entirely inside a studio on sets, referred to as "realistic." The production work is superb in the Metro-Goldwyn-Mayer tradition, yet the use of matte shots and rear projection was obvious even in 1943. Above all, the artificial, expressionistic use of swirling fogs and mists coupled with the almost magical onslaught of the Japanese crawling on their bellies toward their own proscribed enemy gives the film its eerie power. In its own way, *Bataan* is realistic. Its anger, determination, and passion for the fight are very real. It is as if that passion were sealed in the film cans, and to open them is to feel some of what Americans felt at the humiliating defeat of Bataan. This is to suggest not that we feel good about the propaganda *Bataan* contains, or that we believe that propaganda now, or subscribe to it in anyway—but only that we can clearly see and feel what it was at the time. *Bataan* is sure of its task as a film. Everything that the cinema has to offer—lighting, cutting, composition—is placed in service of the main message of propaganda. *Bataan* does not seek to make subtle meaning out of the tools of cinema. It puts them at the service of its message and story. Thus, *Bataan* is indeed an effective work of propaganda, of storytelling, and, as history has proved, of genre. It told a story we would want to hear again and again. It influenced and affected the way the story of World War II combat would be told in the future. *Bataan* has commitment. It is the definition, clarified, focused, and presented with passion.

Bataan is the story of a group of hastily assembled volunteers who, through their bravery and tenacity, hold off an overwhelmingly large group of the enemy long enough to buy important time for the American forces. The raw emotional power of the combat, along with the intense presentation of sacrifice, makes the film a disturbing one. Its format is the hold-the-fort variation of the basic story pattern as opposed to the take-the-objective roving format of such films as *Objective Burma!* (Raoul Walsh, 1945).

Thirteen men are trapped in a situation. They come from different parts of the United States, and from different branches of the service. They are differ-

The men of Bataan *"represent the American melting pot."* Bataan. Courtesy: Photofest

ent in age, background, experience, attitude, and willingness to fight. "They're a mixed group," says the captain. "They've never served together before." In establishing such a collection of misfits (who will be assembled into a coherent fighting group), the film confirms and makes specific the foundation of the combat patrols to follow. These men obviously represent the American melting pot, but the representation is not a simple-minded one. Our strength is our weakness and vice versa. We are a mongrel nation—ragtail, unprepared, disorganized, quarrelsome among ourselves, and with separate special interests, raised, as we are, to believe in the individual, not the group. At the same time, we bring different skills and abilities together for the common good, and from these separate needs and backgrounds we bring a feisty determination. No one leads us who is not strong, and our individualism is not set aside for any small cause. Once it is set aside, however, our group power is extreme.

The group consists of:

1. Sergeant Bill Dane (Robert Taylor). An infantry career man, who has been in the Philippines two years.
2. Captain Lassiter (Lee Bowman). A West Point Cavalry man, who has been in the Philippines four months.
3. Leonard Purckett (Robert Walker). A Navy band musician who used to be an usher in a moviehouse.

4. Ramirez (Desi Arnaz). A private from the 192d Tank Corps. A Californian. Was part of the National Guard.
5. Jake Feingold (Thomas Mitchell). A corporal from the Fourth Chemical Corps.
6. "Barney Todd" (which turns out to be a pseudonym) (Lloyd Nolan). From the Provisional Signal Battalion. Enlisted 5 February 1941 and volunteered for the Philippines on 11 November 1941. Corporal. (His real name is Dan Burns.)
7. Yankee Salazar (J. Alex Havier). A Filipino scout. Former boxing champion.
8. Steve Bentley (George Murphy). An Air Force lieutenant.
9. F. X. Matowski (Barry Nelson). Engineer. From Pittsburgh.
10. Sam Malloy (Tom Dugan). Motor Transport Service. Acts as group's cook. Private.
11. Gilbert Hardy (Phillip Terry). Fourth Medical Battalion private. A conscientious objector who enlisted as a medical aide. Carries no arms.
12. Corporal Katigbak (Roque Espiritu). A Filipino Air Force man. Mechanic.
13. Wesley Epps (Kenneth Spencer). Was studying to be a minister before the war broke out. Third engineer. A demolition expert.

They are, respectively, WASP, WASP, WASP, Mexican, Jew, WASP, Filipino, WASP, Pole, Irish, WASP, Filipino, black. The two Filipinos are subdivided into Philippine primitive (Salazar, the scout, a former champion boxer, who plays the role an Indian would play as scout for a cavalry group) and Philippine nonprimitive (an Air Force mechanic). The WASPs are subdivided into an elite, West Point man (Lassiter), an innocent farm boy (Purckett), an unidentified "gangster" (Todd), a natural, graceful leader of democratic tendencies (Bentley), and a noncombatant (Hardy). They are from everywhere: West Point, Midwest, California, New York, Pittsburgh, the South, and nowhere. They are geographically mixed, as they are racially and intellectually. For purposes of narrative development, each of these men plays a traditional role that defines the internal structure of the combat story.

The Dead Father Figure (Lee Bowman). The officer who originally rounds up the group of volunteers for an important mission is the official ranking officer, and thus the leader or father figure of the group even if, as in this case, he is a young man. As the film opens, he has just secretly wed a young nurse from Kansas, and he is seen saying goodbye to her in a restrained manner. Lassiter represents a kind of American nobility, having gone to West Point (class of 1940). In his brief scenes in the film, he has a generous bearing, intelligence, and grace. His correct sense of things is demonstrated when he tells Robert Taylor, the true and natural leader and the man with the most experience in the group, to "just tell me when I make an error." He also tells Taylor to give orders directly if needed, and not to waste time getting his permission.

The first thing that happens to the group is that this man, their leader and "father" figure, the best educated among them, is suddenly, unexpectedly, and, without much being made of it, killed. "We'll stay as long as we can stand up," says Lassiter, just before he dies. His words are the meaning of the film, but he dies saying them. This becomes a basic unit of the combat genre. The metaphoric meaning is obvious. In war, one will lose security, home, and comfort. A sacrifice will be made, and this initial loss in the story line depicts this for the viewing audience in narrative terms.

The Hero (Robert Taylor). Taylor plays the role of the natural leader, the professional soldier who has already seen two wars. He is a slightly tarnished version of the classic romantic hero, a man of experience and intuition. He is so capable that he "would have been an officer" except that he "trusted a man" who went AWOL from him during his time as a military policeman. As a result of this betrayal, he lost his chance for a commission. However, because of his having been tested and found wanting, this character has learned that the world is not an easy place. He has proved his ability to withstand the hardships that lie ahead, because he has withstood those from his past. Not only is he personally ready for trouble, but he can guide others through difficulties. This man will be the last to die. In fact, the audience does not see him die. Instead, we see the film end in a blur, with Taylor bravely, defiantly continuing to machine-gun the oncoming hordes of the enemy in an image reminiscent of gangster films.

The Hero's Adversary (Lloyd Nolan). This man is the group cynic, an important stand-in for audience doubts and for its unwillingness to face the hardships the war will bring. Such a character becomes an appropriate initiation figure into the change of attitude that will be required for the task at hand. He can voice dismay, disapproval, disgust—anything negative—and siphon off audience ill will. He can *be* unpatriotic. He becomes the foil against which the issues of the film are played. In the plot line of *Bataan,* this character is operating under a false name. He is, in fact, the man Taylor, the hero, once trusted. Thus, they appear in the film operating under a plot conflict from their pasts. It is significant how genre, from the beginning, indicates other films, other stories. Their story might easily be a military service film from the 1930s. The structural device of having a hero and an adversary carrying forward a conflict acts on audience unawareness as a sort of updating of the old familiar service film/training film plots. All that's over now. We must win the war. In this way, one old genre (or formula) is used to help the audience locate itself in the new. There is also the hint that Nolan is that American tradition, the outlaw hero, as he is almost a gangster type.

The Noble Sacrifice (George Murphy). Murphy's character is a brave and good man, who is the most likable and understanding of all the men. He is an officer in the Air Force who, when the official group leader dies, does not take over command but defers instead to Taylor's natural leadership. This man, mortally wounded, elects to die for the group by flying his plane out and crashing it into the bridge between them and the Japanese, to destroy it and buy time. (Note the similarity to the ending of *Flying Tigers* [David Miller, 1942].) Murphy is a WASP type, and thus represents the price white middle-class America will pay in the war.

The Old Man/The Youth (Thomas Mitchell/Robert Walker). The war film inevitably portrayed an older man in the midst of combat, usually one who fought in World War I (the sobriety of such a thought made its own point) and whose feet hurt (as this one's do). The old man character of this group, played by Thomas Mitchell, is Jewish, and a chemical engineer. He is also a kind of comedy relief, and a semi-parental figure to balance the one lost by the death of the original leader. The young man, Robert Walker, represents initiation into battle and the question of bravery/cowardice, as in the novel *The Red Badge of Courage*. Walker's young man is innocent, dreamy, a former movie usher who entered the Navy as a musician. When his ship was shot out from under him, he swam ashore, and joined up with this motley group. Walker's character is naive, but not unwilling or incapable. He talks of his former life ("reminds me of when I was a cowpoke!" or "did I tell you about when I was a cab driver?"), but it is clear it is a life that not only never existed, but under the circumstances, never will. It is the remembered life of the movie usher, a series of filmed touchstones from a Walter Mitty-like youth. Walker plays this character brilliantly, and the poignancy is all the more painful for its comedy. The youth character represents the best of the group, which is to be totally wasted and which, if it would only be allowed to grow and develop, would make us a better nation. The old man, on the other hand, is what we are. We've been through this, and our feet hurt. The contrast of youth and age is both shattering and uplifting for the audience. It shatters us to lose the youth, but on the other hand, maybe we'll live through it, like the old man. (In *Bataan*, of course, everybody dies.)

The Immigrant Representative (Barry Nelson). Nelson plays the man with the unpronounceable name, F. X. Matowski. Such a character (and such characters are almost always Polish) overtly reminds everyone of the melting pot tradition. This man, who is from Pittsburgh (the steel mills?), dreams of his mom's lima bean soup "made with vinegar." (This is a candidate for one of filmdom's worst recipes.)

The Comedy Relief (Tom Dugan). Both the old man and the young man character provide comedy relief. A film of such grim nature requires more than one porter knocking at its door! In this film, the official comedy relief is the cook, played by Tom Dugan, and frequently thereafter, the comedy relief *is* the cook.[1] The man in war who is there to do unwarlike (and thus unmanly) things is a suitable subject for comedy.

The Peace Lover (Phillip Terry). In this film, the man who speaks of peace is an actual noncombatant, a figure seldom seen in the early World War II combat films, for obvious reasons.

The Minority Representative (Desi Arnaz, Kenneth Spencer, J. Alex Havier, Roque Espiritu). A Mexican from California (Ramirez), a jitterbug who loves jive music; Filipinos (Salazar, Katigbak) who are not American citizens; and a black man (Epps) who sings, prays, and delivers himself of such folksy insights as, "You can promise your mind, but you gotta deliver something to your stomach."

Bataan opens with credits that appear against a map of the Philippine Islands. BATAAN! screams the title, jumping out of the frame and coming at the viewer in all its implied horror, defeat, and sacrifice. For the audiences of the day, the word practically dripped American blood and shame. Its impact was directly emotional, linked as it was to a current event that no one in the audience could be unaware of. Seen today, the impact is visual, and it becomes emotional by extension.

The objective of the above mentioned volunteers will be to demolish a bridge and prevent a Japanese breakthrough at all costs. In so doing, they will buy time for MacArthur so the war in the Philippines won't be "over too soon." The film's printed dedication said it all: "When Japan struck our desperate need was time—time to marshal new armies. Ninety-six priceless days were bought for us— with their lives—by the defenders of Bataan, the Philippine Army which formed the bulk of MacArthur's infantry fighting shoulder to shoulder with the Americans. To those immortal dead, who heroically stayed the wave of barbaric conquest, this picture is reverently dedicated."

The Japanese flag being raised is the opening image, and then we are plunged into Manila. In the chaos of war, women and children and soldiers are mixed in a mass of evacuees. This first sequence speaks to us of the horror of World War II—it will be a war waged as much on women and children as on soldiers.

As the band of volunteers is assembled, they are told to join the Twenty-sixth Cavalry for their special detail. The cavalry, a film metaphor of heroism and dashing bravery, is a familiar military group for viewers. They fought the barbaric Indians, as this group will fight the barbaric Japanese. ("Those no tail baboons," says Taylor, "they're no. I skillful. They can live and fight for a month on what wouldn't last you guys two days.") In fighting the "no tail baboons" (also referred to as "yellow skinned, slanty-eyed devils"), the thirteen men will lose their lives. The order in which they die, as well as the methods by which they die, are significant to later narrative structures. After the loss of the leader, the minorities die first, and then the weak and the mentally sensitive. Later genre stages will create new meanings by varying this structure.

The order of death is as follows:

1. The father figure, the captain, as discussed earlier. He is shot in the head as he walks away after giving his volunteers their orders. It is sudden, swift. (The first death must always be a significant one.)
2. The Pole from Pittsburgh. Immediately after the nostalgic conversation about his mother's soup, he climbs a tall tree and is shot by snipers. This is one of the film's most memorable moments, and it is practically axiomatic from then on that he-who-climbs-tree-in-war-film dies. (A further implication is included in the juxtaposition of the climb and the home front conversation. Sink into the past, the film seems to say, and lose your life. No time for warmth and nostalgia here. Keep your mind on war.)
3. The Filipino Air Force man. A mechanic, he is last seen walking back to their camp to get the carburetor repaired. He dies offscreen. He is found in a

swirling, deadly mist, a samurai sword sticking out of his dead body, its ornate top visible in the fog. (This is a horror film image, and a horrible death becomes traditional for minority figures who act as fodder for the film's narrative.)

4. When Japanese planes fly over and bomb their camp, the cook, in a fit of personal rage, picks up a machine gun and brings down one of the planes. Immediately after his joyous triumph, he himself is mowed down. (You can't feel pride and joy in the work of killing. When you take a moment to act as a selfish and prideful individual, they'll get you.)

5. The other Filipino, the former boxer and present scout, strips down to native wear and sets out through the jungle. His body is later seen hanging across the ravine, stripped and barbarically killed. (This man's obvious stripping down to his primitive self invited such a death, and linked the viewing audience to the film tradition of cowboys and Indians.)

6. The Mexican jazz lover, Desi Arnaz, dies of malaria. "He's jitter-buggin' himself to death," observes the black man, as Arnaz shakes and sweats.

7. George Murphy, dying of wounds, crashes his plane into the bridge, making a noble sacrifice.

8. The noncombatant from the medical corps goes mad and runs toward the Japanese, throwing grenades. (His ultimate acceptance of the need for combat is an obvious lesson, with its underlying implication that he was a noncombatant because he just couldn't take it, as his madness overwhelms him.)

9–13. The final section of the film is reserved for a powerful presentation of the ultimate total combat these remaining five men are subjected to. The black man dies first, then the Jewish old man, then the youth, then the hero's adversary, and finally, of course, the hero.

In this thunderous finale of combat, all five men demonstrate incredible bravery, skill, and heroism. They fight fiercely, running up out of their foxholes and charging the enemy in hand-to-hand combat that includes any method of dirty fighting they can manage—throwing dirt in Japanese faces, tripping them, cheating, and both garroting the enemy and beating their dead bodies with rifles after the garroting. They shoot already fallen bodies to be safe, and ruthlessly use a corpse as a decoy. It is not a prettied-up barroom brawl, and the enemy does not lie down and die easily.

In a horrible clash of cultures, the black man runs forward from frame right toward a Japanese soldier, who runs with equal speed toward him, on a diagonal from the left. The black man strikes this oncoming soldier with his rifle, and bayonets him after he falls. As he accomplishes this, a second Japanese soldier runs in full speed from frame right, the upper-right-hand corner, and swings a sword (and/or bayonet—repeated viewings still cannot separate the distinction in the blur), hitting the black man solidly in the back of the neck. The victim's face is seen to respond, contracted in horror, with a scream frozen on his mouth. The blade enters halfway through his neck. Although we do not actually see the head fall, or blood spurt out, this is one of the most graphic and violent killings of the pre-1960s period of film history. Involving us as it does in the swift action, the effect, even today, is breathtaking. This death finishes out the bad news for the minority figures in the film—for them are reserved the most brutish deaths.

A brief respite occurs. The surviving men, Thomas Mitchell, Lloyd Nolan, Robert Taylor, and Robert Walker, gather together. Mitchell walks into their area of shelter, enters his foxhole, sits down, and dies. In this aftermath of battle, the final conversations about why we are fighting occur. The peace and sustaining nature of this interlude is destroyed when they hear on their radio the words, "America! You are beaten." "You stink!" cries out Walker, standing up and demonstrating the famous edict, never stand up in a foxhole. He is shot and dies.

This leaves only the hero and his adversary, Taylor and Nolan. "It's you and me now, Sarge," says Nolan, and "We've been headin' for that for a long time," Taylor replies. Nolan is stabbed in the back by a supposedly dead Japanese body, leaving Taylor alone, standing in the grave he has knowingly dug for himself. "Come on, you suckers. Come and get me." He dies alone, firing his weapon and laughing. "Didn't think we were still here? We'll always be here."

The film's propaganda values are prominently displayed. Not only are the Japanese referred to with insulting epithets, but screen time is devoted to discussions about why we are fighting. When, just before the film's ending, Walker asks Taylor, "Can I write a letter?" the ensuing oral dictation of what he wants to say, put in the form of a letter to his mother ("Dear mum," he begins), is the vocalizing of the youth's fears. "There were thirteen of us, and now there are only three. Maybe there won't be any of us ever to get out of here alive . . ." When he breaks and cries, Taylor takes over, finishing the thought by adding purpose to it: "Maybe it don't seem to do a lot of good, for men to get killed in some place you never heard of, but we figure . . . the men who died here may have done more than we'll ever know . . . to save the world ["He died a long way from home," said the black man in an earlier scene, as he prayed over a grave] . . . it don't matter where a man dies as long as he dies for freedom." A voice-over speaks: "So fought the heroes of Bataan. Their sacrifice made possible our own victories in the Coral and Bismarck Seas, Midway, New Guinea and Guadalcanal. Their spirit will lead us back to Bataan!" (A film called *Back to Bataan* [Edward Dmytryk, 1945] was in the works, albeit made by another studio.)

The Japanese of *Bataan* are an almost invincible force. Not only are there seemingly zillions of them (they keep coming and coming in endless waves of undervalued humanity), but they also have planes, tanks, trucks, ammunition aplenty, searchlights, and everything it takes to make modern war. They are both totally sophisticated with their mechanical skill and up-to-date equipment, and totally primitive, with their barbaric methods of killing. It is significant that when the Filipino scout sets out to go through their territory, he strips down to native dress, a symbolic acceptance of the attitudes he must have to deal with them in what has become their territory. "Get civilized again," Taylor orders the scout, but he slips away into the ravine before this can happen. Taylor constantly warns his men about the strength and cunning of the enemy. He must not be underestimated. At the same time, he speaks of the Japanese in the most brutally racist terms.

The Japanese are seen as an impersonal, faceless enemy. They are a mindless group, as opposed to our collection of strongly delineated individuals. Walker, the beardless youth, wants to prove his worth by killing one of the enemy. "If I could only get ONE Jap for myself," he says over and over. His Jap, the one he bayonets, is the one exception to the facelessness of the players who represent the Japanese army in the film. When Walker hesitates before bayoneting a man on the ground, he is himself tricked, tripped, and thrown. Walker, with skill and cunning, recovers himself and *does* kill this treacherous enemy. It is not only *his* Jap, the one he longed for during the film, but it is also *ours*. His is the only one we see in the film with a real face.

After the volunteers establish their camp on a high shelf of rock, from which they will make their last stand, they undergo periods of night and day, rest and work, combat and noncombat. From time to time, there is mist around them, presumably rising from the heat and humidity of the jungle and the river across which their objective, the bridge, stretches. This eerie white mist provides a sense of danger, coming as it does from images in horror films. It also provides a sense of the mist of myth and of history. The dead die and fall into the mist, tumbling away into legend. It surrounds their graves. Their situation is one of a symbolic act—a few men sacrificing their lives for the many. The misty look does much to enhance their historic importance.

The realities of war were seen and absorbed by viewers: the iconography of the military—guns, helmets, uniforms, quinine tablets, K-rations, planes, radios, and the like. The practicality that is required is spelled out. You don't play taps when a buddy dies, because it alerts the Japanese as to how many of you are dying. And you don't leave his helmet to mark his grave if someone needs to wear it to keep his own head from being blown off. All the action helps both to entertain and to educate the audience.

In summary and in retrospect, it may be said that with the release of *Bataan*, the foundation of the World War II combat film is in place. Using *Bataan* for guidance, these are its generic requirements:

- The group as a democratic ethnic mix, in this case a motley group of volunteers from several service branches who really have no other choice (the basic immigrant identification).
- A hero who is part of the group, but is forced to separate himself from it because of the demands of leadership.
- The objective (hold the bridge, delay the Japanese).
- The internal group conflicts (Nolan versus Taylor, and the need for the men to accept Taylor's hard-nosed ways in combat).

- The faceless enemy (with the one exception).
- The absence of women (after opening scenes).
- The need to remember and discuss home, and the dangers involved in doing so.
- The typical war iconography and narrative patterns of conflicting and opposite natures.
- The journeying or staying nature of the genre: in a last stand, they win or lose; in a journey, they also win or lose.
- Propaganda, the discussion of why we fight and how justified it is.
- The events combatants can enact in their restricted state: writing and receiving letters, cooking and eating meals, exploring territory, talking and listening, hearing and discussing news, questioning values, fighting and resting, sleeping, joking.
- The attitudes that an audience should take to the war are taught through events, conversations, and actions.
- The tools of the cinema are employed to manipulate viewers into various emotional, cultural, and intellectual attitudes, and to help achieve all the other goals.
- Information the audience already has in terms of prior films, stories, newsreels, magazines, comic books, experience, and the like is put to use, as when images associated with horror films surround the death of Espiritu and engulf the five final survivors.
- A location in time, place, and military service is established, aided by, maps, military advisors, and official dedications.
- Death.

All these items are clearly repeated in the films that followed rapidly after *Bataan*.

In film history, *Bataan* is rather like *Citizen Kane* (Orson Welles, 1941). It wasn't that audiences had not seen *Kane*'s devices before: deep focus photography, out-of-sequence narrative, and low ceilings had appeared in Hollywood cinema before. But *Kane* fused them together in one film, and told a powerful story by using all of them to one purpose. *Bataan* is not the work of art that *Citizen Kane* is, but what *Kane* did for form and narrative, *Bataan* does for the history of the combat genre. It does not *invent* the genre. It puts the plot devices together, weds them to a real historical event, and makes an audience deal with them as a unified story presentation—deal with them, *and* remember them.

1943 after *Bataan*

After *Bataan*, the other 1943 combat films that were released were *Destroyer* (William A. Seiter, 2 September), *So Proudly We Hail* (Mark Sandrich, 10 September),

Corvette K-225 (Richard Rosson, 21 October), and three dramatic November releases, *Sahara* (Zoltan Korda, 12 November), *Guadalcanal Diary* (Lewis Seiler, 18 November), and *Cry Havoc* (Richard Thorpe, 24 November). The year ended with the release of *Destination Tokyo* (Delmer Daves), reviewed in the *Times* on New Year's Day of 1944. With these titles, the genre of World War II combat was firmly established and repeated, solidifying the characteristics and attitudes that constitute its core.

Tables 1 and 2 (see end of essay) are comparison tables that contrast *Bataan, Sahara, Guadalcanal Diary, Destination Tokyo,* and *Air Force* (Howard Hawks, 1943) in terms of recurring characteristics. The similarities are striking despite the obvious differences of setting, military force, and enemies faced. The tables could easily have included *Destroyer* and *Corvette K-225*, two minor films that also fit the definition. *So Proudly We Hail* and *Cry Havoc* also follow the *Bataan* format, but they concern themselves with women in war.

In closely observing *Sahara* (desert tank warfare against the Germans and Italians), *Guadalcanal Diary* (jungle war against the Japanese), and *Destination Tokyo* (undersea war against the Japanese) one can see how the basic definition has no difficulty remaining constant whether on land or sea, in dry or wet climate, based on a real event or an imaginary one, against Germany or Japan.

The flexibility of genre, which is seldom discussed, is well demonstrated by these films. As the tables indicate, all four films are the same, yet different enough to please filmgoers. If these films were *exactly* the same, no doubt moviegoers would have turned away. They are instead enough the same to serve emotional needs, match audience expectations, relate to common perceptions about war (and war movies), and yet provide enough variation and singularity to attract new audiences.

Each film maintains an area of uniqueness. *Destination Tokyo* was the first big-budget submarine movie of World War II combat, and it became a famous and fondly remembered film. It lives in people's memories partly because it clearly establishes the dramatic world of the combat submarine. It shows people how men lived in subs and made war. It shows how a submarine works, how it dives, how its machinery functions, and how it defends itself from attack from above as well as from the inevitable crushing danger of the ocean. It presents in detail the harrowing life aboard a tiny sub under combat conditions. The challenge of limited space to be explored by the camera, coupled with the various possibilities for dramatic action—both above and below the sea—make it a natural for the film medium.

In addition to the explicit presentation of the unique submarine world *Destination Tokyo* dramatizes and emphasizes a special element of its own—that of the concept of family. The crew is the traditional representative group of mixed types, but it is also presented as a family. As the sub sets out on its secret voyage, the men sing Christmas carols and exchange gifts and greetings (while Alan Hale, playing the comic cook, dresses up like Santa Claus) and their enclosed world, separate from the one they left behind, is clearly established. These men have a

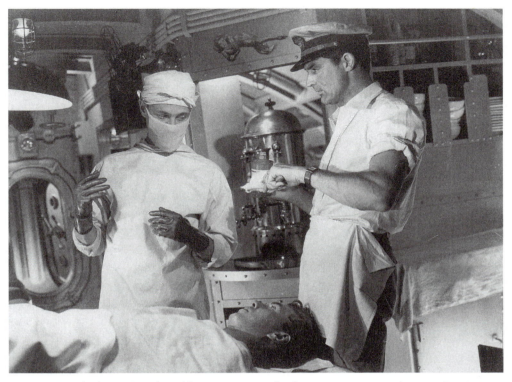

Captain Cassidy (Cary Grant) and his men prepare for the emergency appendectomy. Destination Tokyo. Courtesy: Larry Edmunds Bookshop

kitchen, bedrooms, places to relax and talk. They have a cook who acts as a mother to them, and they have each other. Theirs is the world of combat, but it's a family world. When appendicitis strikes a crew member and there is no doctor on board, the family gathers around. Using American ingenuity, they make the necessary instruments: the cook's knives are ground into scalpels; a tea strainer is used to administer an anesthetic; the cook tells the sick man that, when he comes out of it, he can have anything he wants to eat. "Start cooking a pumpkin pie" is the response. As the operation takes place, one man reads aloud the instructions from the anatomy book and the doctor's manual, to help guide the pharmacist's mate who performs the surgery. The victim (how else can we view him?) recites Psalm 23 as he goes under, and it apparently helps. He survives. Supported by friends and his surrogate family, he *can* survive, a wartime lesson for viewers.

As the sub moves toward Japan, the movie virtually turns into submerged soap opera. The men chat, eat, have coffee together at the kitchen table, listen to the radio, exchange philosophies. Alan Hale gets a haircut. They discuss life after death, and religion. "Pills," their pharmacist's mate, believes in only what he can see, he says. (He'll have plenty of time to find God in his foxhole later, when he has to take out the appendix.) John Garfield tells an anecdote about a girl he tried to pick up and Cary Grant thinks of his son's first haircut. These last two episodes are seen in flashback. The difference between these flashbacks and those in *Immortal Sergeant* (John Stahl, 1943) is the difference in the acceptance of the war. In *Immortal Sergeant*, the flashbacks are themselves a miniature movie, a unified collection of scenes which, if removed from the film and spliced together, would make a traditional romantic comedy. They exist separate and whole, and tell a story the audience waits to have finished. They recur more frequently as the film moves forward. They actually explain the combat portion of the film to us, in that we know the hero must learn to have enough courage to court the girl or he will lose her to the smooth other man. Will he find his courage, asks the film? Combat capability is linked to home, to sex, and to romance. In *Destination Tokyo*, the tiny, fragmented flashbacks are brief, and disappear as the film progresses. They tell us a little bit about the men. That's all. They do not form a complete story on their own.

After leaving the Aleutians, the sub enters maximum danger and the combat begins. The basic units of the submarine film are established: planes attack them up top; an unexploded bomb drops and becomes wedged on the aft deck, followed by a slow and intense sequence of defusing the bomb to save the sub; a burial at sea takes place; they go through nets into the Japanese harbor and sit on the bottom of sea; they hear Tokyo Rose on the radio; a group must go ashore on a mission; the appendicitis attacks; they attack ships with torpedoes; they undergo a destroyer attack with depth charges; they have to sit on the bottom again for a long period of time. These units of story appear over and over again in later submarine films. They represent the need to work against time (defusing the bomb, or emergency diving when someone is still up top); the constant threat of death; the need for patience during long periods of intense helplessness; and the primary importance of working well together.

Although they are indigenous to the submarine film, and dependent on the submarine setting, they are not really different from the basic units of *Bataan*. For instance, in *Bataan* a burial takes place in the ground, instead of at sea. There is malaria instead of appendicitis. The men in *Bataan* have to sit and wait for the Japanese to attack, knowing they will come, as the men in the sub await the depth charges. Both listen to Japanese propaganda on the radio; both work against time; both must repair equipment to survive; both must cook and eat; both must be patient and learn to work well together. The group going ashore on a mission is like the scout who goes out for help in *Bataan*. Precious group members die, and there is the constant threat of death. Combat is different if you are inside a submarine, and so are uniforms, battle conditions, and physical settings. However, key elements are the same. The group, with its leader, must work together setting aside differences to withstand danger. The men share fear, but exhibit grace under pressure. The ideas of why we are fighting the war are discussed, and heavy propaganda is established as to the cruelty and treachery of the enemy, as well as to its intelligence and its worthiness as adversary.

At the beginning of *Destination Tokyo*, Cary Grant speaks to his men as the sub leaves home. The audience sees all the men, meeting them fully for the first time. As the film ends, we see the sub sail back in under the Golden Gate, and each man says what he most wants: "Cold cider back on the farm," "Dinah Shore records," "Green vegetables," "Girls," "Someone else to cook." Order is restored. Watching this triumphant return, with the group intact despite its tragic loss of "Pop," its official father figure who has died in combat, one may feel that *Destination Tokyo* is the family that succeeds because its crew knows how to cohere into a group, how to become a family, whereas *Bataan*'s did not have enough time together to do more than try. Both films say we must fight unto death, and by never giving up we will win. Both tell us that some have to die to win this war. The audience has learned about death and sacrifice, but also about the possibility of endurance and victory.

Sahara and *Guadalcanal Diary* also demonstrate both the maintenance of the basic definition and subtle variations that mark its flexibility. The most interesting comparison between *Bataan* and *Sahara* is in their two groups of thirteen men from representative backgrounds, in *Sahara*'s case a miniature UN, instead of the more common mix of Americans:

1. The tank man hero, Humphrey Bogart, American, former cavalry man, a pro.
2. The American radio man from the tank, Dan Duryea.
3. The tank's American machine gunner from Waco, Texas, Bruce Bennett.
4. A British medic.
5. A Frenchman.
6. A cynical Britisher who has corns and aching feet.
7. Lloyd Bridges, young and naïve, who carries a photo of his girl and shows it to everyone. (With British troops, his accent is Australian.)
8. A black man, a British Sudanese, from the Fourth Sudanese Battalion, who knows the territory—the location of wells and depth of the sand (the Indian scout character).
9. An Italian, whom the Sudanese has taken prisoner and who speaks English— his wife has cousins in America.
10. An Australian.
11. A captured German pilot.
12. A South African originally from Dublin.
13. A Britisher from Sussex.

Where *Sahara* differs from *Bataan* is that it presents a "last stand" that ends successfully. The international group—that is, the two left alive—effect a surrender from hundreds of German troops. (This is a variation of the real-life story of World War I hero, Sergeant York.)

The credits of *Sahara* indicate that it is based on a Soviet novel, *The Thirteen*. Like *Bataan*, however, its plot is very similar to that of *The Lost Patrol* (John

Ford, 1936). The desert setting is the same, and the slow elimination of the group by the enemy fits well with the John Ford film. It is a somewhat more optimistic presentation in that, although only two survive, they have captured what appears to be the entire German Army. Neither *Bataan* nor *Sahara* officially credits the original author of *Lost Patrol*. Neither is officially classified as a remake. Yet the similarities are striking. The *New York Times* review said *Sahara* was "in a class with that memorable picture which it plainly resembles, *The Lost Patrol.*"

In terms of location of combat and general setting, *Guadalcanal Diary* is the most like *Bataan* of these late-1943 films. It is based on the best-selling book of the same name by Richard Tregaskis. Its credits acknowledge its "grateful" appreciation to the military forces that helped make the film. Its title is seen as the cover of the book, and after the cover is lifted, the credits appear as pages in that book. We read about "a new chapter in the history of America by the correspondent who landed on Guadalcanal with the first detachment of U.S. Marines." Then we see drawings of the stars of the film, with their characters' names and ranks underneath their images. After the rest of the credits, the film opens on a troop transport ship in the South Pacific, headed for combat. "Today, Sunday, July 26, 1942," says a narrator, and we are plunged into a filmed re-creation of Tregaskis's diary-like book, a motif that will recur all through the film.

Guadalcanal Diary, like the book, captures a sense of the democratic amalgamation of people going off to fight. It is perhaps the first really conscious mythologizing of the fighting men, characters who are brave, jaunty, funny, and who sing. Oh, boy, do they sing! "Rock of Ages," "Genevieve, Sweet Genevieve," "Bless 'Em All," and many more. It's the combat film Hit Parade.

The opening sequence on board the troop ship introduces the film's group, and acquaints viewers with who and what they are through their conversation. As the action of the film unfolds, it is carefully linked to the reality of the actual event through the device of announcing the dates: "Friday, August 7, 1942." The film seems to work from the assumption that the audience would already know the basic story, from newsreels and newspaper accounts.

A mythology of the men who fight the war for America is beginning to take hold. Here are events we already recognize: mail call, conversations about future plans, talk of women back home, burials, and prayers. Here are the kinds of characters we appreciate as "typically" American: William Bendix from Brooklyn (Bendix qualifies as an icon of the World War II movie, combat or otherwise) and the brave minority figure, Anthony Quinn, as a Mexican. Here is the attitude of humor and resignation, the acceptance of the burden the enemy has laid on us. This represents, says the myth, the American pioneer spirit, the ability to go to a strange land and take hold of it. We show our American character through griping and complaining, but also through singing and praying. We talk bad, but we're really swell!

One sees this mythologizing in the usage of film references. A man wets the end of his rifle with his thumb, as audiences had seen Gary Cooper do in

The soldiers, "linked back to the home front," try to listen to the World Series on short wave radio.
Guadalcanal Diary. Courtesy: Photofest

Sergeant York (Howard Hawks, 1941). "Tex, this ain't no turkey shoot," says a tough old sarge. "Make 'em all count." Later Tex is asked, "Who do you think you are? Sergeant York or Gary Cooper?"

"They were good, too," he replies, and then gobbles like a turkey, which was a diversionary trick of Cooper/York. When a Japanese hears and raises his head, he is shot.

We see the tools of war, and how they are used: guns, machinery, uniforms, and the jaunty jokes our soldiers make, such as the road sign that says, "3380 1/2 miles to Tokyo." We are linked back to the home front in the same ways that "our boys" are linked, through popular culture, baseball games that come in on shortwave radios, and pin-up pictures of Betty Grable. (Bendix shaves before a cover of *Modern Screen* magazine on which her face appears. Grable was the pin-up queen of World War II, and references to her abound throughout the evolution of the genre. Whenever she appears, in name or image, she *represents*—sex, glamour, love, affection, beauty, both attainable and unattainable. Her persona was that of the blonde who was nice enough to meet the folks and sexy enough to inspire dreams. Bendix's act of shaving is practically an obeisance to Grable.)

The combat of *Guadalcanal Diary* is memorable for its amount and its passionate intensity. It is brutal on both sides, culminating in the hideous battle that finally secures the island. A miniature last-stand unit is contained within the action, in which the only survivor, Anthony Quinn, gets away by swimming underwater. There's a bit of a Tarzan feel to this, and the implication that, for once, the minority can endure. The relationship between Indian scout, black man, Indian, and Mexican is a sort of Gunga Din relationship. The white troops have their assistants from the lands they exploit: the fey, imaginative, and in-tune-with-nature creatures that guide them through the jungles and hostile terrains they have set out to exploit in true white-man tradition. On board the troop ship, when the men want ships identified, they summon a black man. Like an Indian scout on a high bluff, he identifies the stuff on the horizon for them.

At the finale, the new troops coming in pass by the old, a ritual that will become a familiar sight in films to come. Unlike *Bataan*, this group survives, although not without losses, of course.

Summary: Elements of the Genre

From these films of 1943 comes a list of elements to be found that repeat and recur in the combat genre. We know *Guadalcanal Diary* to be an on-the-spot-correspondent's account of an actual battle. And yet the story might as well have been brought up in Hollywood by someone who had never been there. Setting aside differences in military uniform and weapons, and thus the attendant differences in mission and type of combat, *Destination Tokyo, Bataan, Air Force, Sahara,* and *Guadalcanal Diary* are the same movie. . . .

Here is the "story" of the universal World War II combat film, with its primary units . . . and indications of how they can be varied without violating the basic definition in brackets.

The credits of the film unfold against a military reference. [A map, a flag, an insignia, a photo or painting of battle, a military song, for example.]

The credits include the name of a military advisor.

Closely connected to the presentation of the credits is a statement that may be called the film's dedication. [It may be printed or narrated. It may be a reference to a military battle of the past or present. It may contain thanks to a military service that cooperated in the making of the film, or an emotional tribute to a gallant fighting force, our Allies, or a quote from a famous World War II figure, with Churchill and Roosevelt being particular favorites.]

A group of men, led by a hero, undertake a mission that will accomplish an important military objective. [The group of men is a mixture of unrelated types, with varying ethnic and socioeconomic backgrounds. They may be men from different military forces, and/or different countries. They are of different ages. Some have never fought in combat before, and others are experienced. Some are intellectual and well-educated, others are not. They are both married and single, shy and bold, urban and rural, comic and tragic. They come from all areas of the United States geographically, especially the Midwest (stability), the South (naïveté but good shooting ability), New England (education), and New York City (sophistication). Favorite states are Iowa, the Dakotas, and Kansas for the Midwest; California and Texas for recognition; and Brooklyn. (In the war film, Brooklyn is a state unto itself, and is almost always present, one way or another.) Their occupations vary: farmer, cab driver, teacher. Minority figures are always represented: black, Hispanic, Indian, and even Oriental.]

This group contains an observer or commentator. [A newspaperman, a man keeping a diary, or a man who thinks in his head or talks out loud.]

The hero has had leadership forced upon him in dire circumstances. [The highest-ranking officer may have been killed, placing him in command. He may have been forced into his role simply by having been drafted or having felt he had to volunteer for the role. He may have been a career military man who received an odious assignment. The assumption of enforced responsibility, however willingly or unwillingly accepted, is present.]

They undertake a military objective. [They may have to hold a fort and make a last stand. They may have to rove forward through jungle, desert, forest, the ocean, both on top and under water, or in the air. But whether holding the fort or journeying to destroy the enemy's fort—or waiting for returning comrades or going out to rejoin comrades—the objective is present. The objective may have been a secret, or it may have been planned in advance, or it may have grown out of necessity.]

As they go forward, the action unfolds. A series of episodes occurs that alternates in uneven patterns the contrasting forces of night and day, action and repose, safety and danger, combat and noncombat, comedy and tragedy, dialogue and action. [The variations are endless, as inventive as the writers can make them.]

The enemy's presence is indicated. [He may appear face-to-face, fly over in airplanes and bomb, sail by in other ships and shoot, crawl forward in endless numbers, assault from trees, broadcast on the radio, whatever. He is sometimes seen in close-up, and is sometimes faceless.]

Military iconography is seen, and its usage is demonstrated for and taught to civilians. [Uniforms, weapons, equipment, insignia, maps, salt tablets, K-rations, walkie-talkies, and the like.]

Conflict breaks out within the group itself. It is resolved through the external conflict brought down upon them.

Rituals are enacted from the past. [If a holiday comes, such as Christmas, it is celebrated. If a death occurs, a burial takes place.]

Rituals are enacted from the present. [Mail is read, and weapons are cleaned. Philosophies of life and postwar plans are discussed.]

Members of the group die. [This has many variations, including the death of the entire group. The minorities almost always die, and die most horribly.]

A climactic battle takes place, and a learning or growth process occurs.

The tools of cinema are employed for tension *(cutting)*, release *(camera movement)*, intimacy and alienation *(composition)*, and the look of combat *(lighting)* and authenticity *(documentary footage)*.

The situation is resolved. [It will be so only after sacrifice and loss, hardship and discouragement, and it can be resolved either through victory or defeat, death or survival.]

THE END appears on the screen. [A "roll call" of the combatants appears, either as cast names or pictures of the actors with their cast names or as a scene in which they march by or fly by or pass by us in some way, living and/or dead.]

The audience is ennobled for having shared their combat experience, as they are ennobled for having undergone it. We are all comrades in arms. Anyone wishing to write a combat film can follow this story and make an appropriate script. Just to show how it can work, here is the first one-third of an imaginary combat film, entitled *War Cry!*

The insignia of the Marine Corps is seen, and "From the Halls of Montezuma" is being sung by a male chorus. *"War Cry!"* jumps out from the screen. The credits appear, including the name of Colonel Marcus B. Everson, technical advisor. As the credits finish, a map of the Solomon Islands is seen, and these words are on the screen: "This film is dedicated to the ferocious fighting men of the American Marine Corps. From the halls of Montezuma to the shores of Tripoli . . . and now to the heat and humidity and horror of the Pacific . . . these men, ordinary people with extraordinary ability to fight . . . guard our American way of life. We owe them our deepest gratitude and greatest respect, because, no matter what, they always do the job with the rallying cry, 'Marines. Let's *Go!*'"

Semper Fidelis . . .

On a troop ship heading into battle on the Pacific is a combat platoon consisting of Feinstein, O'Hara, Thomas Jefferson Brown, Kowalski, Rinaldi, Andy Hawkins, Bruce Martinson, Pop Jorgenson. They are under the command of Captain Charles P. Jenkins, and their tough professional soldier top sergeant is Kip McCormick. With them is war correspondent David C. Davis.

On board ship as they await battle, they talk of their lives and homes. Pop's feet hurt. He tells about the night before his first battle in World War I. Martinson, a Harvard graduate who had planned to go to medical school, is reading *A Farewell to Arms*. Feinstein talks about wishing he was back home going to Ebbetts Field to see the Dodgers, driving there in his cab. Hawkins, a young and unsophisticated boy, has never been away from home before, his home being his father's farm in the mountains of Tennessee. Kowalski and O'Hara hate one another, and are arguing about how to make a good stew. Kowalski says no potatoes, use cabbage. O'Hara says no cabbage, use potatoes. Thomas Jefferson Brown sings "Swing Low, Sweet Chariot," and Jenkins tells him how they always sang "Rock of Ages" at their little church in New England, but he guesses it's all just the same song. Jenkins notices the little dog Hawkins has hidden beside him, but decides to ignore it. Jenkins talks about his wife, a Sunday school teacher, and his two kids. Davis is keeping a diary. His voice-over talks about his fears of combat, and about how brave the other men seem. McCormick says nothing. He keeps his own counsel. Rinaldi is sleeping.

Going ashore, Jenkins is killed, and after their small band is isolated from the main group, McCormick assumes command. To survive, they must rejoin their main forces while avoiding the Japanese patrols. They have only enough salt tablets for half the group. Their maps were lost in the landing. Feinstein has been wounded and cannot walk. Kowalski and O'Hara prepare to carry him. Davis's voice is heard saying, "If we ever get out of this alive . . ."

Here you have the first one-third of a perfect combat movie, based on what you already know.

NOTE

1. A figure my students have dubbed "mom."

Table 1. Comparison of Five Films

Element	Sahara	Guadalcanal Diary	Air Force	Destination Tokyo	Bataan
DEDICATION	Acknowledgment: IV Armored Corps of the Army Ground Forces	"Appreciation is gratefully acknowledged to the Marines . . . Army, Navy." "A new chapter in the history of America: by the correspondent who landed on Guadalcanal with the first detachment of U.S. Marines."	"It is for us the living to be dedicated . . . to the great task remaining before us."—A. Lincoln, Gettysburg Address	"To the Silent Service"	"to those immortal dead . . . the defenders of Bataan"
TIME	June 1942	26 July–10 December 1942	6 December 1941 onward through Pearl Harbor and beyond	Christmas Eve 1941 through Doolittle Raid, 18 April 1942	Just after the evacuation of Manila, which Japan entered on 31 December 1941. Americans and Filipinos then prepared for a last stand in weeks to come
PLACE	North Africa	Guadalcanal, Pacific	San Francisco to Pearl Harbor, Wake, Midway, etc.	San Francisco to Aleutians, Pacific Ocean on to Tokyo	Manila
MILITARY FORCE	IV Armored Corps Also: British, French Sudanese	Marines	Air Force; B-17s	Submarine Service	Mix of services
PRIMARY OBJECTIVE	Survival in retreat	Capture Guadalcanal	To fly to Hickam Field, Hawaii	Put men ashore in Tokyo Bay	"Buy time"

Element	Sahara	Guadalcanal Diary	Air Force	Destination Tokyo	Bataan
SECONDARY OBJECTIVE	"Buy time"	Hold Guadalcanal	To survive	Survive combat entanglements	Survival in retreat
HERO	Career military man Sergeant	The group as a unit	The group as a unit	Not a career man Captain	Career military man Sergeant
STAR	Humphrey Bogart: "A loner from nowhere"	—	—	Cary Grant: An Oklahoman—social, but lonely in leadership	Robert Taylor: "A loner from nowhere"
GROUP	Inexperienced youth High-ranking man who'll die Comedy relief Cynic Medical men — Quirt/Flagg — — Mix of international forces	Inexperienced youth High-ranking leader who dies Comedy relief Cynics Medical men Chaplain who prays Quirt/Flagg Two older men War correspondent —	Inexperienced youth High-ranking leader who dies Comedy relief Cynic — — Quirt/Flagg Old man Correspondent (log keeper) —	Inexperienced youth Father figure who dies Comedy relief Cynic Pharmacist's mate Man who prays Quirt/Flagg Old man Correspondent (log keeper) —	Inexperienced youth High-ranking leader who dies Comedy relief Cynic — Man who prays Quirt/Flagg Old man — Mix of miliary forces
ENEMY	Germany/Italy Personal	Japan Impersonal	Japan Impersonal	Japan Impersonal	Japan Impersonal
WOMEN	None	None	None in central combat story	None in central combat story	None in central combat story

Table 2. Comparison of the Narrative Elements of Five Films

	Sahara	Guadalcanal Diary	Air Force	Destination Tokyo	Bataan
Burial or Funeral	Y	Y	Y	Y	Y
Death	Y	Y	Y	Y	Y
Combat	Y	Y	Y	Y	Y
Enemy Deception	Y	Y	Y	Y	Y
Outnumbered Heroes	Y	Y	Y	Y	Y
Nature as Enemy	Y	Y	Y	Y	Y
Humor among Heroes	Y	Y	Y	Y	Y
Roll Call of Living or Dead at End	Y	Y	Y	Y	N
Need to Maintain Equipment	Y	Y	Y	Y	Y
Talk of Wives and Home	Y	Y	Y	Y	Y
Minority Sacrifice	Y	N	N	N	Y
Discussion of Why We Fight	Y	Y	Y	Y	Y
Journey/Last Stand	Y	Y	Y	Y	Y
Music other than Score	Y[a]	Y[b]	Y[c]	Y[c]	Y[c]
Mail	Y	Y	Y	Y	Y
Big Combat Finale	Y	Y	Y	Y	Y

[a]Harmonica

[b]Harmonica and Song

[c]Radio

Dana Polan

Auteurism and War-teurism: Terrence Malick's War Movie

If this were a movie, this would be the end of the show and something would be decided. In a movie or novel they would dramatize and build to the climax of the attack. When the attack came in the film or novel, it would be satisfying, it would decide something. It would have a semblance of meaning and a semblance of emotion. And immediately after, it would be over. The audience would go home and think about the semblance of the meaning and feel the semblance of the emotion. Even if the hero got killed, it would still make sense. Art, [Private] Bell decided, creative art—was shit.

—James Jones, *The Thin Red Line*

At one point in Terrence Malick's *The Thin Red Line* (1998), just before a battle, we see a shot of a natural world followed by a shot of Colonel Tall (Nick Nolte), who intones a phrase in Greek and then tells his soldiers that it's the "rosy-fingered dawn" phrase from Homer's *Odyssey*. With this reference, *The Thin Red Line* does two slightly different things that suggest the complicated situation of the war film in today's culture. On the one hand, *The Thin Red Line* clearly wants to take up identity as an epic of war, a film of vast sweep with great means and great pretense. On the other hand, the use of the explicit *citation* to *declare* the film's lineage to an epic antecedent seems a resolutely postmodern gesture. Like all major war films today, *The Thin Red Line* is an ersatz work, aware of fictionality, aware of tradition, only able to make itself seem traditionally a war film by fictionally declaring itself to be so. Like a speech-act that brings about a state of affairs by announcing that it is bringing about a state of affairs, *The Thin Red Line* isn't naturally an epic but constructs itself as one. Indeed, is it accidental that so many big war films of recent years emphasize the cost and effort that went into their production as if to reiterate the extent to which they build up narrative worlds and also build up the world they subtend? Not naturally, but through immense creative human effort, they bring their war fiction into being. Even as eventually traditional a film as *Saving Private Ryan* (Steven Spielberg, 1998)— applauded by middle-brow America as a realist work that breaks through conventions to achieve Truth—seems in many respects to be about fictionality. From

Meteor #14. © 1998. Reprinted with permission of the editors of *Meteor* (Vienna: PVS Verleger).

its plays with the rules of genre (for example, the coward who in this case never finds the courage to become a hero) to the very ways it only gradually discovers narrativity out of an experimental opening battle that seems to go on and on, *Saving Private Ryan*, too, is in large part about the war film as a construction, rather than as direct and innocent expression of a national will about war.

Experiments in the revision of established, codified genres such as the war film probably have either (or both) of two intents. On the one hand, the attempt to alter the rules of genre can have to do with issues of content, with a sense that the ways the genre typically structures meaning blocks certain worldviews from achieving representation. A modification of the genre, it is hoped, will enable new experiences, new voices, new realities to come into existence. To take just one example, the shift from classic British detective fiction to American hard-boiled fiction was famously lauded by Raymond Chandler as the replacement of the limited unreality of the British aristocratic view of the world by a modern, bluntly real, experientially authentic one, more attuned to the nature of contemporary urban existence.[1]

On the other hand, experiments in genre can also have as their intent to revise form, to play with it, to uncover its ludic possibilities—to see codes as formal structures that future examples in the genre enact productive permutations upon.

Here, again, we can cite the example of British detective fiction. So generally fixed is the moral universe of this fiction as a sedentary world of privilege into which crime comes as a disturbing stain, an upset that must be put right, that only a revolutionary shift of the sort Chandler announces could change its meaning. Before that revolutionary shift, then, the internal history of the British detective story is one of authors engaging in gamelike formal variations (let's make the narrator the murderer, let's make all the suspects the murderer, let's make a totally incidental character the murderer, let's have the detective be a priest, a . . .) that leave the moral universe itself untouched but create new generic delights for aficionados.

We might grasp the evolution of the combat film as the history of a genre in which experiments in form and in content are both at work, pushing individual works to say new things about the experience of war and to find new forms in which to say those things. Traditionally, the combat film was a highly codified genre with a set structure and set meaning. As outlined by Jeanine Basinger in its World War II paradigm, the model for the combat film deals with a team of soldiers from diverse civilian backgrounds who go off on a mission and, along the way, encounter conflicts both external (fights with the enemy) and internal (for example, outbreaks of cowardice that threaten group cohesion).[2] For the soldiers, the mission can become the occasion for emotional growth and self-discovery but, in the ideology of the World War II film, one discovers what was really there all along—the meaningfulness of nation and national mission, the rightness of one's place, the justification of cause. There can indeed be internal division in the World

War II combat film, but, as I argue in my study of 1940s films, *Power and Paranoia*, the wartime film admits dissension only insofar as such dissension can be tamed, co-opted, converted.[3] Indeed, *conversion* is a central narrative structure and strategy for the wartime film: for a war in which soldiers were told "there are no atheists in the foxholes," conversion to the mission of the combat team—and beyond that, to the war effort as organic whole—takes on directly religious meaning. (See, for instance, Hawks' *Sergeant York* [1941], where the pacifist title character converts after a weekend spent reading both the Bible and the U.S. Constitution and Bill of Rights.) Moreover, conversion works here by suggesting not that the meanings of engagement are imposed onto the subject from without, but that they exist rather as an inner spark that needs to be rekindled, a core of commitment that had been forgotten through cowardice or cynicism. As the opening title of the 1942 *China Girl* (Henry Hathaway) tells us, an American will fight for three things—money, a girl, his country—and the central character of this film is said to be fighting for two of these as the story begins. Conversion, then, brings back into the organic unity of nationhood those individuals who never really left, who had simply forgotten their national being and belonging—not for nothing does *Casablanca* (Michael Curtiz, 1942) tell us that Rick had a past as a freedom fighter; he does not convert to something new, but rediscovers a buried part of himself.

For the wartime World War II combat film, meaning was natural. There was a mission, both the literal mission faced by the soldiers and the national mission of the war effort, and its purpose was evident, inevitable. Hence, the importance of conversion, for in its suggestion that one doesn't learn new things, that commitment isn't imposed on the subject from without but wells up from within, the narrative of conversion makes growth into commitment natural, logical, ordinary. Although the moment of war sows seeds for the dismantling of the classical Hollywood narrative—insofar as the narrative of conversion to war commitment requires a disavowal of a commitment to the private realm of the romantic couple so central to classical Hollywood narrative—and thereby prepares the way for disunified postwar genres of battles of the sexes like film noir and the woman's Gothic film, it is also important to understand the World War II combat film as one of the last perfections or accomplishments of the classical Hollywood cinema. Here is a genre where ease of style, naturalness of narrativity, matches an ease of worldview, a naturalness of mission and meaning—a genre whose philosophy is pre-given (pre-given to the filmic form, to the characters in the narrative, and to the target audience).

But in the recent combat film, unity—unity of form and content, of mission and meaning, of character and moral purpose—frequently comes undone. As cultural theorist Marita Sturken shows in her chapter on Vietnam and post-Vietnam variants of the combat narrative structure in her *Tangled Memories: The Vietnam War, the AIDS Epidemic and the Politics of Remembering*, the manifestations of the genre in these later historical moments adhere to initial meanings of the genre (the mission as process of self-education and accomplishment) while suggesting that the original organic unity of the genre is no longer easily or readily to be had.[4]

Without a coherent ideology to shore it up, the war film becomes directly incoherent: for example, images that are overfilled and chaotically unreadable (the psychedilia of *Apocalypse Now* [Francis Ford Coppola, 1979]), narrative trajectories that fragment into monadic bits *(Full Metal Jacket* [Stanley Kubrick, 1987] with its two major segments and its numerous set pieces), a visuality of baroque tangle (the tunnels of *Casualties of War* [Brian De Palma, 1989], the labyrinthine camera movements of *Full Metal Jacket*), an experimental fascination with a sheer temporality in which pure duration comes to substitute for the progress of narrative (the seeming endlessness of the opening battle in *Saving Private Ryan*, the excruciating torture of the training sequence in *Full Metal Jacket*, the temporally vast minimalism of the assault on the hillside in *The Thin Red Line*).

As Sturken notes, the political divisions of the Vietnam War have bequeathed to the representations of war a legacy of confusion, contradiction, and struggles over meaning rather than assurances of natural meaningfulness. Indeed, if in the classic war conversion we are passive participants in observing a meaningfulness that is naturally and easily recovered—conversion as the light of awareness that grows and glows across the face as the cynic realizes his true mission—by contrast a number of recent war films show meanings being constructed, being tested, offered up as so many tentative hypotheses.

Hence, the sheer sense of discussion or didacticism in the recent war film: meaning does not preexist the characters and, instead, has experimentally to be built up for and by them. Thus, to take one example, *Platoon* (Oliver Stone, 1986) presents itself as a veritable debate—war as a battle for the souls of men, with the young innocent, Taylor, caught between the evil Barnes and the christological Elias. The allegorical weightiness of the film derives no doubt in large part from Stone's sledgehammer conception of cinema as emphatic education, as is even more evident in *Born on the Fourth of July* (1989), where scenes like that of the two vets in the Mexican desert become shouting matches of political position. But it is also necessary to see that this concern with cinema as imposed and obvious instruction or interrogation into the meanings of war seems to be the case of so many recent war films. Thus, to take an example that is often opposed to *Platoon, Full Metal Jacket* is a film of visual bravura but it is also a film of constant debate and discussion. At many moments, the swirl of war (the emphatic sweeps of the camera matched by the frenetic rock music of the 1960s) gives way to intensely static shots in which figures face off against each other and announce positions. For instance, there is the meeting of the war correspondents with their commander, filmed as so many closeups of talking heads; the scene of Joker facing off against the general, who mechanically intones clichés of war patriotism; and the scene of the men being filmed by a TV crew and expressing their often-cynical views of the war. Where *Full Metal Jacket* differs from *Platoon* in this respect is not in its sense that meaning is a construction—since both films argue that—but in its radical, and less reassuring, sense

Another verbal assault by Sergeant Hartman (R. Lee Ermey) on Private Pyle (Vincent D'Onofrio). Full Metal Jacket. Courtesy: Photofest

that the construction of meanings has no end, that there is no morality that is natural, even at the end of a journey of discovery. Where *Platoon*'s Taylor learns of the bifurcation of morality—of the essential and essentially conflictual Nature of Good and Evil—it is not clear that Joker learns anything at all. How much lack of irony, or not, is there in his final declaration that he is not afraid, announced to the background chant of Mickey Mouse? One shot in *Full Metal Jacket* is emblematic of its postmodern refusal of answers: as Sergeant Hartman slaps Private Pyle around once again, we cut to a shot of Private Cowboy watching, but the look on his face offers no clue of moral perspective, of narrational point-of-view.

Given this context, we would easily anticipate that the newest and most ambitious of war films, Malick's *The Thin Red Line,* would readily come off as an incoherent work, but one in which incoherence is less an aesthetic failing than an aesthetic and political inevitability for a film in this cultural moment.

To be sure, there is in Malick a romanticism that seeks to posit a coherent authenticity of nature beyond all subterfuge, beyond all the incoherencies of human conflict. *The Thin Red Line* seems to imagine incoherence as only a contingent situation that one is in danger of falling into, rather than a fundamental condition that one inevitably is always already in: hence, the opening of the film portrays a timelessness of nature and native into which narrative gradually arrives—a white soldier appears, a naval boat appears. But in our postmodern age, such romanticism itself can only appear ersatz, a derivative cliché. Malick's use of natives to portray lost innocence is certainly politically problematic and not at all innocent; similarly, his use of femininity as memory—trace of a joy lost in the ravages of war—the intercut shots of a woman, especially of her breasts, that posit her as an essential purity outside the fall into war/culture—seems awkwardly out of time. (As a friend of mine says, "Where has Malick been for the last twenty years? In a cave somewhere?!?") Not for nothing do so many later reminders in the film of the purity of nature come as reminders precisely—obtrusions that arise from shock editing (cuts to animals, jumps into flashbacks of femininity) that turn into emphatic declarations by means of the mechanical art of montage enacted upon a realm of the supposedly natural.

In this respect, it is important to note that for many moviegoers, *The Thin Red Line* will be viewed as the film of an auteur, its images of nature not naturally and spontaneously arising before us but seen to be articulated for us by a strong creative voice, the images brought into being by his authoring of a cinematic universe. The stories of the time it took Malick to come back to filmmaking parallel in this way the stories of the complicated production histories behind so many recent war films, reminding us of their constructed nature.

Now, auteurism certainly has long had a bad reputation in the critical study of film, and my own intent in talking of Malick's authorial presence is not to revive mythologies of creative genius. Quite differently, and with an emphasis on the hypothetical and tentative nature of this, I would want to posit contemporary auteurism as one of the effects of the same political climate that led to the incoherencies of the contemporary Vietnam film. Authorial voice is a product of its time. The classic auteurs—the auteurs of the Hollywood studio system—may have had personal voices, but increasingly we see how many of them were pure Hollywood Professionals (to use the title of a series of books on the classic auteurs), their own coherence as filmmakers merging easily and logically and, dare we say, naturally, with the organic world of Hollywood narrative. A good Howard Hawks film, for instance, is generally good both as a Hawks film and as a Hollywood film. But as the organicity of American consensus disappears in the 1960s—along with the coherence of the studio system—a new auteurism, more contemporaneously American in nature, arises, and by the end of the 1960s it is about the isolation of lone creative voices that spring up against the bland conformity of establishment and system.[5] Not for nothing does a book at the very cusp of the end of the 1960s encapsulate in its title the notion of authorial voice as personal vision—Joseph Gelmis's *The Film Director as Superstar*—and the late years of the Vietnam War will also be the years of a rampant auteurism, a Hollywood renaissance that so many cinephiles still think back on with deep fondness.

The point to make in an analysis of such auteurism is not that it is somehow a force of creativity that arises magically against the social and political conditions of the nation, but that it is itself a force generated by those conditions, personal creativity becoming one of the ways in the 1970s and after to live out issues of constraint and conformity. Not for nothing, then, are so many Vietnam films auteur films, not so much films about the war but about this or that director's take on the experience of war and, more often, on the experience of filming war—Coppola's Vietnam, Kubrick's, De Palma's, and perhaps Stone's, and now definitely Malick's World War II. In this respect, there is little possibility of reading the natural images of *The Thin Red Line* naturally; they come to us as voiced, as authored. To take just one example, how, when an auteur has not made a film for twenty years, is it possible to read just the nature in the new film's opening shot (an alligator that immerses itself in murky swamp water up to its eyes) and not also read for authorial voice, visual talent, this director's take on the war movie?

Indeed, for all its romanticism for an Eden before the human fall, before the inscription of the human onto the surface of the world (as ostensibly is the case in the opening shot), *The Thin Red Line* is also very strongly a writerly film, a film of voice and narration and inscription, a film whose processes of construction are rendered manifest. As with other auteur war films, *The Thin Red Line* is a film of discussion and debate. There are numerous set pieces of verbal sparring, such as those between Welsh and Witt, between Tall and Staros, between Tall and Quintard. For all of the film's modernist emphasis elsewhere on private voices (men caught in their own agony, men given in to personal obsession), *The Thin Red Line* is also very much a film about conversation and interchange, albeit one in which no closure of position is brought to the debate.

Indeed, cutting between the social world of public communication and the private world of personal obsession or fantasy, there runs through the film the experimentalism of its voice-over narration. Reviews just after the film's release tended to treat this narration, which moves around various characters, as an expression of inner thought, but the actual functioning of the narration seems more complicated, more incoherent than that, for it is in no easy way a direct expression of character thought. Like the infamous *style indirect libre* of *Madame Bovary*, which offers both the character's perception and an intelligent comment on her perception that Emma herself could never have had, the narration in *The Thin Red Line* both originates in various characters and goes beyond them, creating a floating perspective in keeping both with the film's epic pretense and its poetic ambition to represent unities of the human and of the natural beyond all artificial divisions. Not only does the narration say things we do not necessarily imagine the particular characters to be capable of saying, but it also seems to waft beyond any particular character's perception, becoming a virtually pan-individual disquisition on war and existence. Indeed, many reviewers have noted, and criticized, the fact that several characters resemble each other and have similar styles of narration, but what for the reviewers is generally a failure of the film can also be read as part of the film's ambition, one of the things it is impelled to do as contemporary war fiction by an auteur.

But if intellectualizing is one of the things we can expect auteurist cinema to quest after, a very different experimental goal of such cinema has to do with its desire to achieve what we might term a pure experience, an experience outside debate and discussion. What I mean by this is not that experience *of war* that certain films try to offer up as their achievement of realism, their claim to Truth. That mythology has been pinpointed by Sturken, who talks of the ways *Platoon*'s claim to "'experience' was contingent on its following certain codes of cinematic realism—portraying the details of a patrol, the boredom, the confusion of combat, the presence of the jungle. The heightened 'naturalized' sound of the jungle at night, rapidly edited combat scenes, and on-location shooting."[6]

Beyond that documentary realism that claims to capture Experience, there is in the works of several Vietnam auteurs the glimpsing of experientiality itself, a pure immersion in temporality, in a duration that only vaguely adds up to either meaningfulness or anything resembling realism. I think, for instance, of the opening of *Full Metal Jacket,* where narrativity only eventually emerges to give some sense to an experience at the limits of tolerability, a cinema of cruelty not unlike extremes of theatrical experiment. In the enclosed space of the barracks, the shaven-head men seem to come from some ritual theater laboratory on the edge of being, à la Artaud or Peter Brook or Jerzy Grotowski. Similarly, though its fall into narrative is all the more traditional, the battle sequence at the beginning of *Saving Private Ryan* also catches some of the experience of a temporality outside of narrativity, a viscerality that only partially has to do with the horrific content within individual images.

In this respect, one of the most ambitious experiments in *The Thin Red Line* has to do with its rendition of its central battle, a set piece that takes on epic lengths but that is only ambiguously epic in meaning.[7] Strangely, for all its violence and explosions and action, the battle is also intensely minimalist, moving toward that sparse cinema, that cinema of silence, that also captivates Vietnam auteurs.[8] The legacy of the new war film comes not only from earlier forms of the genre but also from other 1960s forms, such as the structural cinema of Warhol or Michael Snow. As in the excruciating beginnings of *Full Metal Jacket* and *Saving Private Ryan* (discounting the latter film's kitsch prologue at a war cemetery), much happens but little happens, and action is emptied out to give way to blockage, repetition. The training that goes on and on In *Full Metal Jacket,* the assaults that keep happening with new troops endlessly replacing the wounded and the dead in *Saving Private Ryan* and *The Thin Red Line* are rendered as noncumulative explosions of violence that lead nowhere and mean nothing. And where *Saving Private Ryan* portrays battle as a messy chaos—the beach cluttered with war paraphernalia, the focus that blurs backgrounds against Tom Hanks—*The Thin Red Line* renders action sparse even in its look. The long waves of grass so beloved by Malick become here a pure space of experience as we see nothing but endless fields with no advance, no logic, no fixities of point of view.[9]

Like the narration that can go anywhere but never adds up to a final meaning, the field of battle in *The Thin Red Line* is a space of floating, of meaningless violence that can come from anywhere, but also of the effect of just waiting, of

"We see nothing but endless fields with no advance." Sergeant Welsh (Sean Penn) leads his men. The Thin Red Line. Courtesy: Photofest

living with nonaction. One might want to imagine that this is the experience of war, but it is also an experience of cinema, a comment on modern cinema's narration, its rediscovery of what Gilles Deleuze famously termed the "time-image," a confirmation of modern cinema's ambitious and auspicious inability to find a clear way to recount war today.

NOTES

1. See Raymond Chandler, "The Simple Art of Murder," in *The Simple Art of Murder* (New York: Vintage, 1988).

2. Jeanine Basinger, *The World War II Combat Film: Anatomy of a Genre* (New York: Columbia University Press, 1986).

3. Dana Polan, *Power and Paranoia: History, Narrative, and the American Cinema, 1940–1950* (New York: Columbia University Press, 1985).

4. Marita Sturken, *Tangled Memories: The Vietnam War; the AIDS Epidemic and the Politics of Remembering* (Berkeley: University of California Press, 1997).

5. Andrew Sarris writing on American film for the experimental journal *Film Culture* is the key figure here.

6. Sturken, *Tangled Memories*, 99.

7. Depending on how one segments, it goes on for more than an hour.

8. See, for instance, the influence of Bresson on Paul Schrader.

9. See his fetish for wheatfields in *Days of Heaven* (1978).

Race

Robert Burgoyne

Race and Nation in *Glory*

In resurrecting the forgotten story of a black Union Army regiment and its white leader, Colonel Robert Gould Shaw, *Glory* (1989) conveys a particularly complex understanding of the way racial and cultural identity is both bound up with and competes with the forces of national construction. Examining the historical construction of racial and national identity in the United States at a moment when concepts of nation were being fundamentally redefined, *Glory* emphasizes the tension between a civic ideal of nation conceived as a community of equals and the powerful appeal of ethnic and racial identities based on what Michael Ignatieff calls "blood and belonging."[1] Far from mediating or subduing ethnic concepts of nation, the Civil War, the film suggests, pulled potent structures of racial identification into visibility, promoting a sense of racial mobilization in white as well as in black America. *Glory* thus departs from the traditional themes of Civil War narratives, which typically focus on the emancipation of the slaves and the rebirth of national ideals of community and equality, to explore a subject that D. W. Griffith first considered from a rather different perspective: the struggle between competing ideals of nation, ethnic and civic, and their equally potent claims to recognition and belonging.

At first glance, *Glory* appears to be primarily concerned with the relation between what Cornel West has described as identity from above—identification with the nation-state—and identity from below—racial and ethnic identity. These two forms of identity, as West points out, are both defined by the most elemental concerns; they are fundamentally about desire and death. The desire for affiliation, for recognition, for visibility, is one of the most significant and visceral forces shaping both national and racial identity. But the construction of identity also involves the recognition of death, being willing to die for that identity, or being willing to kill others for it.[2] In *Glory*, this concept is dramatized in a strikingly literal way, as the struggle for racial visibility and recognition culminates in the spectacular assault and massacre of the film's final sequence, foregrounding the almost suicidal costs of aligning identity from below and identity from above. Underlining the theme of collective martyrdom with the sounds of choral music, the film idealizes the sacrifice of the black soldiers as the price of national affiliation, as if identity from above were in some way a mystical compact, authorized and conferred only in death. By invoking what Paul Gilroy calls "a mystic nation-hood that [is] only revealed on the battlefield," the film further suggests that racial difference is dissolved in warfare, valorizing war as the defining moment when racial and national self-realization coalesce.[3]

But this thesis, in which national identity is presumed to dominate and dis-place the lived identity of race, is complicated by another, competing message in *Glory*. In counterpoint to the ostensible subject matter and theme of the film, which might be summarized in humanistic terms as the mutual reshaping and redefini-tion of identity from below and identity from above, the film also explores the more fractious subject of the failure of social movements to cut across racial identities, emphasizing the fear and hatred of the other as the constant feature of national expe-rience. Although the central importance of national identity is asserted strenuously in the closing moments of the film, the body of the text seems to be concerned mainly with what I am calling identity from across: the nonsymmetrical relation-ship between white identity and black identity that defines points of tension in *Glory* that have little to do with the unifying rhetoric of nation or the traditional Civil War topics of liberty, equality, and self-determination. And it is here that the film illuminates the hard kernel of historical truth that is slowly working its way through the various revisions of the dominant fiction that are currently being offered: the recognition that the achievement of new forms of collective coherence will require something other than an updated narrative of nation, and that only a historical narrative that, as the historian Peter Dimock writes, "is explicitly a col-lective narrative of social loss" will be able to address the present crisis of social belief.[4]

This secondary theme is articulated chiefly through the story of the white commanding officer, Colonel Robert Shaw, which serves in large part as a means of registering the dissonance between white racial identity and the imagined com-munity implied by emancipation. Rather than merging whiteness and nation into a single myth, the film suggests that the historical coalescence of black identity during the Civil War forced apart the formerly seamless narrative of white iden-tity, separating it from its traditional one-to-one correspondence with the concept of nation. With emancipation redefining the meaning of national community, the voice of white racial privilege could no longer be heard as the exclusive voice of national ideals. By inverted yet strangely similar paths, *Glory* comes to the same conclusion as D. W. Griffith's *Birth of a Nation*: white identity is defined and clar-ified by black identity, which forces "whiteness" into the open and compels it to speak in a language of its own.

As Richard Dyer has explained, white identity is an exceptionally elusive and difficult subject to analyze, for it represents itself not in terms of particular characteristics and practices, but rather as a synthesis of all the attributes of humanity. "The strength of white representation . . . [is] the sense that being white is coterminous with the endless plenitude of human diversity."[5] Just as the color itself is defined as a combination of all the other colors, white racial identity seems to have no substance of its own: "White power secures its dominance by seeming not to be anything in particular. . . as if it is the natural, inevitable, ordinary way of being human."[6] The invisibility of whiteness, its lack of specificity, masks it as a category; so thoroughly identified with the norm, white racial identity becomes difficult, especially for white people, to see and to represent.

One of the ways white identity does become visible, Dyer suggests, is in the contrast between white and nonwhite in narratives marked by ethnic or racial difference, narratives in which nonwhite characters play significant roles. In order to represent white identity, a "comparative element" seems to be required, for "only non-whiteness can give whiteness any substance." In such texts, the characteristics of whiteness can be inferred if not defined, understood by way of contrast with the stereotypes associated with nonwhite modes of behavior. In the films Dyer analyzes, the "presence of black people . . . allows one to see whiteness as whiteness." And the sense of whiteness is accentuated, Dyer notes, in films centering on situations where white domination is contested.[7]

These ideas offer an instructive approach to the representation of racial identity in *Glory*. The film uses the drama of the Fifty-fourth Massachusetts Infantry, the first black regiment to be raised in the North, partly to pull white identity into visibility, detailing the practices and characteristics of the white Union military, emphasizing the "psychology" of whiteness, as seen through Shaw, and placing in relief the internal complacency and self-interest of the white establishment. The effective display of white identity, however, depends on a relation of rigid contrast with black identity, a contrast that recalls the absolute binarisms of racist thought. Stiff formality, an emphasis on individual agency and responsibility, and links to historical tradition are set out as clear markers of whiteness and explicitly set against the exuberance, collectivity, and sense of historical emergence that characterize the black soldiers. In keeping with the film's liberal themes and contemporary perspective, however, many of the features associated with whiteness are held up to scrutiny and subjected to criticism, partly through the voice-overs of Shaw himself. Ultimately, however, the traits identified as white are restored to dominance as Shaw overcomes self-doubt and gains the approbation and respect of the black troops.

As Dyer observes, the ability to resolve this kind of crisis of identity can also be seen as one of the attributes of whiteness; here, the hero restores his own fading sense of authority by appropriating the emotional intensity associated with the black soldiers, displaying an uncharacteristic passion in a series of scenes in which Shaw ferociously confronts the military establishment, dresses down his own officers, and, in an expression of solidarity with his troops, rips up his pay voucher to protest the unequal pay the soldiers have received, taking his cue directly from the black soldier Trip. In a subtle way, however, the emotional intensity common to the black soldiers is recoded in these scenes as part of human nature, latent but still accessible to the white Colonel Shaw. In contrast, when the black soldiers take on the rigor and discipline associated with the whites, it is a cultural attitude, not nature, that is absorbed. Where Shaw seems to require an infusion of natural passion to complete his character, the black soldiers require, in the logic of the film, the armature of certain cultural values associated with whites. Here, the film appears to reiterate conventional notions of blacks possessing more "nature" than whites, whereas whites command the sphere of culture. Thus, despite the superficial impression the film gives of a fluid crossing over of characteristics, the overall marking of racial differences is such that the boundary between black and white appears to be more fixed than permeable, and where mutual reshaping of identities does occur, the traits that are exchanged often play into well-worn stereotypes of racial difference.

Glory provides an especially good map of contemporary liberal thinking about race. In stressing the ways that white identity has been historically conferred, the film displays with exceptional precision the traditions, psychology, and behavior and practices of the white establishment during the Civil War period, underscoring the different ways whiteness, in both its progressive and reactionary aspects, has been shaped by the reality of an emergent black racial identity. In contrast, however, the film offers a portrait of black identity that is affirmative, but resolutely ahistorical, as if black history had to be remade by white hands and according to white ideas in order to release its most powerful messages.[8] Despite the positive accent the story of the black troops receives, the film's erasure of its actual historical figures, compared with its detailed reconstruction of the milieu of Colonel Shaw, ensures that the relations of racial identity here remain nonsymmetrical.

In general, the film uses two different paradigms to define racial identity, one of which is historical, the other folkloric and stereotypical, which are folded together or superimposed upon one another throughout the film. At several points in the narrative, the particularities of historical experience assert themselves in a powerful fashion, conveying a clear message that history has shaped racial identity in incommensurably different ways. For example, the film foregrounds the different meanings that blacks and whites assign to features of military life and specifically to the war against the Confederacy: military training and discipline, marching, and the climactic battle itself are viewed from a bifocal perspective that makes explicit the distinct optics that racial difference confers. At other points, however, this self-aware and careful dialogical principle gives way to a simple binarism in which racial difference is defined not in terms of historical experience but in terms of intrinsic differences, a tendency that rehearses essentialist patterns of racial representation. Seen in the most positive light, the film makes visible the way identity is constructed transitively, from across, using the binarisms of racial representation in a critical fashion and drawing from the dialogic encounter of black and white a reconsideration of the issues and traditions of national identity. But from another angle, the film hews uncomfortably close to old stereotypes, especially in its folkloric approach to black identity, which diminishes the actual historicity of black experience and identity.

In the pages that follow, I analyze the representation of racial identity in *Glory* from three different perspectives. First, I notice the contrast in the way the participants in the drama are defined and authenticated, a contrast that can be broadly described as historical versus folkloric. Second, I show how the film, despite its occasional lapses into stereotype, extends the dialogic principle discussed above—the foregrounding of the distinct viewpoints that racial difference entails—to encompass the historical process itself, represented in terms of two distinct historical trajectories, two competing narratives of history that are brought into conjunction in the imagery of the road and the march into the South. Third, I consider the messages the film conveys about racial identity and the national narrative from the perspective of the present, arguing that its seemingly traditional message of military valor and sacrifice opening up the "iron gate" to equality is counteracted by another message, signified by the closing shot of bootless corpses, which projects, like a kind of afterimage, a narrative of a nation imprisoned by its past as much as empowered by it.[9]

History versus Folklore

By placing difference and conflict at the center of the national narrative, the film's approach to racial and national identity substantially changes the meaning of the story as it was known in the nineteenth century. Celebrated as one of the most renowned figures of the Civil War, Shaw, along with the Fifty-fourth Infantry, had captured the imagination of the general public as well as the interest of the literary and political leaders of the period. Shaw's posthumous stature was such that Ralph Waldo Emerson and William James, among others, commemorated his "martyrdom" in verse and prose.[10] The recent treatment of the story, however, highlights Shaw in a different way, using him as a medium for registering the pointed racial animus of the Union military, as his idealism seems to bring into the open the underside of white racial identity, its basis in racial exclusion and fear. In large part, the text divides its affirmative and critical messages regarding racial identity in such a way that the Shaw narrative becomes the locus of a critical interrogation of white identity, now disjoined from its usual central position. The story of the black troops, on the other hand, who had been marginalized to such a degree that the "Shaw Memorial" in Boston had originally been designed with no black soldiers represented, is made the positive focus of the narrative, which treats the sacrifices of the Fifty-fourth as the genesis of a black narrative of American history.[11]

In many respects, *Glory* reverses the usual codes of racial representation, portraying white identity for much of the narrative in an expressly critical way, while representing the narrative of the black soldiers as a drama of origins, the tracing of a heroic lineage. But in other ways, the film recapitulates many of the traditional stereotypes of race.

Whereas the character of Shaw is heavily psychologized in a manner that emphasizes his self-consciousness and awareness, the black soldiers are portrayed in a resolutely nonpsychological fashion, and are associated instead, as if by way of compensation, with a kind of spirituality and resilience. Additionally, the historical dimensions and traditions of white identity are stressed: Shaw's actual historical existence is underlined by specific references to his abolitionist family and to the political and military leaders of the day and through the use of his correspondence, rendered in the form of several first-person voice-overs scattered throughout the film. The black soldiers, on the other hand, are represented as bereft of historical tradition: the actual historical figures who served in the Fifty-fourth, which included Frederick Douglass's two sons, are replaced by entirely fictional figures. Whereas the historical individuality of Shaw is underlined, the black soldiers are represented in the form of an ensemble of stereotypes in which the "Wild Tom," the "Uncle Tom," the "Buppie," and the rural hick are plainly represented.

Another striking difference in the way white identity and black identity are portrayed is in the dissimilar styles of language that characterize the two groups. In the voice-over that opens the text, for example, Shaw draws direct links among language, history, and national identity. Comparing the Civil War to the War of Independence, he says: "How grand it is to fight for the country, like the old fellows did in the Revolution. Only this time we must make it a whole country so that all can speak." The voice-over continues over images of life in the military camp and scenes of dispossessed blacks on the road, at which point we hear that the war is being fought "for a people whose poetry has not yet been written, but which will presently be as renowned and enviable as any." The character finishes the monologue with a quote from Emerson, whose words, he says, provide him with strength and comfort. These lines are typical of the discourse of the white officers. The refined speech of Shaw and his colleagues connotes class privilege, a sense of social obligation, and a long, stable, and unified tradition, one that assumes a perfect congruence of white racial identity and national identity.

In contrast to the unified tradition of Shaw, the black soldiers exhibit a range of dialects, verbal patterns, and rhetorical styles; the "poetry" to which Shaw alludes conveys a diverse sense of origins and a loose, patchwork form of connection. Thomas, for example, the eastern-educated black volunteer, must have the patois of a Sea Island black translated for him by another black soldier. Similarly, the exaggeration and deadpan humor of Trip proves incomprehensible to Jupiter, a rural black. Moreover, the motley regiment comes equipped with a mute drummer boy, whose practice and mastery of his instrument serves as a kind of synecdoche for the unit's growing sense of cohesion. Whereas Shaw's voice-overs, together with the speech patterns of the white officers in general, are clearly marked as "historical," the black soldiers' speech patterns are marked as geographically diffuse, underlining the film's strategy of treating the story of the Fifty-fourth as a narrative of emergence.

One of the consequences of this strategy, however, is the elimination of all but the most glancing references to black participation in the established political and social traditions of the period. A case in point is the portrayal of Frederick Douglass, who is depicted at the beginning of the film in a way that promises to counterbalance the traditional emphasis accorded Lincoln in stories of the Civil War. Contrary to expectation, however, Douglass appears only in the company of the white establishment, and is never mentioned by the black soldiers, who appear to be wholly unfamiliar with him. This aspect of the film contradicts the view of historians who aver that Douglass was widely known and revered among the black population of the Civil War period. The bracketing of Douglass from the portrait the film offers is compounded by its overlooking the fact that Douglass's two sons, Lewis and Charles, served in the Fifty-fourth, with Lewis becoming sergeant major. Moreover, the film fails to indicate that the first black Medal of Honor winner was a member of the Fifty-fourth.[12] Although it tries to make racial struggle a "formative and necessary part of the story" of American history, to use the words of Nathan Huggins, the film provides only fictional "types" among the black soldiers, rather than the actual historical figures, whose presence would certainly lend its historical portrait a heightened degree of authority.[13] Another omission is the role played by the black intellectual Charlotte Forten, who worked as a teacher and nurse in the area where the Fifty-fourth was encamped in South Carolina, and who had gained the admiration of Shaw. To some degree, the film treats the black soldiers and citizens of the period as bereft of historical tradition, understood in the conventional sense. The story of the Fifty-fourth is instead constructed as the genesis, the mythic origin, of black historical consciousness.

But the history of black identity during the Civil War period that *Glory* suppresses with one hand it restores with the other; what Frederick Douglass called the "fleshly diploma" of slavery—the whip marks and other signs of physical abuse inflicted on the slave's or the ex-slave's body—comes to express another kind of tradition, another kind of history, one that functions in counterpoint to the dominant tradition.[14] Although the film erases much of the actual history of the Fifty-fourth, it succeeds in creating a picture of a historical world that is shaped by radically different historical experiences, implying that there are potentially many histories embedded in a given historical moment. Moreover, the film suggests that black history and white history in the United States determine and shape one another. At certain points, it illuminates with surprising subtlety the deep, structural connections between the dominant tradition and the suppressed and marginalized history of racial domination, a theme that allows us to glimpse the outline of a more fundamental rewriting of the narrative of American history than we might have expected from this film, a rewriting that works against the convenient myth that, as Huggins puts it, "American history—its institutions, its values, its people—was one thing and that racial slavery and oppression were a different story."[15] By articulating these stories together, the film echoes the approach of historians such as Huggins, whose words could almost serve as an epigram to certain sequences: "whereas the master narrative detached . . . slavery and the slave experience from the central story . . . there can be no white history or black history, nor can there be an integrated history which does not begin to comprehend that slavery and freedom, white and black, are joined at the hip."[16]

These ideas are powerfully expressed in the flogging scene in *Glory*, as Trip and Shaw reenact a historical pas de deux that suggests that the stories of white and black in America are inseparable and mutually defining. Trip, the black soldier whose defiant character has already called forth particularly intensive disciplinary procedures, has slipped out of camp to acquire some decent leather boots. Caught and assumed to be a deserter, Trip is brought before Shaw and the assembled company to be flogged. Shaw insists on this punishment, over the protests of his second in command, determined to show his control over the men as well as his control over his own emotions. As Trip is readied for the punishment, the drill sergeant pulls the shirt off of Trip's back to reveal a torso covered with scars from previous whippings. Despite his evident shock and dismay, Shaw sticks to the order he has given. As the whipping commences, however, a certain reversal takes place. In a series of close-up reverse shots, Trip's self-discipline and control over his body are underlined, as he receives the flogging without "breaking down." Shaw, on the other hand, appears to lose authority with each stroke of the whip, as his rigidity is coded not as a form of strength but as inflexible adherence to a code that has suddenly been revealed to have two different meanings, one having to do with military discipline, the other with racial domination.

The flogging scene in *Glory* departs from actual history—flogging was banned in the Union military—to make a larger point about the way the historical past marks black and white differently, but with the same pen. The whip marks on Trip's body are the signifiers of the other national narrative, a history that, although suppressed and marginalized, challenges the master narrative itself. Here, the film uses the imagery of scarred and lacerated flesh as a historical text to be read in counterpoint or, better, to be read interlinearly with the dominant narrative, like a coded message in which every other line carries the principal meaning, a meaning that often explicitly contradicts the text taken as a whole.

The commonality of these two histories is underlined by the physical mirroring of Trip and Shaw. Consider the following passage from Frantz Fanon on the way master and slave, colonizer and colonized, act out a kind of mirrored identification:

> A world divided into compartments, a motionless, Manichean world, a world of statues. . . . The first thing the native learns is to stay in his place and not go beyond certain limits. . . . he finds he is in a state of permanent tension. . . . The symbols of social order—the police, the bugle calls in the barracks, military parades and waving flags—are at one and the same time inhibitory and stimulating: for they do not simply convey the message "Don't dare to budge"; rather

they cry out "Get ready to attack." The impulse . . . implies the tonicity of the muscles. . . . The settler . . . keeps alive in the native an anger which he deprives of an outlet; the native [is] inwardly in a state of pseudopetrification.[17]

The flogging scene in *Glory* corresponds in an almost uncanny way to this description: the overall quality of motionlessness in its mise-en-scène, emblematized in the statue-like posture of Shaw versus the tensed, tight, muscular tonicity of Trip; the stiff formation of the soldiers; the trappings of military authority; the bugle call and the drum roll, which evoke here the contradictory emotions that Fanon describes—"Don't dare to budge," as well as "Get ready to attack"—producing an adrenalized stasis that is plainly represented in the body postures of Trip, the soldiers, and Shaw himself. Although the "symbols of social order" clearly mean different things for blacks and whites, the effects of power position Trip and Shaw in similarly fixed and inflexible roles. In an instructive analysis of Fanon's imagery, Homi Bhabha points out that the play of polarities in his description of colonial relations—Subject/Object, Self/Other, Oppressor/Victim, Power/ Powerlessness—places both oppressor and victim in exceptionally similar predicaments: both are "pseudopetrified" in their antagonism.[18] In a similar fashion, Trip and Shaw become, in a sense, mirror images; in Trip, a continuous physical tension marks the conflict between the proscriptions of social reality ("Don't dare to budge") and the impulses of psychic reality ("Get ready to attack"), whereas in Shaw, the immobilizing effects of authority seem to mummify the character, marking his features and his body posture with a kind of rictus as he resolves to exercise the power of his office.[19]

Flogging scenes are a familiar staple of narratives set in the Civil War period; what sets this sequence apart is its dialogic quality. Rather than simply appealing to the masochistic or moral propensities of the viewer, the sequence is explicitly staged as a challenge to the dominant historical order and its way of perceiving race. Trip, a "graduate of the peculiar institution with [his] diploma written on [his] back," to apply the words of Frederick Douglass, has in effect "educated" Shaw about a history he had been insulated from, a history that transforms the punishment of Trip from the singular event that Shaw perceives it to be to the replaying of a historical pattern.[20] In a striking and pointed reversal, the scene suggests that it is Shaw's understanding of the historical past—and, by extension, white America's—that is mythological and folkloric. The dominant tradition, with its idealized conception of the American past, is itself a form of mythology insofar as it represses the history of race. As Huggins writes:

> The story of the United States is of the development of the North (read Puritan New England) rather than the South. It is of whites unrelated or unengaged with blacks. It is of freedom and free institutions rather than of slavery. It is as if one were to write a history of Russia without serious consideration of serfdom: a history of India ignoring caste. The distortion would be jarring did it not serve so well the national mythology and an idealized national character.[21]

Although the film appears at first to draw the most extreme contrast between the historicity of the white tradition and the folkloric nature of its version of black history, these terms end up being reversed, as one kind of historical knowledge confronts another.

Two Historical Trajectories

With the flogging scene, *Glory* produces a striking impression of "turning the tables" on the dominant tradition. But the overall thrust of the film—which is, I think, focused even more closely on white identity than on black—also channels the message of the sequence, in another direction, bringing it back to the question of whiteness, to how the white hero will respond. The film uses this scene to instill in Shaw a layer of guilt that will be played on throughout the film. The linked themes of guilt, reparation, and reconciliation are from this point forward used to define the narrative of whiteness in a way that is distinct from the story of the black troops. Partly, this is a consequence of the psychologizing of Shaw, the focus on his emotions and sense of self-doubt. But it is also an aspect of the deeper fault line in the film, which configures the black narrative and white narrative along two different historical plot lines.

Like a painting with conflicting vanishing points, the film sets out different historical teleologies for blacks and whites. The narrative of collective emergence that characterizes the story of the African Americans is explicitly inverted in the story of Shaw, who we see discovering for the first time the hypocrisy of the white establishment. Continually confronted with venality, corruption, and lack of commitment in the military establishment, Shaw as a character becomes a way for the filmmaker to foreground the attenuation of the enlightenment narrative of history, of history unfolding in the service of liberty. With his continual wrestling with ethical dilemmas, and with the explicit message communicated through Shaw that the battle to be fought is not against an external enemy but rather against the internal complacency and self-interest of the whites, the Shaw narrative takes on the moral chiaroscuro more typical of the Vietnam film than the Civil War genre.

Nonetheless, Shaw is constructed as the hero of the narrative. Usually shown on horseback, often pictured in solitary contemplation of some distant horizon, Shaw is vested with the unmistakable iconography of the heroic. However, the film changes the meaning of his heroism from what it meant in the nineteenth century, for in *Glory* Shaw is constructed principally as a redemptive image of whiteness, a sacrificial figure who counteracts or "cleanses" the racial bias among the whites detailed throughout the film. Through Shaw, the narrative of whiteness becomes associated with social guilt and with the repayment of a historical debt. The theme of martyrdom, which dominated the Shaw legend in the nineteenth century, is here recoded to express a very different message of guilt and expiation.

In the scenes set on the road, the sense of a nation moving in two different historical directions is brought into relief. For example, one of the first shots in the film shows a mass of black families walking on the road near Antietam. As the film progresses, and as the soldiers of the Fifty-fourth become increasingly disciplined and united in their resolve, the road is converted from an image of displaced drifting to a symbol of racial striving, with synchronized marching replacing images of wandering and admiring comments from bystanders supporting a sense of growing racial identity. One of the ways the film underlines the importance of the road motif is through its repeated use of close-up shots of running, marching, and bloodied feet. In a famous line, Frederick Douglass wrote, "My feet have been so cracked with the frost that the pen with which I am writing might be laid in the gashes."[22] The film reworks this image of wounded flesh, with its links to memory, into its own representational logic to signify the coalescence of a historical force and the beginnings of a new historical epoch, as the march of the black troops through the South clearly evokes the civil rights marches of the 1960s. From this perspective, the film corresponds closely to Mikhail Bakhtin's description of the "novel of historical emergence," in which the hero "emerges along with the world and . . . reflects the historical emergence of the world itself." The soldiers of the Fifty-fourth Infantry of *Glory* are represented "at the transition point between two historical epochs," a transition that is accomplished, to paraphrase Bakhtin, in them and through them.[23]

The motif of the road conveys a very different sense of historical meaning, however, when viewed in terms of the character of Colonel Shaw. Rather than an image of collective emergence, the road represents something like a religious *via crucis* for Shaw, one that stretches from his near brush with death at Antietam to his actual death at Fort Wagner. The construction of Shaw as a purificatory figure culminates in the scene on the beach immediately prior to the assault on Fort Wagner. Here, in a solemn moment of poetic introspection, Shaw is shown gazing out to sea, in the company of his horse. In this scene, marked by solitude, interiority, and a sense of an approaching "end," there is little suggestion of an impending social transformation on the horizon. Instead, Shaw becomes the locus of a critical, post-Vietnam-style interrogation of individual and collective morality, especially the morality of white America. The message of historical emergence associated with the black troops thus meets a sense of historical closure in the character of Shaw, as the film projects a dualistic image of nation, one in which scenarios of continuity or dissolution seem equally available as possible futures that might be generated from the events of the past.

Racial Identity into National Identity

In what is clearly the summit of the film's aspirations concerning the recovery of African American history, *Glory* provides a long, detailed treatment of the collective religious ceremony called the shout, in which the black soldiers of the Fifty-fourth define their own sense of collective identity. The filmmaker, Edward Zwick, has said that discovering the "voice" for this sequence was particularly difficult, and that he relied on the black actors and their experience of contemporary churches to fashion it.[24] Here, the film shifts to a different rhetorical style and mode of address—Zwick claims that it was done in an almost improvisational way—to underline the black "authorship" of the scene. And despite Zwick's seeming disclaimer as to its historical authenticity, both the imagery and the call-and-response pattern of the shout accurately render the communal practices of black people during the Civil War years, including black Union soldiers preparing for battle.[25] Music and religion, as Paul Gilroy notes, were the two resources of communication and struggle available to slave cultures: "The struggle to overcome slavery, wherever it developed, involved adaptations of Christianity and politically infused music and dance, which, in Du Bois's phrase, comprised 'the articulate message of the slave to the world.'"[26]

But the significance of this scene lies less in its historical authenticity than in the way it opens to larger themes of racial and national identity, especially the translation of racial identity into national identity. The shout in many ways functions as a kind of nerve center of the text, bringing the issues of race and nation, of identity from below and identity from above, into vivid conjunction. As the camera focuses on the troops assembled around a campfire, a lead vocalist is seen singing lyrics that communicate a double message: the story of Noah's Ark as an allegory of the slave ship. Certain lines of the song make this relation explicit: "He packed in the animals two by two; / ox and camel and kangaroo; / He packed them in that Ark so tight / I couldn't get no sleep that night." The song underlines the themes of diaspora and wandering that will be played up throughout the sequence, and poetically converts the experience of slavery and displacement into a message of survival and providential guidance.

As the scene continues, the historical analogies encoded in song and testimony also continue, with each character's testimony accenting the themes of history and identity in a different way. Jupiter, for example, an illiterate field hand at the beginning of the film whose tutoring by the well-educated Thomas has been subtly insinuated into several scenes, speaks of going into battle with "the Good Book in one hand and the rifle in the other." The link between the Bible and the rifle calls to mind the particular accent black people of the period gave to the image of Jesus. As Lawrence Levine notes, Jesus was ubiquitous in the spirituals, but it was not the Prince of Peace of the New Testament that was celebrated but rather a Jesus transformed into an Old Testament warrior: "The God I serve is a man of war."[27] Jupiter's words also imply an image of a future that will be made with both the rifle and the book; the book, the film suggests here, is a weapon as powerful as the rifle and can serve as an agent of community, in this case bringing the rural field hand and the educated easterner together.

Another character, Rawlins, also makes a comparison to the Bible when he says that he has left his young ones and his kinfolk "in bondage." The phrase calls up images of the Israelites and the historical affinity of the black slave narrative with the story of Exodus. Finally, Trip gives a statement about the value of collective endeavor, couched in terms of family. Bereft of kin, continually on the run, Trip here redefines his tragic past through his identification with a larger collective endeavor. At the end of the sequence, Thomas, the cultured friend of Shaw, becomes the focus of the camera's attention. Although Thomas doesn't speak in this scene, he begins singing the chorus of the spiritual, clearly marking his identification with his fellow volunteers. As the film has progressed, Thomas has taken on an increasing understanding of a specifically black consciousness. When he is wounded in battle, for example, he vehemently insists that he "is not going back." The phrase conveys a double meaning. Not only does he refuse to be sent back to Boston and a life of comfort, "a cup of decent coffee, sitting by a warm fire, reading Hawthorne," as Shaw reminds him, but he refuses to go back to being a favored black man in an all-white culture. Thomas here seems to have fully embraced a black identity.

Stuart Hall has written of black identity as something that must be constructed: "The fact is 'black'. . . has always been an unstable identity, psychically, culturally, and politically. It, too, is a narrative, a story, a history. Something constructed, told, spoken, not simply found. . . . Black is an identity that had to be learned and could only be learned in a certain moment."[28] The sequence of the shout strongly conveys this sense of identity being learned "in a certain moment"; black identity is "told" and narrated in such a way that a form of community emerges out of polyphony: a collective identity is here constructed from diverse voices and distinct trajectories. With Shaw manifestly excluded from the scene, the shout becomes a way for the potency and value of black collective life to pass directly to the spectator, as if the spectator were being invited to join in a dialogic ritual that, as Gilroy says, breaks down the division between spectator and performer. The signifiers of decline, isolation, and melancholy affixed to Shaw are directly countered by the vitality and exuberance of the black soldiers.

But as the film moves to its final, climactic scenes of battlefield carnage, this initial message of black identity as a dialectic of displacement and belonging is overlaid by the unifying paradigm of nationhood, in which the suicidal attack on Fort Wagner is configured as a necessary moment in the progressive unfolding of a plenary narrative characterized by racial and social advancement. In the ensuing scenes, the expressive form and language of the shout, which explicitly articulates a narrative of black diaspora, a narrative of dispersal, is, placed in the service of a restored narrative of nation. Imagery that was used to express a fragmented,

The Fifty-fourth Regiment of the Massachusetts Volunteer Infantry fighting the losing battle at Fort Wagner. Glory. Courtesy: Photofest

diaspora history is converted here to the expression of a coalescing nationalist sensibility. The variety of linguistic practices and the sense of geographic diffusion that have been associated with the black troops throughout the film are, in its closing scenes, renarrativized in terms of an exodus whose point of resolution is the nation-state. Although strong traces of African tradition can be found in the imagery and structure of the shout, the overall message that emerges is of a translation: vernacular black culture writing itself into, or being written into, the discourse of American nationalism.

The convergence of the theme of African American emergence with the theme of national identity is staged in a remarkably direct way. In the sequence that immediately follows the shout, the soldiers are depicted in tight, parallel formation, forming a corridor through which Shaw walks as he inspects the troops. After Shaw pauses to receive a Roman-style rifle salute from Jupiter, the film cuts to a high-angle close-up of the Stars and Stripes that literally fills the screen.

Earlier, the symbolic meaning of "carrying the colors" had dominated a conversation between Trip and Shaw; Trip's refusal of this "honor" placed him on the far end of a continuum of identification and resistance that included Jupiter's eagerness to "wear the blue suits" and Rawlins' ambivalence about accepting the rank of sergeant major. But in the climactic attack on Fort Wagner, Trip has something like a battlefield conversion, seizing the colors and leading the charge—and immediately paying the price.

The "symbolic repertoire" of the community formed by the black soldiers has been portrayed in the film as relatively unfixed and still evolving, combining elements of Christianity, African tradition, local culture, and the codes of military life. But in the translation of this discontinuous history into a nationalist narrative, the film attempts to fix these symbols into universal meanings, capable of binding the whole "national community" together.[29] It attempts to assert, under the banner of the national, a sense of black and white "having a common story and necessarily sharing the same fate," an awareness of commonality that for Huggins, the author of this phrase, entails nothing less than a wholesale challenge and overturning of the master narrative of American history.[30] *Glory* takes this ideal as its goal, but stops far short of Huggins's conclusions, tying identity, instead, all the more securely to identification with the nation-state.

In the final scene, in which Trip and Shaw are buried together in a mass grave along with the other dead troops, the film refers to Griffith's *Birth of a Nation* and its very different tableau of racial brotherhood—the dying embrace of two white soldiers fighting for opposing sides. Seen as a dialogic response to Griffith, *Glory* can be said to push the question of race back into history; rather than seeing the persistence of racism and the legacy of slavery as forces that complicate or diminish the central American story, *Glory* treats them instead as necessary parts of the story, a point that is underlined by the ominous ending of the film, in which the Confederate flag is shown being raised over the bodies of the defeated troops. The overall political and historical context of emancipation is dramatized, then, not from the perspective we might expect, not as a privileged moment of decisive social change in which black and white came together, but rather from the viewpoint of the present, with its awareness of the relapses, resistance, and reactions that continue to plague the course of the struggle for racial equality in this country.

For all of the ways that *Glory* could be said to challenge racist ideology, however, its most resonant appeal is to forms of nationalism that are themselves "colored with racial connotations," reinforcing some of the ideologies the film seeks to challenge.[31] Although it restores, to some degree, the historical dimensions of black life in the United States, it also refurbishes national symbols of authority that require the renunciation of cultural particularity. And the links the film establishes among patriotism, militarism, and nationalism, its endorsement of a "mystic nationhood" revealed only on the battlefield, reinforce the dominant fiction at the site of its greatest potential harm, where it can have the most lethal consequences. Nevertheless, in its interstices, the film retains a quality of skepticism about the power of what Raymond Williams calls the "artificial order" of the nation-state in comparison to the more complete order of "full social identities in their real diversity."[32] In its unusually direct examination of identity from across—the particularities of white and black identity defined in relation to one another—the film makes evident the limits of its own nationalist solution to racial difference and antagonism, projecting in its closing images a message not about the end of slavery, but about the end of the nation as we know it. In the shots of the mass burial of the soldiers of the Fifty-fourth that end the film, the national narrative is hauntingly evoked not as a triumphal story of social progress, but as a collective narrative of social loss.[33]

NOTES

1. Michael Ignatieff, *Blood and Belonging: Journeys into the New Nationalism* (New York: Farrar, Straus & Giroux, 1993).

2. Cornel West, "A Matter of Life and Death," *October* 61 (Summer 1992): 20–23.

3. Paul Gilroy, *There Ain't No Black in the Union Jack* (London: Hutchinson, 1987), 52.

4. Peter Dimock, "Towards a Social Narrative of Loss," *Radical History Review* (Winter 1991): 54–56.

5. Richard Dyer, "White," in *The Matter of Images: Essays on Representations* (London: Routledge, 1993), 145.

6. Ibid., 141.

7. Ibid., 144.

8. Edward Zwick, the director of *Glory*, is probably best known as the co-creator of the TV series *thirtysomething*. In an interview in *Film Comment*, he describes the "anachronistic" scene in which Trip and Shaw converse about their parallel purposes as containing "a certain degree of liberal fantasy." See Armond White, "Fighting Black," *Film Comment* (January–February 1990): 26.

9. Frederick Douglass, *The Life and Writing of Frederick Douglass*, vol. 3 (New York: International, 1953): "The iron gate of our prison stands half open . . . one gallant rush . . . will fling it wide" (123).

10. Gary Scharnhorst, "From Soldier to Saint: Robert Gould Shaw and the Rhetoric of Racial Justice," *Civil War History* 34, no. 4 (1988): 308–322.

11. Ibid., 317–318.

12. See Peter Burchard, *One Gallant Rush* (New York: St. Martin's, 1965): on Douglass's sons, see 84, 139; on Charlotte Forten, see 116–117, 145–146. In the film, the black woman standing near Shaw in the Port Royal scene is, according to the screenwriter, Kevin Jarre, meant to represent Charlotte Forten.

13. Nathan Huggins, "The Deforming Mirror of Truth: Slavery and the Master Narrative of American History," *Radical History Review* (Winter 1991): 37.

14. Frederick Douglass, *My Bondage and My Freedom*, ed. William L. Andrews (Urbana: University of Illinois Press, 1987), 218–219.

15. Huggins, "The Deforming Mirror," 25.

16. Ibid., 38.

17. Frantz Fanon, *The Wretched of the Earth* (New York: Grove Weidenfeld, 1968), 51–53.

18. Homi K. Bhabha, "A Question of Survival: Nations and Psychic States," in *Psychoanalysis and Cultural Theory: Thresholds*, ed. James Donald (London: Macmillan, 1991), 98–99.

19. Ibid., 99.

20. Douglass, *My Bondage*, 218–219.

21. Huggins, "The Deforming Mirror," 31.

22. Frederick Douglass, *Narrative of the Life of Frederick Douglass, American Slave, as Written by Himself*, ed. Houston A. Baker Jr. (New York: Penguin American Library, 1982), 72;

quoted in Stephanie A. Smith, "Heart Attacks: Frederick Douglass's Strategic Sentimentality," *Criticism* 34, no. 2 (1992): 197.

23. Mikhail Bakhtin, quoted in Gary Saul Morson and Caryl Emerson, *Mikhail Bakhtin: Creation of a Prosaics* (Stanford, Calif.: Stanford University Press, 1990), 411.

24. See White, "Fighting Black."

25. See Lawrence W. Levine, "Slave Songs and Slave Consciousness: An Exploration of Forgotten Sources," in *Anonymous Americans: Explorations in Nineteenth-Century Social History,* ed. Tamara K. Hareven (Englewood Cliffs, N.J.: Prentice-Hall, 1971), 99–130.

26. Gilroy, *There Ain't No Black,* 159.

27. Levine, "Slave Songs," 120.

28. Stuart Hall, "Minimal Selves," in *Identity: The Real Me* (London: ICA, 1987), 45.

29. Gilroy, *There Ain't No Black,* 236.

30. Huggins, "The Deforming Mirror," 38.

31. Gilroy, *There Ain't No Black,* 26.

32. Raymond Williams, *Towards 2000* (Harmondsworth: Penguin, 1983); quoted in ibid., 50.

33. Variations of this phrase appear in Huggins, "The Deforming Mirror," and the separate "Responses" of Peter H. Wood, Peter Dimock, and Barbara Clark Smith, *Radical History Review* (Winter 1991): 25–59.

Michael Rogin

Home of the Brave

Do gender and regional differences explain the divergence of *Pinky* from *Gentleman's Agreement*, or is the black/Jewish contrast more fundamental? A thought experiment would imagine changing the black protagonist (like the heroine of *Pinky*) from woman to man, moving him north instead of returning her south, and transforming the gentile as Jew (like the hero of *Gentleman's Agreement*) into a Jew as black. Stanley Kramer and Carl Foreman carried out that experiment as *Pinky* was being filmed when, turning black the Jewish protagonist of Arthur Laurents's Broadway play, they made *Home of the Brave* (Mark Robson, 1949).[1]

Why did Kramer and Foreman black up Laurents's Peter Coen? For one thing, it looked like better box office . . . to shift from Jews to blacks. In addition, to "daringly substitute a Negro" for a Jew, in the prose of *Time* magazine, was, so the *Saturday Review* thought, to make a more radical choice.[2] However vicious, American anti-Semitism was not the racism that organized the society. While the United States was defeating Nazism with a Jim Crow army, there was growing recognition that American Negrophobia was the counterpart of European anti-Semitism. The NAACP journal, *Crisis*, warning against the "kernel of fascism" in the South, exposed "Southern Schrecklichkeit." "These are not wrecked Jewish establishments in Nazi Germany, but Negro businesses in democratic America," ran the caption under pictures of a "Kristallnacht" in Columbia, Tennessee. *Crisis* exposed antiblack and anti-Semitic appeals in the successful 1946 reelection campaign of Detroit mayor Edward Jeffries. The *Jewish Frontier* showed that the Cicero, Illinois race riot a few years later was fed by rumors that "Jews were planning to move Negroes into Cicero." Both *Crisis* and *Commentary* campaigned against discriminatory college admissions policies and restrictive covenants that excluded Jews and blacks from white Christian neighborhoods, the plot device on which *Gentlemen's Agreement* turns.[3]

These parallels served the black/Jewish civil rights alliance. The most virulent racists were also anti-Semites, *Crisis* reminded its readers. Racists blamed Jewish judges for tolerating black criminals. Reporting a Klan revival in the South and an increase in southern anti-Semitism, *Crisis* quoted Tennessee kleagle Jesse M. Stoner's pronouncement, "Anti-Semitism and white supremacy go hand in hand." *Commentary*, founded by the American Jewish Committee (AJC) after the destruction of European Jewry, made the fight for civil rights in the United States a central concern of the magazine's first five years. Kenneth Clark, the African American social psychologist on whose research the Supreme Court would rely in *Brown v. Board of Education,* wrote for *Commentary.* James Baldwin's first two published short stories, the only *Commentary* fiction of the period not to center on Jewish experience, appeared in the AJC organ.[4]

But although shared opposition to racism generated the civil rights alliance of the two diaspora peoples driven from their homelands, African Americans and Jews, that alliance also exposed the more privileged position of Jews, both in society and in the civil rights organizations themselves, where most of the money, legal resources, and social scientific expertise (though, crucially, not all) was in the hands of Jews, and where integrationist goals and legal means would work better for Jews than for blacks.[5] Kramer's film marked that difference when, in painting its Jewish soldier black, it turned its doctor into a Jew—not explicitly, but by replacing his gentile name with no name at all, giving him a Jewish nose and appearance, photographing him from angles and in close-ups that emphasized his facial look, and, unlike the play, hinting at his own experience of racial prejudice.

One massive social fact, however, ought to have made impossible the transformation of victim from Jew to black, even in Hollywood—and yet not a single reviewer named it, not even those most critical of the film for avoiding the real character of racial oppression in the United States. In the Jim Crow American Army of World War II, no black soldier could have been in the company of whites. The American Armed Forces were entirely segregated during the war, and the postwar debate over integration could not have been missed by anyone concerned about civil rights. A 1946 Army report proposing that an occasional Negro technician enter white units "where Negro personnel with special skills can be utilized to advantage as individuals" might have explained the black soldier's presence among whites, since he is brought in as the only available surveyor. That report not only postdated the war, however; it was also never implemented. Civil rights forces pressed for military integration in the year before *Home* was filmed, and A. Philip Randolph and the NAACP threatened black draft resistance if the Army remained Jim Crow. When, under pressure from black militance and the Henry Wallace threat, Truman finally issued his executive order in 1948 looking forward to military integration, the Army dragged its feet. It did not place black and white troops together until the Korean War.[6]

By blocking out Jim Crow . . . *Home* took its lone black man out of a black milieu. Textually the African American alone is vulnerable to racial hate, subtextually, as with blackface, to racial love. In the film's plot, Peter Moss (Peter Coen in the play, played in the movie by James Edwards) has suffered partial amnesia and a hysterical paralysis after his best friend, white, is killed on a mission to map a Japanese-held island. Through drug-induced narcosynthesis and flashback, the doctor elicits the story of racial tension among the five soldiers on the island. *Home* thereby does what the Office of War Information wanted and most war films failed to do: unite combat to the larger issue of why we fight. How can America be the home of the brave, the film asks, if it is not the land of the free?[7]

A government official had proclaimed during World War II, "By making this a people's war for freedom, we can help clear up the alien problem, the negro problem, the anti-Semitic problem."[8] This New Dealer's guilt by association aligned African Americans and aliens, not white supremacists and nativists, alongside anti-Semites. *Home of the Brave* also inadvertently makes visible the political unconscious that infected even those supporting civil rights.

Stanley Kramer named his black soldier for Carleton Moss, the Hollywood journalist who, having attacked *Gone with the Wind* (Victor Fleming, 1939) in the *Daily Worker,* had then written and starred in the World War II Army film *The Negro Soldier* (Stuart Heisler, 1943). Acknowledging the "evils which still hinder complete integration," Moss nonetheless urged black troops to resist Japanese propaganda about American Jim Crow. Once the war ended Moss had served his purpose, and the Army dropped him, as he put it, for "my un-American past." Three years later Moss promoted the film on race prejudice in the war against Japan made by his leftist friends.[9]

To accomplish Carleton Moss's goal of promoting democracy, however, the film cripples Peter Moss; it humiliates him in extended and visually intrusive ways. Although the announcement that Moss cannot walk is made at the beginning of the film, the camera first shows him, in flashback, as arguably the first dignified, erect, nonstereotyped, intelligent black leading man to appear on the Hollywood screen. Moss, unlike the white soldiers, has already volunteered for the mission in the scene where he meets them. As the white men hunch over, fearful and vacillating, not wanting to join the mission but afraid to refuse, he towers above them.

That opening scene projects the painfulness of Moss's fall. Most of the movie analyzes him as a man brought down by racism. But the film does not show what it tells, for Moss can close himself off to racial insults. Made abject by the Jewish doctor's interventions, he becomes abject again, in flashback, through his love for and loss of his white friend. The doctor injects him, forces tears from his eyes and words from his mouth, hovers over him while he's lying in bed, lectures him, berates him, sneaks behind his back to scare him with the voices of members of his mission (T. J., his persecutor, and Finch, his dead friend), holds him, cures him, and is finally the recipient of his devotion. The film puts blackvoice imitations and racist stereotypes, including a reference to Finch and Moss as Amos and Andy, into T. J.'s mouth. That method of distancing itself from blackface allows *Home* to do its own blackface on a far more powerful, because loving, level.

A fundamental contradiction runs through this film. Its ideology is "Jewish" on the *Gentleman's Agreement* model: northern, male, and integrationist, the film insists there is no difference between black and white. But its spectacle, its affect, enforces black difference as bodily excess. Assimilated to Jew at the high level of mind, Moss is made emotion-ridden and female at the low level of body. As hysterical body, Moss (née Coen) blackened an anti-Semitic stereotype that troubled the assimilating Jew. Was it integrationist identification with the victim of racial oppression that made the film so powerful a viewing experience for two white male adolescents, one Jewish, one not, watching the film a continent and a decade apart?[10] Was it aspiration to the position of power in which Jew/white helps black? Or was it male adolescent anxiety about tears, the open body, and gender confusion—brought again into play when these now grown men watched the film together with a leading (and female) film authority on cross-gender identification?

In forcing words and tears from the black face, the Jewish doctor, imitating the jazz singer before him, is effectively putting on blackface. He is making the black face and body perform emotions forbidden to his (male, Jewish) self. In turning Moss into an infant and mammy, he also joins the doctors who invade women in innumerable postwar psychological films, doctors who heal women's divided identities, as this doctor heals Moss. As a doctor film, *Home* participates in the postwar turn to psychology and the faith in the professional expert to solve the country's postwar maladjustment.[11]

Home belongs with the postwar focus on psychology in advertising, industrial relations, and child rearing, when the production of private desire motivated consumption and served regulatory functions for corporate, state, and professional institutions. The turn to psychology, to reestablish the home front division of labor interrupted by depression and war, targeted women in particular. But damage repair began with the soldiers themselves. Soldiers are ubiquitous in post–World War II films, and they typically have home front adjustment problems. Al Jolson ends up in a hospital bed in *Jolson Sings Again* (Henry Levin, 1949), victim of a lung collapse while entertaining World War II troops. The entertainer-as-war-casualty reminds us that *Home* is a combat film. The war film's effort to intensify immediate experience, through combat semantics and the documentary effect, moves into the social problem film by way of passing and psychological invasion. The combat wounds of returning veterans, in such films as *Best Years of Our Lives* (William Wyler, 1946) and *The Guilt of Janet Ames* (Henry Levin, 1947), signified internal disturbance. They were read both through the psychological tests administered to soldiers during the war and through the pervasive wartime discourse about the psychological disabilities that made so many soldiers unable to fight. Old-fashioned, moralistic condemnations of cowardice were displaced during and after World War II by attention to psychosomatic disorder. The poetic line that is *Home*'s leitmotif, "Coward take my coward's hand," asks what it means when, in the home of the brave, soldiers are rendered unfit for combat.[12]

But if psychological disablement is a universal problem of the World War II fighting man, what does race—the land of the free—have to do with it? It is in the space between the specificity of racial disablement and the universality of male lack (exhibited, for example, by the armless veteran in *Best Years*) that *Home* locates itself. The doctor's psychological detective work makes Moss and the audience experience how race prejudice has turned the black soldier into "half a man"

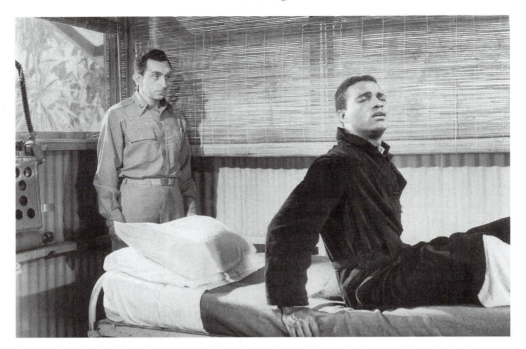

The psychiatrist (Jeff Corey) tries to get Moss (James Edwards) to walk. Home of the Brave. Courtesy: Photofest

(the title of NAACP leader Mary Ovington's book on the Negro problem). In the claustrophobic mise-en-scène of jungle and hospital room, camera angles crowd and decenter the frame, cut off body parts, and merge the Japanese menace with the pervasive racialized surround. Racial slurs, by T. J. in the Pacific and from Moss's memories of his prewar past, are brought home when Finch, having left behind the maps, starts to call Moss a "yellow-bellied nigger" for arguing against Finch's return for them. The film seems to be saying that, unable to respond aggressively to racial intimidation, Moss unconsciously wanted his best friend to be hit. When Finch dies, the analysis would go, Moss turns his racial anger inward. This psychology of the oppressed, anticipating Frantz Fanon's *Wretched of the Earth* by a decade, seems confirmed when the doctor finally gets Moss to walk by calling him a yellow-bellied nigger. Moss, exemplifying the Fanonian solution, moves forward in anger.[13]

Fanon's goal, however, is rebellion, race-conscious and violent, a direction in which *Home* can hardly go, both for political reasons and because it would acknowledge the legitimate anger blacks feel toward sympathetic whites.[14] Finch wants Moss's reassurance that he is not like all the others; it turns out that he is. Having exposed black rage, *Home* must dissolve it. On the one hand, not Moss but the invisible Japanese enact the violence of people of color. On the other hand, between the diagnosis and the walking cure intervenes the rejection of the analysis on which the film depends. The doctor has told Moss he was glad when Finch was shot, not because of the racial slur, but because all soldiers are relieved when the man next to them takes the bullet. . . .

Home consciously shifts to survivor guilt so that Moss can share with white soldiers a common humanity; the unconscious desire is to evacuate the divisive racial ground. Washing Moss white is insufficient to wipe away white guilt for his suffering, however, and when the film elicits African American forgiveness, racial stereotyping returns. The first part of *Home* deprives Moss of his black milieu as racial specificity . . . (there are no other blacks either in the neighborhood where Moss grows up or in his Army), but insists on the racial specificity of the wound to his psyche. By the film's end this distribution has been reversed. As the message deprives Moss of his difference as caused by racial prejudice, by a compensatory logic the story restores his racial difference as less than whole. The racist source of his disability is denied only after the movie turns Moss into the racially abject.

Home subjects Moss to three primal scenes of abjection. The first brings Finch and Moss together after Finch has been tortured by the Japanese. In the first shot the camera closes in on Moss alone, as Dimitri Tiomkin's mysterious, menacing wartime music mixes with the strains of "Sometimes I Feel Like a Motherless Child." Moss falls on the ground and cries, "Nigger, nigger, nigger, nigger." Supposedly a sign that he has been broken by racist slurs, the incantation announces the racist stereotype that, however sympathetic, is about to take Moss over. The dying Finch crawls through the mud to Moss, who gathers his mutilated white friend into his arms. An extended series of close-ups shows Moss babbling to Finch and listening for signs of life. His head on Finch's chest, Finch's head on his chest, hysterically rocking and cradling his friend's dead body, Moss is enacting a black and white pieta. . . . Moss is thereby . . . playing mammy. The abject is gendered feminine, writes Carol Clover.[15]

The second scene, consummating the cure through tough love, shows the doctor supporting Moss and calling him Peter after his racial insult has finally provoked the paralyzed soldier to walk. No one in the Army has ever called him Peter, Moss gratefully tells the doctor, but the first name that the doctor now incessantly repeats is no advance over "Mossie," the name given the African American in dialogue and on the cast list; no white soldier, after all, is ever called by his given name.

Moss's final abjection ends the movie, as he goes off to open a bar and restaurant with Mingo, the white soldier who, doubly castrated in the film's symbol system, has lost both his arm and his wife. Moss knows in his head that the doctor is right, that his survivor guilt makes him like other soldiers, but he only believes it in his heart when Mingo describes a similar feeling of relief. By reaching Moss's racial anger, the doctor has gotten him to walk; only interracial camaraderie, though, can lift his depression.

In bleeding black man into white, against the traditional model of closed-off and invulnerable manhood, *Home* provoked nervousness about homoeroticism among white male reviewers. *Crossfire* (Edward Dmytryk, 1947) had replaced the murdered homosexual of the book from which the movie was made with a vaguely effeminate Jew. *Home*, completing the circle, turned its Jew into an African American homoerotically bonded with a white. The movie and Leslie Fiedler's essay "Come Back to the Raft Ag'in, Huck Honey!" appeared at the same time. As Ralph Ellison responded to Fiedler, however, the scandal lay not in interracial male love but in its route through black humiliation, not in cross-gender liminality but in the need to color black the bearer of the identificatory wound. The maternal black man would offer a less contaminated healing were he not invented to care for whites. Tying Moss to the disabled veteran, the movie intends to dissolve the stigmas attaching to racial difference and amputation (and, subliminally, homosexual love), but in proclaiming that two damaged men could make a postwar life together, the movie was allying the black man with the cripple.[16]

NOTES

1. [*Editor's Note: Pinky* (Elia Kazan, 1949) is about a black woman, played by Jeanne Crain, who passes for white. *Gentleman's Agreement* (Elia Kazan, 1947) concerns a gentile reporter, played by Gregory Peck, who pretends to be Jewish in order to experience anti-Semitism.] Arthur Laurents, *Home of the Brave* (New York, 1945). Laurents would go on to write the libretto for *West Side Story*.

2. *Time*, 9 May 1949, 100; John Mason Brown, *Saturday Review of Literature*, 11 June 1949, 26–27. For the contrary view, see Manny Farber, *Nation*, 21 May 1949, 590. See also *Variety*, 4 May 1949, in *Variety Film Reviews*, 8.

3. Daniel James, "A New Coalition in U.S. Politics," *Jewish Frontier* 19 (November 1952): 5–9; Ted Poston, "The Race Riots in Cicero," *Jewish Frontier* 18 (August 1951): 5–10 (6 quoted). See, from *Crisis*, Jacob Panken, "A Northern Judge Looks at the South," 54 (February 1947): 42; untitled, 53 (September 1946): 276; "What Happened at Columbia," 53 (April 1946): 110–111; Joseph H. Genrie, "Roosevelt College and Democracy," 55 (February 1948): 45–46; untitled, 54 (October 1947): 297. And from *Commentary*, see Felix S. Cohen, "The People vs. Discrimination," 1 (March 1946): 17–22; Malcolm Ross, "The Outlook for a New FEPC," 3 (April 1947): 301–308; Charles Abrams, "Homes for Aryans Only," 3 (May 1947): 421–427; Maurice J. Goldbloom, "The President's Civil Rights Report," 4 (December 1947): 559–567; Felix S. Cohen, "Alaska's Nurenberg Laws," 6 (August 1948): 136–138; James A. Wechsler and Nancy F. Wechsler, "The Road Ahead for Civil Rights," 6 (October 1948): 297–304; Charles Abrams, "The Segregation Threat in Housing," 7 (February 1949): 123–126.

4. Panken, "A Northern Judge Looks at the South," 60; Harold P. Reese, "The Klan's 'Revolution of the Right,'" *Crisis* 54 (July 1946): 202–203; Kenneth Clark, "Candor About Negro-Jewish Relations," *Commentary* 1 (February 1946): 8–14; James Baldwin, "Previous Condition," *Commentary* 6 (October 1948): 334–342; James Baldwin, "The Death of the Prophet," *Commentary* 9 (March 1950): 257–261. Baldwin's first story addressed the problem of friendship between an African American and a Jew; in the second story, a Jewish boy, by introducing the protagonist to the movies, initiates his rift with his fundamentalist preacher father. (Baldwin retells that story as autobiography, indicating his father's anti-Semitism, in *The Fire Next Time* [New York: Dial, 1963], 53–54.) The deathbed confrontation between unforgiving father and terrified son offers an unredemptive version of *The Jazz Singer* (Alan Crosland, 1927).

5. See David Levering Lewis, "Parallels and Divergencies: Assimilation Strategies of Afro-American and Jewish Elites from 1910 to the Early 1930s," *Journal of American History* 71 (1974): 543–564.

6. Roy Wilkins, "Still a Jim Crow Army," *Crisis* 53 (April 1946): 106–108 (quoting Army report); Richard Polenberg, *One Nation Divisible: Class, Race, and Ethnicity in the United States Since 1938* (New York: Penguin, 1980), 76, 112–114. However, blacks and whites did work together in the Army Corps of Engineers, and *Bataan*'s black soldier among whites was prece-

dent for *Home*. See Thomas Cripps, *Making Movies Black: The Hollywood Message Movie From World War II to the Civil Rights Era* (New York: Oxford University Press, 1993), 72. Challenged by white southern support for the segregationist States Rights Party, and by African American and Jewish support for Henry Wallace, Truman owed his 1948 victory to massive black majorities in Cleveland, Chicago, and Los Angeles. See Polenberg, *One Nation Divisible*, 108.

7. Tom Schatz, presentation on the war film to the Film Group, Humanities Research Institute, University of California, Irvine, 11 November 1992; Clayton R. Koppes and Gregory D. Black, *Hollywood Goes to War* (New York: Macmillan, 1987).

8. Quoted in Polenberg, *One Nation Divisible*, 47.

9. Cripps, *Making Movies Black*, 22, 106–108, 125, 222–223.

10. The two adolescents were Tom Schatz and myself. Watching *Home of the Brave* again forty years later with Tom Schatz and Carol Clover decisively influenced my understanding of the film. See also Clover, *Men, Women, and Chain Saws* (Princeton, N.J.: Princeton University Press, 1992).

11. Mary Ann Doane, *The Desire to Desire: The Woman's Film of the 1940s* (Bloomington: Indiana University Press, 1987); Siegfried Kracauer, "Psychiatry for Everything and Everybody," *Commentary* 5 (March 1948): 222–228. James Agee (*Nation*, November 19,1946, 536–537) reviewed a doctor/female-divided-self film, *The Dark Mirror* (Robert Siodmak, 1946), alongside *The Jolson Story* (Alfred E. Green, 1946), perhaps sensing the invasive doubling that doctor/female patient movies share with blackface. Doane associates *Home of the Brave* with the medical discourse subgenre of the postwar woman's film in "Dark Continents," 295.

12. Schatz, seminar on the war film; Rebecca Plant, "The Menace of Momism: Psychiatry and the Anti-Woman Backlash in the Post–World War II Era" (seminar paper, Johns Hopkins University, 1992), 16–21; Dana Polan, *Power and Paranoia: History, Narrative and the American Cinema* (New York: Columbia University Press, 1986); Kaja Silverman, *Male Subjectivity at the Margins* (New York: Routledge, 1992), 52–90.

13. Silverman, *Male Subjectivity at the Margins*, 52–54, 63–90; Mary Ovington, *Half a Man* (New York: Longmans, Green, 1911); Manny Farber, "Films," *Nation*, 21 August 1949, 590–591; Frantz Fanon, *The Wretched of the Earth*, trans. Constance Farrington (New York: Grove, 1961). During the black/Jewish Crown Heights conflict of the early 1990s, there were New York City police who called Mayor David Dinkins a "nigger" and who carried signs announcing that his "true color" was "yellow-bellied" (see Elliot Cose, *The Rage of a Privileged Class* [New York: HarperCollins, 1993], 28).

14. Although Fanon interprets racial oppression psychoanalytically, he cites *Home of the Brave* to illustrate his distrust of most "talk of psychoanalysis in connection with the Negro" (*Black Skin, White Masks*, trans. Charles Lam Markmann [New York: Grove, 1967]). Fanon had yet to develop his *Wretched of the Earth* alternative. "Whites don't want you to be angry," observed Basil Paterson half a century after *Home of the Brave* (quoted in Cose, *Rage of a Privileged Class*, 31).

15. Clover, *Men, Women, and Chain Saws*, 18.

16. Richard M. Clurman, "Training Film for Democrats," *Commentary* 8 (August 1949): 182; Robert Hatch, "Good Intention," *New Republic*, 16 May 1949, 22; Leslie Fiedler, "Come Back to The Raft Ag'in, Huck Honey!" (*Love and Death in the American Novel* [New York: Criterion, 1960]); Ellison, *Shadow and Act* (New York: Random House, 1964), 51. Two critical and popular successes that offer variations on the caretaking and feminizing theme are *Driving Miss Daisy* (Bruce Beresford, 1990) and *The Crying Game* (Neil Jordan, 1992).

Brian J. Woodman

Represented in the Margins: Images of African American Soldiers in Vietnam War Combat Films

Of the numerous Vietnam combat films that have been released by Hollywood since the late 1960s, most have focused on understanding the experiences of America's combat troops in Southeast Asia. According to David James and Rick Berg, "almost all Hollywood films have proposed the experience of the GIs, either in Vietnam or on their return to the U.S., as the most authoritative guide to the war's meaning."[1] These films often attempted to reveal to U.S. audiences the "authentic" war experiences of the American soldier in Vietnam, or, the way Vietnam "really was" for American soldiers fighting there.

It is doubtful that any film could ever create an absolutely authentic cinematic image of Vietnam, as total fidelity to history is only an unattainable ideal. The difficulties that movies have had in demonstrating authentic images of American soldiers are reflected in the representations of African American troops in Vietnam War films. During Vietnam, the experiences of black soldiers were unique. These soldiers were more likely to be drafted, faced discrimination both at home and abroad, and made up a disproportionate amount of the casualties.[2] Despite the singular experiences of many black veterans, Hollywood Vietnam War films have tended to marginalize their stories, either through stock treatment or vast underrepresentation of their numbers.[3]

Although Hollywood Vietnam War films have fallen far short of the ideal of authenticity regarding the images of African American combat soldiers, some things can still be learned about black troops from these Vietnam War films. The authentic may be impossible in these films, but Vietnam War films can, in some cases, still deliver insights into what the war was like for those who fought there. These insights can be defined as cinematic representations that, although incapable of fully expressing the nature of the Vietnam War for black soldiers, are able to at least give a glimmer of truth regarding the conflict, whether by demonstrating broad historical trends of the war on film or by recounting an individual

Journal of Film and Video, 53:2–3 (Summer/Fall 2001): 38–60. © 2002 by the University Film and Video Association. Reprinted with permission of the University Film and Video Association.

soldier's story. Maybe the authentic representation of "the way it really was" for black soldiers will forever be elusive, but through the insights gained from some Vietnam films, we can at least view the shadow of the authentic experience of African American soldiers.

When examined, five Vietnam War combat films, namely, *The Green Berets* (1968), *The Boys in Company C* (1978), *Apocalypse Now* (1979), *Platoon* (1986), and *Hamburger Hill* (1987), are revealing in terms of both their insights and their misrepresentations of black Vietnam War soldiers. Films such as *The Green Berets* have done the disservice of relegating black characters to small, often stock, supporting roles. The subsequent films have delivered increasingly fascinating depictions of African American soldiers that are able to grant important insights concerning black war experiences, even though these representations are often problematic in their own ways and are usually confined to the margins of the cinematic text.

In order to investigate how Vietnam War films can misrepresent or stereotype African Americans as well as give significant insights into black experiences in Vietnam, the interplay of various factors will be examined. Ways in which the films' narrative strategies add or detract from potential insights contained within each film will be explored. These strategies include the use of voice-over narration, and what such narration, or lack thereof, suggests regarding racial representation. Specific plot situations, whether conversations between characters or actions while in the heat of battle, also have much significance. Aspects of genre formula, specifically, of the World War II combat film, are also of paramount importance in comprehending how genre conventions have contributed to both the marginalization and the development of black soldiers' stories in Vietnam films. Finally, characterization will be investigated in order to understand how black characters either reinforce traditional black stock portrayals and stereotypes, or how they manage to give insights into the African American war experience. The frequency of African American appearances in these films will also be taken into consideration, as will the number of black soldiers' deaths. Through this study, it will be demonstrated that some Vietnam War films avoid telling the story of the African American Vietnam soldier, while other films are able to grant some insight into the uniqueness of black experiences in Southeast Asia. Such an examination of the images of African American soldiers in these Hollywood Vietnam combat films can thus serve the goal of saving these often-overlooked black characters from being forgotten in the margins of the Vietnam experience.

The Relegation of Blacks to Stock Status in *The Green Berets* (1968)

John Wayne's *The Green Berets* has the distinction of being the only major Hollywood studio picture made during the Vietnam War directly concerned with the war and combat. During the late 1960s, the Vietnam War was becoming increasingly unpopular with the public. As a result, Hollywood shied away from the conflict, fearing bad box-office returns. Also, the studios knew that every night the average person could turn on the television and get the latest updates and footage from the front, thereby lessening the attractiveness of Hollywood representations of the war.[4] It took the nerve of ultra-conservative icon John Wayne to get Vietnam into theaters.

Toms and Ebony Saints

Wayne's hawkish Vietnam film depended upon the old studio formula of the World War II combat film, a genre that had served his career well in the past. According to Jeanine Basinger, the World War II combat genre is characterized in part by faceless enemies, war iconography such as fatigues and rations, climactic battles, and deaths. All of these elements are present in *The Green Berets*. World War II combat films also tend to follow a "melting pot" of stock characters from various ethnic and socioeconomic backgrounds. The stock characters are always a "mixture of unrelated types" such as married and single, educated and uneducated, or shy and bold, and are usually from different parts of the country.[5] Obeying the genre rules, the stock characters of *The Green Berets* include the goofy kid, the "good old Sarge," the country boy, and the beefy soldier.[6] In the trailer for the film, these formulaic characters are embraced. The trailer enumerates every one of the major supporting characters complete with a short description of his "stockness." For example, the trailer lists Colonel Mike Kirby as "the pro," Sergeant Provo as "the humble," and Sergeant Kowalski as "the killer." Among the characters listed in the trailer is the token black soldier, Doc McGee, played by Raymond St. Jacques. This *Green Berets* version of the token black is labeled simply in the trailer as "the dependable." According to Basinger, such a token minority character is a requirement of the genre that was present in combat films as early as *Bataan* (1943), in which Kenneth Spencer played demolition expert Wesley Epps.[7]

In *The Green Berets*, Doc is, as the name suggests, the medic of the group. Jeremy M. Devine points out that a black actor was cast as the medic in various other Vietnam War films in order to "provide a certain self-conscious racial balancing to the Nam equation."[8] Such a position, after all, would require some education, thus allowing for the appearance of social advancement for African Americans on the screen. It is important to note, however, that despite some basic medical training, Doc is still not really a doctor; it is more of an honorary title. One possible way of understanding black medics such as Doc in war films is as what Donald Bogle referred to as the stereotype of "the tom." Toms are black male characters who are first and foremost, socially acceptable, "good" blacks who never "turn against their white massas, and remain hearty, submissive, stoic, generous, selfless, and oh-so-very kind."[9] Although many of these characteristics of "the tom" do fit Doc, it would be misleading to suggest that Doc is a tom in the same sense as the naive and contented "faithful souls" portrayed in D. W. Griffith's *The Birth of a Nation* (1915).[10] Doc might be better understood as a variation on the "ebony saint" roles of actor Sidney Poitier. According to Ed Guerrero, Poitier's ebony saint characters are "sterile paragons of virtue completely devoid of mature characterization or of any political or social reality."[11] In such films as *Guess Who's Coming to Dinner?* (Stanley Kramer, 1967), Poitier "portrays a black who diligently strives to be white."[12] Whether characterized as a tom or as Poitier's ebony saint, Doc is just another in a line of nonthreatening black film characters. Doc has been put into this film to show that indeed African Americans did nobly fight in the war. The film, however, refuses to demonstrate that this black character has any purpose other than serving as a token "dependable" black man who selflessly looks after local Vietnamese children and serves at the pleasure of John Wayne's character. He exists, in short, to show that in fact yes, a good black soldier or two did serve in supporting U.S. interests in Vietnam.

Interestingly, however, African Americans were far more common than the token black character in *The Green Berets* would seem to suggest. In fact, the number of black soldiers serving in combat far exceeded their percentage of the population. The Vietnam War draft, which was biased according to income level, conscripted twice as many poor young Americans as wealthy Americans, and of these draftees, the poor were twice as likely to be assigned to combat units. Given that young black men were more likely to be poor than young white men, black men were disproportionately sent to Vietnam to face combat.[13] According to Thomas A. Johnson's "Black Servicemen and the War: 1968," African American soldiers made up 9.8 percent of all U.S. military forces in 1968, and yet black men made up almost 20 percent of combat troops in Vietnam.[14] Blacks were also poorly represented on draft boards. In 1966, although African Americans made up 11 percent of the population, only approximately one percent of draft board members were black, and seven states did not have a single black board member.[15] This discrepancy may also have contributed to black Americans' increased likelihood of being conscripted.

Despite the reality that blacks served in Vietnam in disproportionate numbers, John Wayne had no desire to give *The Green Berets* more African American characters. Wayne, answering a question about whether he limited the number of black characters in his films, acknowledged his token treatment of African Americans, while also inadvertently displaying some of the racism that has often made it difficult for African American actors to get roles in Hollywood. In this interview, Wayne stated, "I've directed two pictures and I gave the blacks their proper position. I had a black slave in *The Alamo,* and I had a correct number of blacks in *The Green Berets.*"[16] Apparently for Wayne, the correct number of African Americans in a film about a war that was made up of a disproportionate amount of minority soldiers is one major black character, and maybe a walk-on cameo.

Further examination of Wayne's political opinions adds additional layers to the understanding of the representation of African Americans in his film. In the same interview as above, Wayne said, "I believe in white supremacy until the blacks are educated to a point of responsibility. I don't believe in giving authority and positions of leadership and judgment to irresponsible people."[17] In other words, to borrow from the terminology of Bogle and Guerrero, Wayne believes in white supremacy except for the case of the toms or ebony saints. This belief of Wayne's is reflected in the characterization of Doc in *The Green Berets*. In the film, Doc is the loyal and obedient soldier who fails to express any concern for black men in Vietnam. In fact, there is no indication in the film that he is even black, other than the obvious color of his skin, as is common with ebony saint characters. He is the idealization of Wayne's black man, the trustworthy one who serves as a right-hand man to Wayne himself, never expressing any sort of independent identity. As a "dependable" black, Doc is worthy of some responsibility as the medic of his outfit, but he is still always subordinate to Wayne, and he serves for the betterment of his white leader.

Doc, who is properly educated into the beliefs of the U.S. military, also serves an important propaganda function in *The Green Berets*. Discussions about whether involvement in a war is justified are another common characteristic of the World War II combat film genre.[18] According to Vietnam scholar Milton J. Bates, black soldiers are often portrayed by white literature writers as assimilationist noble savages (such as the tom or the super-soldier) who are examples of pure patriotism.[19] This is true of Doc in *The Green Berets*. In fact, Doc's primary role in this film is to give speeches explaining why the military's involvement in Vietnam is just. He is a good black man explaining what other good black men should think. At the beginning of the film, Doc is used as the mouthpiece for why the United States must intervene in Vietnam in order to protect the South Vietnamese from the brutality and savagery of the communist enemy. According to Doc, if the atrocities committed by the North Vietnamese had occurred in America, "every teacher that you'd ever known would be tortured and killed, every professor you ever heard of, every governor, every senator, every member of the House of Representatives and their combined families all would be tortured and killed, and a like number kidnapped." That is why Doc insists the South Vietnamese "need us [. . .] and they want us." Thus, Doc is never allowed to develop into anything more than a hybrid of the tom serving at the side of John Wayne, and the purely intentioned, patriotic ebony saint who extols the right-wing propaganda that Wayne wished to disseminate in his film.

The Response to The Green Berets

The Green Berets brought in close to $20 million at the box office, nearly a $14 million profit, thus making it a financial success.[20] Nonetheless, it was universally panned by critics for its anachronistic dependence upon World War II film ideas and its right-wing politics. In one scathing *New York Times* review, Renata Adler proclaimed: "*The Green Berets* is a film so unspeakable, so stupid, so rotten and false in every detail that it passes through being fun, through being funny, through being camp, through everything and becomes an invitation to grieve, not for our soldiers or for Vietnam (the film could not be more false or do a greater disservice to either of them) but for what has happened to the fantasy-making apparatus in this country. . . . It is vile and insane. On top of that, it is dull."[21] A 1968 *Variety* review added to the torrent of derision, stating that the script "is so loaded with corn and cardboard that 'hawks' may be embarrassed, while 'doves' will be embarrassed for the hawks."[22] As controversy surrounding the war increased, Hollywood avoided another venture back into the terrain of the Vietnam War film for another decade. When Hollywood studios finally did produce more Vietnam War films in the late 1970s, they were sure to treat them with more complexity than did Wayne. Although images of African American soldiers in Vietnam War films after *The Green Berets* were far from perfect, they were never again so wretched.

The World War II Film Turned on its Head: *The Boys in Company C* (1978)

It took most of the decade of the 1970s before another film portrayed combat in Vietnam. Hollywood avoided the subject of Vietnam because of the controversy and lingering doubts about the war, as well as the concerns about whether or not Vietnam would sell at the box office. According to Peter McInerney, "how could films succeed which reminded audiences of military stalemate if not outright defeat, generated guilt about suffering inflicted on Vietnamese and Americans, or caused bandaged cultural wounds to bleed afresh?"[23] Such fare was not considered a safe box-office bet. It was not until Sidney J. Furie's *The Boys in Company C* that combat in Vietnam was turned into movie material again.

Just Another Combat Film?

To some film scholars, *The Boys in Company C* merely rehashed World War II combat film conventions. According to Albert Auster and Leonard Quart, *The Boys in Company C*'s "World War II film clichés are carried even to the extent of following the adventures of a melting pot platoon of young marines, updated for the 1960s to include a young, idealistic hippie . . . and an urban black . . . from basic-training innocents to hardened combat vets."[24] From this description, it seems that *The Boys in Company C* falls into the same patterns as *The Green Berets*. As Terry Christensen notes, however, this film avoids *The Green Berets'* simplicity by showing that this platoon is like nothing seen before in a combat film. One soldier is addicted to heroin, while another deals drugs, and yet another destroys Army property for fun.[25] Such nihilistic behaviors by stock characters are a tremendous deviation from the actions of characters in *The Green Berets*.

Similarly, it would seem that the presence of only one African American character as a stock black soldier limits the amount that the film can say regarding the issue of race in Vietnam. This assumption seems even more relevant when one recognizes that the film is narrated by a white soldier, which suggests a predominantly white perspective for the film. Initially, the single black character, Tyrone Washington, played by Stan Shaw, seems like a simple stereotype. Tyrone is a young black hustler from the south side of Chicago. He is an outsider from the streets that has been transplanted to the training grounds of the Marine Corps. He is a man who will not participate in call-and-response exercises, and he pushes other, slower troops out of the way on the obstacle course. He is even initially seen trying to work out a method for drug trafficking. Early in the film, this hardened man from the inner city threatens his fellow trainees, "Don't mess with me. Don't mess with me. Don't bring no heat down on me. You're all headed for a fall, and I ain't taken the ride. Do you dig?" Tyrone seems to be a stereotypical street hustler, complete with loner posturing and an inner-city lingo, who doesn't yet know the combat film value of teamwork. If the story of Tyrone's character is not examined further, *The Boys in Company C* appears to be just another film in the World War II style about the rebel recruit who falls in line for the sake of the troop.

In *The Boys in Company C*, however, things are not always what they seem. Four new recruits arrive at the training grounds. These bigoted men spout racial epithets at Tyrone while he works at a menial painting task. One says to Tyrone: "They got more niggers in this platoon than the Oakland fuckin' Raiders. Hey Sambo, why don't you get some of that whitewash on your black ass there. Hey boy, what you goin' inside for there, boy? I thought the hot sun don't bother you cannibals none."

This short scene exemplifies the rampant racism that black soldiers frequently faced in Vietnam. In Wallace Terry's collection of interviews, *Bloods: An Oral History of the Vietnam War by Black Veterans*, there are various personal accounts of similar racial confrontations. Staff Sergeant Don F. Brown recounted how one white soldier responded to a television report on the assassination of Martin Luther King Jr. by stating, "I wish they'd take that nigger's picture off."[26] Radarman Dwyte A. Brown remembered how some white soldiers flew Confederate flags and burned a cross.[27] Sergeant Major Edgar A. Huff even recalled having hand grenades thrown at his house on base by white soldiers who did not like his level of success in the military.[28] Although the racial slurs hurled at Tyrone are not physically threatening, as are the personal accounts of cross burnings and grenade attacks, *The Boys in Company C* has made it clear that it will not skirt over the issue of race in the fashion of earlier combat films such as *The Green Berets*.

Tyrone: Angry Leader or Black Urban Stereotype?

Upon viewing *The Boys in Company C*, it quickly becomes apparent that Tyrone Washington is one of the most significant voices in this film. In fact, he is quickly transformed into the platoon's heroic leader. Tyrone is the man who kills the Viet Cong snipers who are cutting American soldiers to pieces during one particularly

Tyrone (Stan Shaw) and the men in company assault the enemy; Tyrone is aiming at a cruel American commander. The Boys in Company C. Courtesy: Photofest

horrible firefight while others remain frozen, pinned down by their own artillery fire. He is the one who looks out for a drug-addicted comrade after he overdoses. It is also Tyrone who leads the men in the climactic soccer game against the South Vietnamese and scores the winning goal, thus defying the wishes of the military brass who expect them to throw the game. Such idealization of Tyrone and his abilities runs the risk of seeming to be false overcompensation to prove just how good black men can be in service of the white man's Army, a possible positive stereotype. The filmmakers, however, are smart enough to also show a more personal side to Tyrone. At the end of the movie, Tyrone, thinking of the well-being of one of his fellow soldiers, Pike, tells a medic that Pike has brain damage from a battle. This is a lie, but a lie meant to return Pike to the United States to his newborn child. Likewise, after the narrator, Al, throws himself on a grenade to save his fellow men, Tyrone embraces Al's best friend, the hysterical Vinnie, and says to him, "You're a man. You can cry any goddamn time you get ready." Tyrone is not just a stock black soldier serving his country; in fact, he is the group's leader, the cohesive glue holding the men of the unit together.

Although Tyrone is the leader of this predominantly white platoon, his character does not lose touch with the concerns of African American soldiers in Vietnam. In a move away from the ebony saint stereotype present in *The Green Berets*, Tyrone is allowed to comport himself actively and aggressively. In some ways this change in black representation seems to pull from the evolution of the

World War II genre. In World War II films of the 1960s, such as *The Dirty Dozen* (John Sturges, 1967), all of the members of the melting pot units are more angry and assertive. In *The Dirty Dozen,* in fact, each man is a criminal, and the token black character is no exception. In the film, Jim Brown's black character has killed two white men who attacked him.[29] In *The Boys in Company C,* Tyrone is also an angry misfit lashing out at racism, a strong voice of black rage. When an officer executes a Vietnamese villager, Tyrone stands up to him and says, "You wouldn't have done that if that was a white boy back there. Yeah, but to you he's nothin' but a gook. I mean he's just a yellow nigger." Tyrone has not only under-scored the bigotry he has experienced in Vietnam, but also the racism inherent in the war against the Vietnamese. In *Bloods,* black veteran Emmanuel J. Hollo-man made a similar observation. Holloman noted that generally black soldiers got along better with the Vietnamese. He claims that "the majority of the people who came over [to Vietnam] looked down on the Vietnamese. They considered them ragged, poor, stupid. They just didn't respect them. I could understand poverty."[30]

Through the character of Tyrone Washington, *The Boys in Company C* thus has begun to explore the vast polarization of the races that was taking place in Vietnam by the end of the 1960s.[31] It would be remiss to say that this connec-tion between black soldiers and the Vietnamese is an absolute truth of the Viet-nam War; such a statement is difficult to prove. Nonetheless, as demonstrated in *Bloods,* some black soldiers did indeed feel a kinship with the Vietnamese based on poverty and a subjection to the racism of white soldiers. In *The Boys in Com-pany C,* Tyrone lets this perspective be known.

Although *The Boys in Company C,* through the character of Tyrone Wash-ington, is able to give greater insight into the black experience in Vietnam than *The Green Berets,* the film does on occasion resort to stereotyping. For example, in a confrontation between Tyrone and a white drill instructor, the DI reveals his stereo-typical assumptions. In this argument, the drill instructor yells at Tyrone, "I got eight fuckin' weeks to teach these goddamned people what it took you twenty years to learn on the streets." The drill instructor believes that growing up in the south side of Chicago automatically means that a person is a trained warrior, an assump-tion that the film seems to share. This assessment falls back on an exaggerated image of the tough inner-city streets, and suggests that growing up in a poor, pre-dominantly black neighborhood is somehow tantamount to combat experience in Vietnam. Obviously, life in Chicago and life during the Vietnam War are not com-parable experiences, despite the hardships that inner-city life may bring. Likewise, although the film does develop Tyrone's character, this movie could still be criti-cized for falling back on stock characters and the classic rebel-turns-good war story. Ed Guerrero asserts that the strong black character of Jim Brown in *The Dirty Dozen,* for all his potency and assertiveness, still always served white authority.[32] Similarly, Tyrone acts heroically and expresses his rage at discrimination in Viet-nam, yet in the end he serves to bind together the remaining white men of Company C. Also, the film still only portrays one major black character, thus following the rather limited World War II combat genre conventions.

Despite these problems, *The Boys in Company C* should be applauded for what was a major advance in the portrayal of African Americans from the tom and ebony saint characterizations of *The Green Berets*. According to Ed Guerrero, during the 1970s, Hollywood produced ever-decreasing numbers of black-focused films. In 1977, only four of 311 films produced were black-centered, and throughout the rest of the decade, Hollywood averaged only six or seven black-focused productions a year.[33] At a time when Hollywood was regrettably silent both on issues regarding race and on the Vietnam War, the strong black lead of Tyrone Washington in *The Boys in Company C* seems exceptional. This film took the World War II film formula and applied it to Vietnam, then shook it apart, making it into what Peter McInerney called "an upside-down version of *The Green Berets*." It entered unchartered territory in its portrayal of Vietnam as "a breeding ground for imperialism, racism, corruption, and death."[34] Viewing the film from the comfortable distance that two decades afford, it is not difficult to find imperfections in its representations of African Americans, and it is easy to complain that such failings render this film as innately inauthentic. Nonetheless, The *Boys in Company C* took a step forward, seemingly against the tide of the rest of Hollywood, by focusing attention on a black soldier and by exploring how issues of race infiltrated men's experiences in Vietnam. Although *The Boys in Company C* is occasionally problematic in its representations of African Americans, looking to the margins of the film allows for significant insights into black war experiences.

Race and the Surreal:
Images of African Americans in *Apocalypse Now* (1979)

When Francis Ford Coppola arrived at the Cannes film festival with his epic Vietnam War film, *Apocalypse Now*, the director made the grandiose claim that he had created an authentic representation of the Vietnam War on celluloid. Coppola asserted to listeners at a press conference, "My film is not a movie; it's not about Vietnam. It *is* Vietnam. It's what it was really like; it was crazy."[35] Although this statement smacked of pretension to many, it does bring up a significant concern. What exactly does Coppola mean when he says that his film "is Vietnam"? In what way is this film "authentic"? Obviously he does not believe that *Apocalypse Now* is historically accurate in a literal sense. This film, loosely based on Joseph Conrad's *Heart of Darkness*, is not literal at all. It is a film steeped in surrealism, a film that takes its protagonist, Captain Willard, down a mythic river where he encounters individuals and events that can only be viewed as metaphoric. Coppola's movie does not seek textbook realism; rather, it strives for the "feel" of Vietnam: the violence, confusion, and nihilism of the war.

Given the film's penchant for the surreal, how can its images of African American soldiers be fairly evaluated? It would be inadequate (and not necessarily accurate) to view the film's representation of black soldiers only according to the frequency of screen appearances or their ability to advance the plot, the elements that often define a character as "central" to a film. In this movie, it is Willard's journey to find the insane Kurtz that is of paramount importance; all other characters exist only to symbolize some aspect of the war. After all, Coppola's agenda in making this movie was to give the bare essence of many facets of the Vietnam War, not just images of the soldiers. At Cannes, Coppola explained his approach to selecting film content. He stated: "So I made a list of all the things you would have to touch on to make an honest film about Vietnam, and there were 200 things. Like the use of drugs, the fact that black soldiers were up at the front line, the fact that American officers lived in affluence."[36]

Recognizing Coppola's broad intentions and the general lack of development of all the characters, the representations of black soldiers should therefore be evaluated according to how the characters are "typed" in their limited appearances, and according to what facets of the war experience they represent. Thus, the development, although limited, of these black characters in the film's margins can perhaps be a useful ground for gaining insights into the African American Vietnam War experience.

Crewmen and Casualties

William J. Palmer notes the significance of *Apocalypse Now* in its representations of African Americans in Vietnam. According to Palmer, "blacks are everywhere in *Apocalypse Now*," whether as important supporting characters or soldiers fighting on the front lines.[37] It is true that the depth of the major black roles in the film is limited, but no more limited than the other roles in the film, excepting Willard and Kurtz. In a 1979 interview in *Rolling Stone*, Greil Marcus questioned Coppola about the inscrutability of the film's supporting characters. In response, Coppola admitted that he did not give these characters much development. He stated, "I did not feel that was what my mission was. I didn't want to spend the time it takes to develop a real group of comrades—I didn't think that was what it was about. . . . I just didn't feel right about giving more than I did."[38]

Although there is little development given to any of the supporting roles, the film gives the most attention to the four-member crew of Willard's boat. Of this vessel's crewmen, two members, Clean (Larry Fishburne) and Chief (Albert Hall), are African American. Clean is a teenager from the South Bronx. Although he comes from a inner-city background similar to that of Tyrone Washington in *The Boys in Company C*, Clean is not as defined by his "inner city-ness." He may be from a poor, urban background, as many African American soldiers were, but his character is not developed with its emphasis solely on this fact. Instead, he is portrayed as a kid who loves rock and roll, motorcycles, and the freedom that Vietnam gives him. His human side is further revealed in an audiocassette from his mother that is played while on the boat. His mother speaks of the family's excitement regarding his eventual return home, and she says they are saving up to give him a car when he gets back. She finishes the message by asking him to "bring your hiney back home all in one piece, 'cuz we love you very much." Clean is portrayed as one of the many kids fighting in Vietnam, complete with a loving family and a lot of life left to live upon returning home. This representative of lower-class minorities that were present in Vietnam is not simply defined by his black urban background.

The other black member of the crew is Chief, the boat's captain. Chief is a strong, disciplined, no-nonsense man. In the words of Willard, "It might have been my mission, but it was sure as shit Chief's boat." Chief sees himself and his crewmates as having a job to do in Vietnam, and he works to fulfill that responsibility. He has little patience for Willard or the mysterious mission that endangers his men and prevents them from fulfilling their duties. At one point, Chief states to Willard, "Until you reach your destination, Captain, you're just along for the ride." Chief is also a man who first and foremost cares about the men on his boat, particularly Clean. He halts an altercation between Clean and a fellow member of the crew, berating the other crewman for the tension. Chief also calms Clean's nerves when they see two men blown off of a bridge, assuring the youngster that he will be okay. When Clean is killed during an attack on the boat, Chief weeps for the young boy, suggesting that Chief feels as if he has lost a son. Thus, although his role is not thoroughly developed, Chief is not a token character. Looking at the subtleties of Chief's character reveals a strict but caring man whose primary loyalty is to his comrades.

Outside of the characterizations of these two African Americans, the marginal characters of *Apocalypse Now* also have much to offer regarding issues of race in Vietnam. Indeed, the film quietly points out some of the injustices experienced by African American soldiers in Vietnam. During Colonel Kilgore's helicopter assault on a Vietnamese village, the first American is wounded in the film. The victim is an anonymous black soldier who lies on the ground, screaming in pain as a medic treats his bloodied leg. Although a very small moment, the wounding of this man in the film and his status as the first casualty suggest the unfortunate reality of Vietnam that black soldiers made up a disproportionate number of American casualties. During the period from late 1966 to early 1967, black casualties peaked at as high as 25 percent of the total number of casualties, even though African Americans only made up 11 to 12 percent of the U.S. population as a whole.[39] The death of Clean is a further comment on the rampant black casualties in Vietnam. In this context, Chief's grief for Clean takes on particular significance. According to Gilbert Adair, "What may be interpreted as the natural and understandable expression of [Chief's] grief is, however, transformed by lighting and framing into a maudlin Pietà of racial oneness and brotherly solidarity. . . . Clean becomes almost a symbol for the wrongs committed by America's white establishment against blacks" and other minorities in the war.[40] Likewise, Chief is killed by a spear during an attack on the boat. Thus, the first two of the boat's crewmen to die are African American. These short but revealing moments connote the fact that blacks serving in Vietnam had to deal with the very real concern that they were more likely to be killed in combat than whites.

Race at Do Lung Bridge and Beyond

Another event in *Apocalypse Now* underscores significant racial realities in Vietnam: the battle at Do Lung Bridge. In this scene, black soldiers struggle to hold the bridge, discharging their weapons at an unseen enemy. In screenwriter John Milius's first draft of the story, the U.S. soldiers at the bridge were not specified to be of a particular race. According to biographer Jeffrey Chown, however, in the final film, Coppola made a conscious decision to make all the American combatants at the bridge African American in order to underscore the reality that a disproportionate number of the front-line troops in Vietnam were black and from impoverished neighborhoods.[41] Christopher Sharrett reiterates this view of black soldiers at Do Lung Bridge when he says: "The abandoned black soldiers firing wildly into the night are the images of minorities used as cannon fodder."[42] This scene thus subtly reflects a harsh reality of Vietnam: black soldiers were more readily put into platoons that saw action on the front lines.

Although *Apocalypse Now* in many ways succeeded in quietly presenting the problems of African American soldiers, the film has not gone without criticism concerning its representations of race. One such criticism concerns the portrayal of one particular black soldier, Roach, at the Do Lung Bridge. Roach is an expert killer who has a Zen-like ability to pinpoint the location of the enemy and exterminate him. He is outfitted in war paint and a necklace of teeth that resemble the garb of an African warrior.[43] Even his grenade launcher is painted in a tiger pattern. This representation of a black soldier as some sort of latter-day African warrior might seem problematic, possibly suggesting the racist stereotypes of "primitive" Africa present in *Heart of Darkness*. The words of Coppola suggest that this interpretation of Roach may have some validity; in an interview he revealed that beginning with Do Lung Bridge, the film began "moving back in time" in order to "imply that the issues and the themes were timeless."[44] By revealing this intention of the film to move metaphorically back in time, Coppola indirectly admits that he is making this connection between a black soldier and the "primitive" Africa of *Heart of Darkness*. This problematic representation of an African American in *Apocalypse Now*, however, must be qualified by the fact that all characters of all races seem to be moving backward in history after the Do Lung Bridge sequence. One white American soldier, Colby, the man who was sent up the river before Willard to dispose of Colonel Kurtz, also has acquired a more "primitive" look. A shirtless Colby stands guard over Kurtz's compound, a shrunken head hanging from his rifle. Thus, although it is possible to take issue with the representation of Roach as a "primitive Africa" stereotype, it should be noted that Coppola's move toward the primitive was applied to many characters, regardless of race. Of course, Roach may still seem problematic in that he is the only character whose "primitive" garb seems distinctly African.

In *Apocalypse Now*, Coppola attempted to use metaphoric means to reveal the essence of what the Vietnam experience was like. If the film is viewed literally, this effort to get at the "truth" of Vietnam is missed. One African American vet who viewed *Apocalypse Now* in such a literal way, Reginald Edwards, did not feel that this surreal film represented the Vietnam that he experienced. Edwards stated, "*Apocalypse Now* didn't tell the truth. It wasn't real. . . . It didn't remind me of anything I saw."[45] If the film is read on a more surrealistic and symbolic level, however, some interesting insights into the nature of African Americans' Vietnam War experience can be gleaned. Although the film has few developed characters, the portrayals of Clean and Chief, two black soldiers, come about as close to being complete as any supporting characters in this movie. Small moments in the film, such as the multiple African American casualties and the battle at Do Lung Bridge, serve as powerful symbols of the inequities of the war that often led to high rates of black casualties, where fighting was heaviest. *Apocalypse Now* is not without its potential problems regarding the representations of the experiences of black combat soldiers in Vietnam, especially with its inherent limitations in characterization and its occasional flirtation with primitive stereotypes. Despite these weaknesses, by viewing the film as the surrealistic piece that it is meant to be, an interesting thumbnail sketch of the lives and problems facing African American soldiers in Vietnam does emerge from the film's margins.

The Way It Really Was: Race, Realism, and *Platoon* (1986)

Apocalypse Now may have professed to "be Vietnam," but the film's dependence on myth and symbolism to communicate the insanity of the war hindered audiences from believing that they were seeing Vietnam "the way it really was." Through the first half of the 1980s, America still awaited a film that would be *the* authentic rendering of the experience of the Vietnam soldier. With the release of Oliver Stone's *Platoon* in 1986, many proclaimed that the first "true" Vietnam film had been made. In a 1987 article for *Time* entitled *"Platoon:* The Way Viet Nam Really Was, on Film," David Halberstam, who had reported in Vietnam, was quoted as praising *Platoon* for being "the first real Viet Nam film [. . .] and one of the great war movies of all time." He went on to say, "the other Hollywood Viet Nam films have been a rape of history. But *Platoon* is historically and politically accurate."[46] This praise stemmed largely from the film's relentless focus on the common combat soldier and his experiences, as well as the naturalistic quality of the film's images. Journalist Peter Blauner of *New York Magazine*, writing about the film at the time of its release, stated that "unlike *Apocalypse Now* or *The Deer Hunter*, which used the Vietnam War as a metaphor, *Platoon* is about the real place and the real time. Stone shows what soldiers went through on a day-to-day basis in Vietnam and how the war turned them against one another."[47] Some supporters suggested that the film was able to convey the complex tensions inhabiting the United States in the 1960s. Richard Corliss credits director Oliver Stone with making a Vietnam film that demonstrates the fact that "in Vietnam [. . .] GIs re-created the world back home, with its antagonisms of race, region and class."[48]

Clearly many individuals in the 1980s thought that *Platoon* was an authentic representation of the Vietnam experience. Such opinions, however, raise the question, What makes this film more authentic than others? How much closer does it come to allowing the audience to understand what the Vietnam experience was like for the American soldiers? In addition, if the function of the film, in Oliver Stone's words, is that it "reminds us what war is really like," then we might ask if *Platoon* is able to present the war as it was perceived by African American soldiers fighting in Southeast Asia.[49]

Much of *Platoon*'s claim to authenticity comes from the fact that it was written and directed by Oliver Stone, a Vietnam veteran. Stone, in an essay about the making of *Platoon*, states that "I wrote it as straight as I could remember it."[50] This staging of his Vietnam memories on film is complete with "battles and incidents he had been involved in," as well a re-creation of "the strife within his original platoons—between the redneck 'juicers' and the 'heads,' pot smokers who were just trying to get out alive."[51] As noted by Stone biographer James Riordan, even the characters used in *Platoon* were largely based on people Stone had known in the service.[52] Unfortunately, the fact that the film reflects Stone's personal memories of the war does not automatically make the film an authentic representation of the way Vietnam really was for other GIs, particularly minority GIs. What it does do, however, is give very real insights into his individual experiences in Vietnam.

Stone, as a veteran writing from his own experience, certainly does have a strong grasp of what he remembers of the war, but it is important to qualify his representations with the fact that they are indeed memories. The view of the war in this film is inescapably colored by the fact that it is being told from Stone's perspective, the perspective of a white man from a middle-class background who is peering back at his experiences. His memories, like those of anyone, are inevitably swathed in a thick layer of subjectivity. The way that he remembers the war may not necessarily be the way that all servicemen perceived it, especially minority soldiers who were drafted into the war. This is in no way a criticism of Stone. After all, Stone admitted that these war memories come from his own perspective when he created a screenplay for *Platoon* that has a narrator and protagonist that is clearly intended to be himself, a white, middle-class kid who volunteered for Vietnam. Therefore, when viewing representations of African American soldiers in *Platoon*, it should be kept in mind that the black troops are being represented in the shards of memory of a white soldier. African Americans are not representing themselves.

Race, Class, and Politics

Although the film is told from the perspective of a white character, in his Vietnam recollections, Stone did not exclude African American soldiers. Stone remembers that in all of his Vietnam units, there was a distinct division "on the one hand, the lifers, the juicers, and the moron white element . . . against, on the other, the hippie, dope smoking, black, and progressive white element."[53] Within this platoon dichotomy, Stone places all but one of the film's six black soldiers within the outcast "hippy, dope smoking" contingent to which he belonged. Granted, these black characters are still supporting players in this film, but "Stone grants them just enough individuality to avoid turning them into characterless abstractions even though the film's prime focus, as in most Vietnam films, is on the experience of white, not black soldiers."[54] The film is also successful in that it avoids turning most black soldiers into stereotypes or stock characters. In a review for the *New York Times*, Vincent Canby said of the cast of supporting characters, "The other members of the platoon don't wear labels that immediately characterize them," and he recognized that "Mr. Stone appreciates the singularity of the grunts without italicizing them."[55] African American soldiers may not be put into the foreground of *Platoon*, but at least most avoid stock treatment.

Although Stone does not make black grunts his primary focus, he allows his black characters to address some of the political concerns of African American troops in Vietnam. The African American soldiers that reside in *Platoon* are well aware of their race and the position in which it puts them while in the service. As recognized by Specialist 4 Robert E. Holcomb in *Bloods*, most black soldiers "were put in the jobs that were the most dangerous, the hardest, or just the most undesirable."[56] Reflecting this fact in *Platoon*, one black soldier, Junior (Reggie Johnson), complains to another black man that they are always put on dangerous ambush patrols. Junior laments, "God damn, man. You break your ass for the white man. There's no justice around here." Another black soldier, Francis (Corey Glover), has a cynical answer for why they are given this treacherous responsibility. He intones simply, "'cuz it's politics, man. Politics." These African American soldiers know that they are in the most dangerous combat situations simply because they are black. Later in the film, Big Harold (Forest Whitaker) angrily vents his frustration at his inability to get a job away from the fighting. Harold says, "Hell, I got to paint myself white just to get me one of those fuckin' jobs." Harold, too, is aware of the fact that, more often than not, black soldiers are sent into combat. This inequity is underscored by the fact that at the end the film, of the six black characters in *Platoon*, only King and Francis return to the United States without serious injury. The high black casualty rate in this film reflects the fact that half the soldiers in combat-rifle companies that saw action in the field were minorities.[57]

When facing questions of race in *Platoon*, Stone is also perceptive enough not to reduce these issues to simple matters of black and white. Stone connects the film's racial tensions to issues of class, particularly the fact that many blacks

Taylor (Charlie Sheen) bonds with King (Keith David). Platoon. Courtesy: Photofest

who fought in Vietnam were poor draftees. In one scene, the film's white protag-onist, Chris (Charlie Sheen), bonds with a black character, the poor, rural-born King (Keith David), while they perform latrine duty, a task they have been assigned because of their status as outsiders. King asks Chris why he is in Viet-nam. Chris reveals that he dropped out of college and volunteered for combat. The exchange continues:

> KING: You'se a crazy fucker. Givin' up college?
> CHRIS: It didn't make much sense. I wasn't learning anything. I figured why
> should just the poor kids go off to war and the rich kids always get away
> with it.
> KING: Oh, I see. What we got here is a crusader [. . . .] Shit, you gotta be rich
> in the first place to think like that. Everybody know the poor always
> bein' fucked over by the rich. Always have. Always will.

In this exchange, Stone is able to make a very sly maneuver. He connects race and class in a way that suggests why black soldiers were sent to Vietnam in disproportionate numbers, and he also demonstrates how such poor blacks, once in Vietnam, are given the worst jobs. More important, however, Stone, through his white protagonist, effectively acknowledges the film's white perspective. He reveals through Chris, who represents the young Stone in the film, the classist assumptions of many whites toward blacks in Vietnam. In a well-meaning recog-nition of racial and class inequities, Chris volunteered for the war. But in doing so, he gave up college, an opportunity many poor African Americas could never even imagine, without a second thought. Through this exchange, Stone underscores the serious race and class issues underlying the involvement of blacks in the Vietnam War, while simultaneously recognizing that, try as they might, the white middle class were unable to understand the extent of black problems.

Platoon's African American soldiers, although only supporting players, do not appear in the film only to symbolize the plight of black troops in Vietnam. A few are given a hint of multidimensionality. After the platoon has committed an atrocity against a Vietnamese village not unlike the My Lai massacre, many of the black men in the platoon congregate to discuss their feelings about their complicity in the killings. Some of the men are haunted by what was done by the platoon, while others throw their support behind the chain of command that allowed the atrocity to go on. These black soldiers do not all share a common point of view. What they do share is camaraderie and a sense of racial cohesion that allows them to function amid the horrors of Vietnam.

Criticisms of Black Portrayals in Platoon

Although *Platoon* is filled with material that emphasizes the inequities of Vietnam for African Americans, a handful of critics have taken exception to Stone's representation of his black characters. Richard Corliss, for example, bemoans the presence of what he sees as a passive racism in the movie. He claims that "the black soldiers are occasionally patronized and sentimentalized; they stand to the side while the white soldiers grab all the big emotions."[58] More scathingly, Clyde Taylor feels that *Platoon*, having removed blacks from their exile in the background, has still avoided putting them in the foreground, relegating them "off its center." He also feels that the main black character, King, "is a convention, a soulful, downhome, church-mothered brother" that veers toward a stereotypical version of a black male mammy. Taylor further contends that the character of Junior is portrayed as a petty, cowardly, whiny, black Nationalist buffoon, a throwback to old African American stereotypes such as the coon and Sambo.[59] Taylor concludes that *Platoon* only portrays blacks in a positive light when they reinforce the colonial power of the United States and identify with traditional Western values.[60]

Despite Taylor's correct assessment that King identifies with Western values, his categorization of King as a male mammy ignores many of the positive aspects of this character in representing dissenting African American views. Taylor oversimplifies when he asserts that King is characterized by "brotherly accommodationism." Although King does act as a teacher for the white Chris, he educates the naïve Chris in the complexities of race and class. As quoted above, while King and Chris perform latrine duty, King references the historic mistreatment of the disadvantaged, while pointing out Chris's well-meaning condescension when Chris reveals that he volunteered for war. Later in the film, when Chris complains about the senselessness of Vietnam, King expresses the frustration of poor blacks. Irritated, King explains that if the wealthy, white Chris can just make it out of Vietnam, then "it's all gravy, every day of the rest of your life—gravy." Although, as Taylor states, King does serve as a father figure for the young, white Chris, he is not simply a "black male mammy to innocent white youth" who lacks any moral authority.[61] In fact, he is the man in *Platoon* who most clearly expresses the unjust discrimination faced by poor black men.

Taylor's charges against the character of Junior, however, seem to have significant merit. In the film, Junior falls asleep on an ambush, then tries to lay blame on Chris. Later, during the village massacre scene, Junior can be seen participating in the rape of a young Vietnamese girl. Near the end of the film, Junior, in an attempt to avoid battle, sprays his feet with insect repellant to make them swell. Finally, Junior is killed while running away from his foxhole, leaving another soldier there alone. Junior clumsily rams his head into a spear that has been placed in a tree, knocking him down. This less-than-dignified event allows an enemy soldier to stab Junior to death with a bayonet. Such a representation of a black man as an irresponsible, inept, and cowardly sexual predator is difficult to rationalize as being anything more than a negative stereotype. It should be noted, however, that given the dependence of this screenplay upon the experiences of Oliver Stone, it is difficult to know whether Junior was based on a soldier that Stone knew, since so many of the characters in *Platoon* are based on real people. Nonetheless, Taylor makes a fair criticism when he claims that the noble King and the infantile Junior "are made attractive or repulsive on the strength of their acceptance of Western preeminence and values—the good nigger/bad nigger schema of characterization."[62]

Thus, the representations of African Americans in *Platoon* are limited by the film's dependence on the memories of a white veteran as well as the stereotyping of a few black soldiers. Nonetheless, through the presence and deaths of many black soldiers, the recounting of racism in duty selection, the recognition of class issues, and the demonstration of solidarity among black troops, the margins of this film still offer many insights into the African American war experience. The high presence of black characters in this film is also significant because representations of African Americans were so rare during the 1980s, a period when black characters were pushed to the side and issues of race and inequality were rarely addressed in Hollywood films.[63] *Platoon* may not be an "authentic" representation of the black experience in Vietnam, but at least multiple black characters in the film's margins are finally given a voice to express their dissatisfaction with the war, a rare occurrence during Reagan's 1980s.

Leveling the Narrative Playing Field in *Hamburger Hill* (1987)

In some ways, John Irvin's *Hamburger Hill* picks up where *Platoon* left off. This film also attempts to show what war was really like for the average soldier serving in the field in Vietnam. According to William J. Palmer, *Hamburger Hill* "is a fine film because its slow, relentless repetition of the events of life in the war, its emphasis upon the disposability of its characters, its verbal outbursts of bitterness and racial hurt, its final images of men constantly fighting an uphill battle, all expand into metaphors for the war itself."[64] This is a film that hopes to approach the unattainable gauntlet of authenticity by avoiding any strong narrative threads or structure, thus demonstrating the randomness, weariness, and confusion of a soldier's life in Vietnam. The film is based on an actual battle that took place in the Ashau Valley in 1969, but it does not overemphasize its real-life antecedent. In fact, the first half of the movie does not even involve the battle for the hill referenced in the film's title; instead, the movie takes the audience through a series of small, seemingly throwaway exchanges between the various men in this fighting unit. The lack of traditional film structure in *Hamburger Hill*, although not guaranteeing authenticity, does grant some insights into how African American soldiers fighting in Vietnam spent their day-to-day lives.

The most interesting step taken by *Hamburger Hill* in trying to achieve a sense of authenticity in its representation of Vietnam is the fact that it avoids identification with any single protagonist. The multiple-protagonist format is underscored by the lack of a narrator in the film. This fact alone is a significant step forward for the representation of African Americans in Vietnam War combat films, simply because it is the first film not to be narrated by a white character or told solely through identification with a white soldier. There are also no stars cast in the film to encourage viewers to connect with a particular character. The result of these narrative and casting decisions is that *Hamburger Hill*, for better or for worse, "winds up with the members of its platoon being largely interchangeable."[65] Although this comment by Vincent Canby suggests that such a narrative leveling could be detrimental to all characters, the effect is that the four black characters in the film are no longer marginalized by the spotlight of a more determined narrative structure, and are thus allowed to express themselves. Thus, as *Variety* noted, "the joke, here, however, is on the whites, since the majority of them are very thinly differentiated from one another."[66]

Racial Conflict in the Day to Day

Hamburger Hill's focus on the mundane serves its representation of African Americans well. The film's embrace of everyday tensions among the men allows for the expression of much of the soldiers' frustrations regarding the war. More specifically, black characters are allowed to discuss how their race handicaps them in this war, especially when they are at their base away from the fighting. One black man, McDaniel (Don James), talks to his sergeant about the possibility of being assigned a job at headquarters, since it is almost time for him to be shipped home. Another black character, Doc (Courtney B. Vance), explains that this will never happen because "They don't take niggers back at headquarters, brother. All the white mother fuckers are back there." This comment, similar to the one made in *Platoon*, speaks directly to the discrimination that African American soldiers experienced in the meting out of less dangerous job assignments. Also the film displays the racial tensions that historically tended to mount while the soldiers were back at base, such as when Doc and a white character, Languilli, engage in a drunken fistfight after having a heated racial exchange about the fact that African Americas are stuck in Vietnam fighting the war because they are black and uneducated.

Hamburger Hill's emphasis on the daily frustrations of soldiers also reveals some of the racial tensions felt while fighting in the field. For instance, McDaniel, the black soldier waiting to go home, is killed while serving in the dangerous position of the point man, the soldier who walks some distance ahead of the platoon in order both to spot the enemy and to draw the fire of hidden enemy before the remainder of the platoon is in enemy range. Doc, questioning the reason for his death, suggests that the only explanation for why the man was put on point while he was so close to going home was because he was black. In order to calm the racial anger of Doc, another black soldier, Motown (Michael Patrick Boatman), leads Doc in a chant of "It don't mean nuthin'. Not a thing." This message of "It don't mean nuthin'," which reoccurs throughout the film, is for William J. Palmer a "chant of nihilism" that cleanses the soldiers' minds of the random and purposeless death of the black comrade.[67] Interestingly, after this death, it is the new black soldier, Washburn (Don Cheadle), just in from the States, who is put on point in McDaniel's place, a gesture that suggests that in the field, new black soldiers simply replace the dead black soldiers in the most dangerous positions.

Another significant event that underscores racial tensions in the field occurs when Beletsky (Tim Quill), a white soldier, borrows a tape recorder from Motown in order to listen to a tape from his girlfriend. After Motown complains that Beletsky used up all of the batteries, Beletsky, emotional from hearing about his loved ones back home, exclaims, "It's that goddamn nigger music you listen to." This racist comment leads to a fight. This exchange is particularly significant because it is a rare example of a racist comment uttered by a major white character in a Vietnam film. Other than the exchange between Tyrone Washington and the racist new recruits in *The Boys in Company C*, it is difficult to pinpoint other instances of outright racial animosity. In *Hamburger Hill*, the comment does not originate with some stereotyped, token redneck as in *The Boys of Company C*; instead, the slur comes from a young, inexperienced soldier who has let the tension get to him. The lack of stereotyping of either character in this scene makes the racial exchange seem all the more real. Thus, *Hamburger Hill* gives examples of heated racial incidents that suggest the tensions of Vietnam without making them seem calculated for the sake of plot.

Bonds Forged by War

Hamburger Hill does not use black characters exclusively as mouthpieces for the frustration of African American soldiers in Vietnam. It also takes time to briefly explore the more personal side of these men. For example, while relaxing on base, McDaniel, Doc, and Motown discuss the problems associated with going home. Although the conversation alludes to the animosity that Americans felt toward vets and the fact that blacks had "been fightin' for the fuckin' United States of white America," the chat centers on how they will act when they return to the United States. Motown relays a story about briefly visiting home. He describes the perfect homecoming where all his family gathers for a good, old-fashioned, home-cooked meal. Motown continues: "So my whole family is there, and I say to myself, 'Motown, you got these people fooled. I mean the day before that we were humpin' the Ashau Valley, and now I'm home with my family.' And I'm skatin', man, no problem. Number one. I smile at my momma. 'Great meal, ma. Would you please pass the fuckin' potatoes. The ham, the ham is fuckin' A, mom. You don't know how fuckin' great it is to be home.'"

This small exchange is one of the few times in a Vietnam War combat film where the black character is allowed to speak to personal concerns that reflect a life outside of Vietnam, a life not just defined by his "blackness." This conversation about the embarrassment of going home and acting like a crass soldier in front of family gives a rare glimpse of the personal lives of black soldiers.

Hamburger Hill, although interested in giving a small window into the experiences of black soldiers, also wants to make larger connections between the plight of African Americans and Vietnam War soldiers of all races. In the film, various references are made that suggest that Doc, and therefore blacks in general, feel that "they're all on the same side in the same mess, but the blacks feel they have had no choice but to come, whereas somehow it's different for the white boys."[68] After being wounded in combat, however, Doc makes a startling comment. On going home, Doc says, "That's just what the world needs. Another nigger with a limp. [Speaking to a white soldier] I'm not omitting you, blood. We all no good, dumb niggers on this hill. Blood and soul type." On his deathbed, Doc, the main voice of black resentment in Vietnam, now feels that the plights of black men and the other soldiers are not dissimilar. They are all outcasts and rejects to the world back home. This comment makes a significant statement about the unappreciative way Vietnam veterans had been treated by the nation to which they returned. It is arguable, however, that framing the experiences of blacks as being similar to that those of white soldiers may have inadvertently undermined the film's success in finally giving voice to many of the racial tensions and frustrations that compounded the black experience in Vietnam. J. Hoberman makes a strong point when he says, "*Hamburger Hill* allows a taste of black rage, albeit focusing on microincidents of racial tension rather than addressing the essentially racist underpinnings of the war."[69]

Nonetheless, despite this potential flaw, *Hamburger Hill*'s leveling of the narrative playing field through the focus on small tensions and events instead of easily identifiable lead characters does make it, according to William J. Palmer, the Vietnam combat film that comes closest "to presenting a true black point of view on the Vietnam War."[70] These narrative moves may not have created an authentic Vietnam War film, but through subtle insights into the African American experience in the film's margins, *Hamburger Hill* is the best cinematic representation of African American Vietnam soldiers that has yet to emerge from a major Hollywood studio.

Conclusion

Since the release of *The Green Berets* in 1968, representations of African American soldiers in Vietnam have changed dramatically. In *The Green Berets*, black soldiers were treated as tokens with little voice of their own. Following that film, however, there has been a slow but steady development of black roles into more autonomous characters. *The Boys in Company C* featured a prominent black character that was aware of his race and the racism to which he was subjected in the military. *Apocalypse Now* was the first Vietnam War film to demonstrate that African American soldiers were not the exception in Vietnam, but rather made up a disproportionate number of the fighting men at the front. *Platoon* and *Hamburger Hill*, on the other hand, show networks of black soldiers who feel anger and frustration due to discriminatory policies and lack of opportunities in the military.

Although there has been a steady development in the images of African American soldiers in these Vietnam War combat films, these films have not been without their problems. Many of these films fall back on stock characterizations from the genre of the war film and African American stereotyping. All of the films, excluding possibly *Hamburger Hill*, have been told from a white perspective, whether through the use of a white narrator or through identification with a white movie icon, such as John Wayne. Related to this issue, all of these Vietnam War combat films, to varying degrees, have relegated African Americans to the background. The story of the African American combat soldier may have begun appearing in the margins of Vietnam War films more often, but these margins only give a glimpse of the unique frustrations of the black soldier. Such explorations of race in Vietnam films were the exceptions in a Hollywood that largely ignored African Americans. These problems with Hollywood filmmaking have prevented the Vietnam War combat films, films that have often pursued the unattainable goal of an authentic vision of this controversial conflict, from describing a specifically African American perspective of the war. It is doubtful that a truly authentic version of the war exists for African American soldiers (or white soldiers, for that matter). However, given that thousands of black men served, each having a different tale, it is still unfortunate that Hollywood has been unwilling and unable to focus squarely on the stories of black fighting soldiers in order to try and understand what was experienced by these men. Hopefully in the future, Hollywood will tell such a story. It is also possible that with the increase in independent filmmaking, especially among minorities, an alternative voice for the black war experience will emerge. One small independent film, *The Walking Dead* (Preston A. Whitmore, II, 1995), has already succeeded at telling a black-centered Vietnam combat story, and hopefully Hollywood films will follow. Until such a day, however, it will be necessary to examine what few images of African Americans Hollywood Vietnam War combat films hold. By looking to the margins of these Hollywood productions, it may be possible to derive some semblance of what this tragic war meant to black combat soldiers.

NOTES

1. David James and Rick Berg, "College Course File: Representing The Vietnam War," *Journal of Film and Video* 41, no. 4 (1989): 61.

2. Wallace Terry, *Bloods: An Oral History of the Vietnam War by Black Veterans* (New York: Ballantine, 1984), xiii–xv.

3. Linda Dittmar and Gene Michaud, "America's Vietnam War Films: Marching Toward Denial," in *From Hanoi to Hollywood: The Vietnam War in American Film*, ed. Linda Dittmar and Gene Michaud (New Brunswick: Rutgers University Press, 1990), 9.

4. Lawrence Suid, "The Making of The Green Berets," *Journal of Popular Film* 6, no. 2 (1977): 119.

5. Jeanine Basinger, *The World War II Combat Film: Anatomy of a Genre* (New York: Columbia University Press. 1986), 73–75.

6. *Variety*, review of *The Green Berets* [12 June 1968], in *Variety's Film Reviews* (New York: Bowker, 1983).

7. Basinger, *The World War II Combat Film*, 53.

8. Jeremy M. Devine, *Vietnam at 24 Frames a Second* (Austin: University of Texas Press, 1995), 41.

9. Donald Bogle, *Toms, Coons, Mulattoes, Mammies, and Bucks: An Interpretive History of Blacks in American Films*, 3d ed. (New York: Continuum, 1997), 5–6.

10. Ibid., 15.

11. Ed Guerrero, *Framing Blackness: The African American Image in Film* (Philadelphia: Temple University Press, 1993), 72.

12. Ibid., 77.

13. Loren Baritz, *Backfire* (Baltimore: Johns Hopkins University Press, 1985), 284.

14. Thomas A. Johnson, "Black Servicemen and the War: 1968," in *Reporting Vietnam: American Journalism 1959–1975* (New York: Library of America, 1998), 354.

15. Baritz, *Backfire*, 287.

16. "Interview," *Playboy* 18, no. 5 (1971): 82.

17. Ibid., 80.

18. Basinger, *The World War II Combat Film*, 62.

19. Milton J. Bates, *The Wars We Took to Vietnam: Cultural Conflict and Storytelling* (Berkeley: University of California Press, 1996), 67–68.

20. Devine, *Vietnam at 24 Frames a Second*, 45.

21. Renata Adler, review of *The Green Berets* [20 June 1968], in *New York Times Film Reviews: 1913–1968* (New York: New York Times and Arno, 1970).

22. *Variety* review of *The Green Berets* [12 June 1968].

23. Peter McInerney, "Apocalypse Then: Hollywood Looks Back at Vietnam," *Film Quarterly* 33, no. 2 (1979–80): 22.

24. Albert Auster and Leonard Quart, *How the War Was Remembered: Hollywood and Vietnam* (New York: Praeger, 1988), 55.

25. Terry Christensen, *Reel Politics: American Political Movies from Birth of A Nation to Platoon* (New York: Basil Blackwell, 1987), 151.

26. Terry, *Bloods*, 167.

27. Ibid., 259.

28. Ibid., 152.

29. Basinger, *The World War II Combat Film*, 206.

30. Terry, *Bloods*, 83.

31. Bates, *The Wars We Took to Vietnam*, 56.

32. Guerrero, *Framing Blackness*, 79

33. Ibid., 120.

34. McInerney, "Apocalpyse Then," 28.

35. G. Roy Levin, "Francis Coppola Discusses *Apocalypse Now*," *Millimeter* 7, no. 10 (1979): 136. Emphasis in original.

36. Ibid., 194.

37. William J. Palmer, *The Films of the Eighties: A Social History* (Carbondale: Southern Illinois Press, 1993), 103.

38. Greil Marcus, "Journey Up the River: An Interview with Francis Coppola," *Rolling Stone* (1 November 1979): 55.

39. Bates, *The Wars We Took to Vietnam*, 55.

40. Gilbert Adair, *Vietnam on Film: From The Green Berets to Apocalypse Now* (New York: Proteus, 1981), 160.

41. Jeffrey Chown, *Hollywood Auteur: Francis Coppola* (New York: Praeger, 1988), 134.

42. Christopher Sharrett, "Operation Mind Control: Apocalypse Now and the Search for Clarity," *Journal of Popular Film and Television* 8, no. 1 (1980): 39.

43. Chown, *Hollywood Auteur*, 135.

44. Marcus, "Journey Up the River," 56.

45. Terry, *Bloods*, 13.

46. Quoted in Richard Corliss, "Platoon: Viet Nam, the Way it Really Was, on Film," *Time* 129, no. 4 (1987): 57.

47. Peter Blauner, "Coming Home: Director Oliver Stone Relives his Vietnam Nightmare in Platoon," *New York Magazine* 19, no. 48 (1986): 62.

48. Corliss, "Platoon," 56.

49. Blauner, "Coming Home," 62.

50. Oliver Stone, "One From the Heart," *American Film* 12, no. 4 (1987): 17.

51. Blauner, "Coming Home," 75.

52. James Riordan, *Stone* (New York: Hyperion, 1995), 42–56.

53. Stone, "One From the Heart," 19.

54. Auster and Quart, *How the War Was Remembered*, 134.

55. Vincent Canby, "*Platoon* Finds New Life in the Old War Movie," *New York Times Film Reviews: 1987–1988* (New York: Times Books and Garland, 1990), 5.

56. Terry, *Bloods*, 213.

57. J. Hoberman, "America Dearest," *American Film* 13, no. 7 (1988): 39.

58. Corliss, "Platoon," 58.

59. Clyde Taylor, "The Colonialist Subtext in *Platoon*," *Cineaste* 15, no. 4 (1987): 8.

60. Ibid., 9.

61. Ibid., 8.

62. Ibid., 9.

63. Guerrero, *Framing Blackness*, 113–115.

64. Palmer, "Coming Home," 49.

65. Vincent Canby, review of *Hamburger Hill*, "Uphill Battle," *New York Times Film Reviews: 1987–1988* (New York: Times Books and Garland, 1990), 118.

66. *Variety* review of *Hamburger Hill* [12 August 1987], *Variety's Film Reviews* (New York: Bowker, 1991).

67. Palmer, "Coming Home," 49.

68. *Variety*: 12 August 1987.

69. Hoberman, "America Dearest," 51.

70. Palmer, "Coming Home," 70.

Gender

Guerric DeBona, O.S.B.

Masculinity on the Front: John Huston's *The Red Badge of Courage* (1951) Revisited

John Huston's original version of Stephen Crane's nineteenth-century naturalistic Civil War novella, *The Red Badge of Courage,* had every chance of becoming one of the finest prestige pictures in the late studio era. A fruitful discussion of the film has already been provided in Lillian Ross's shrewd production history, published in the *New Yorker* in 1952.[1] But a distance of fifty years gives us further insights. In retrospect, the film clearly belongs to one of the more turbulent periods in the history of entertainment; it was made during the Korean War, at the height of the Red Scare, when the old studio system was in deep economic trouble because of the rise of television. Thus, *The Red Badge of Courage* straddles two important cultural movements, one identified with New Deal politics and the other with Cold War anxiety about the Russian acquisition of the atom bomb, leading to what William Graebner calls "a more sober and conservative male look."[2] The former attitude guided Huston's director's cut of *Red Badge*; the latter informed MGM's revision. Interestingly, the film arrived on a fault line beneath very shaky political ground—indeed, it was literally broken up and reconstructed by the producers.

Huston's premier release print—which will be partially reconstructed here from archival script material—exemplifies the liberal, communal attitudes of the 1930s and 1940s, while also offering a strong indictment of war and an ironic treatment of martial heroism. The revised (studio) version displays the conservative politics of the early 1950s, it presents the enemy other as fearful, and it uses the literary canon to reinforce patriarchal values.

Stephen Crane and Cultural Capital

Jim Cullen has argued that there has long been a connection between American popular culture and the Civil War, which he describes as a very "reusable past."[3]

Cinema Journal 42:4 (Winter 2003): 57–81. © 2003 by the University of Texas Press. Reprinted with permission of the University of Texas Press.

Stephen Crane's 1895 novella about a young soldier facing cowardice during the heat of the Battle of Chancellorsville, in May 1863, was undergoing a popular rediscovery by the early 1950s. By the time Huston proposed adapting the book to producer Gottfried Reinhardt in 1950, the novel had attained canonical status in the academy.

It is well known that canonical fiction like *The Red Badge of Courage* was long esteemed as literary capital in Hollywood, even as a potential prestige motion picture for MGM, a studio that was attempting to alter its direction under a new administration. "We must sell this picture as an important picture, in the great tradition," Reinhardt said. "Like *Mutiny on the Bounty*. Like *The Good Earth*."[4]

Crane's realism and penetrating interest in the human psychology of a young soldier were also appealing to the liberal Dore Schary, who had made his reputation by writing and producing social problem movies at MGM, then briefly at RKO (as executive vice president in charge of production). Now back at Metro, this time as vice president, Schary had paid Howard Hughes $100,000 for the rights to produce a project he had already begun at RKO. The film, William Wellman's *Battleground* (1949), was hugely successful for Metro. According to Thomas Schatz, from Schary's point of view, *Red Badge* was the natural successor to *Battleground*.[5] Certainly, Schary was no longer interested in Louis B. Mayer's dream machine, with its glossy reputation for glamour and stars. And Crane's fictional depiction of the psychological events of battle functioned as symbolic capital for a certain American audience who may not have been familiar with Crane but was with the kind of noir realistic style that the novel evoked.

Shortly after *Red Badge* went into production, Mayer was out of the studio, in "retirement" and replaced by Schary. As Huston would later tell Reinhardt, "We combined our efforts not only to reenact the Civil War . . . but we unleashed a civil war of our own at MGM. Louis B. Mayer was the first casualty."[6] But far from initiating what Schary and others hoped would be a new, liberal trend for Metro, *Red Badge* proved Mayer correct that there was a deeply conservative mood in the country and the American audience would lack interest in an antiwar version of the Civil War. Schary had not counted on the problem of releasing a potentially allegorical period piece about the Northern and Southern conflict in America when a civil war was raging in Korea with American troops at the helm. Thus, Schary, as well as Huston and almost everyone else, were crushed at the preview at the Pickwood Theater:

> When "The Red Badge of Courage" flashed on the screen, there was a gasp from the audience and a scattering of applause. As the showing went along, some of the preview-goers laughed at the right times, and some laughed at the wrong times, and some did not laugh at all. When John Dierkes, in the part of the Tall Soldier, and Royal Dano, in the part of the Tattered Man, played their death scenes, which had been much admired before, some people laughed and some murmured in horror.[7]

Bowing to economic interests and conservative cultural tastes, Schary swiftly set about making changes. The film was recut then released while Huston was in Africa shooting *The African Queen* (1951). The original footage has been lost forever.[8] Along with the removal of key scenes (such as the death of the Tattered Man and the second battle scene), Schary and MGM made significant modifications, including adding a voice-over narration that not only contained portions of the novel but that also introduced Stephen Crane as an omniscient author with mythic, masculine superiority. According to the new framing narration, the publication of the novel *The Red Badge of Courage* "made [Crane] a man." The story we see on the screen is of a conventional initiation into manhood, guaranteed by the canonical author himself. By contrast, Huston had imagined the picture would be the story of the human subject in crisis.

Only sixty-nine minutes of Huston's original film have survived from its original length (approximately two hours and fifteen minutes). And when the movie was finally released with all its changes in the summer of 1951, it vanished in a matter of weeks.

In the context of the 1950s, Huston was a better match to adapt Stephen Crane's novel than he was to conform to MGM's changing politics. Major John Huston had experience both editing and writing cinéma verité-style films for the War Department, whose focus, like that of Crane's young Henry Fleming, was the mental plight of soldiers. According to Lillian Ross, "Huston, like Stephen Crane, wanted to show something of the emotions of men in war, and the ironically thin line between cowardice and heroism."[9]

The world Crane shares with Huston and American culture was a noirish one in which "dread and fascination are to a considerable degree shared by the narrator and reader."[10] Thus, Huston and Crane formed an important relationship in postwar America, precisely because they were able to explore the gritty realistic conditions behind human psychology and what produced them.

Trained as a journalist, Crane had written *The Red Badge of Courage* thirty years after the Civil War and three years before the Spanish-American War, during the height of the militarization of the 1890s. Joseph Conrad once said that Crane's novel was a masterpiece in part because of "the imaged style of the analysis of the emotions in the inward moral struggle going on in the breast of one individual."[11] Indeed, Linda H. Davis says in her biography of Crane that the novelist pictured "Henry Fleming's battle as a psychological and spiritual crisis."[12] And, in 1965, a clinical journal published a long article on Crane's novel as "a study of anxiety-defense mechanisms working under pressure to establish some tolerable adaptation to a dangerous reality."[13] Crane's penetrating representation of a young Union soldier's profound fear in the heat of battle and his subsequent urge to free himself of that neurosis seemed like a prophetic utterance for post–World War II America fifty years later, what with that culture's growing interest in the psychodynamics of the human mind—particularly that of former soldiers.

Gritty psychological realism was a common idiom Huston and other film-makers used to explore the dark side of the postwar human consciousness. Guided by his documentary experience during World War II, when he had explored the spiritual terror of battle, Huston was a better choice to produce the work of an established American author than most Hollywood auteurs. Andrew Sarris said that Huston's "protagonists almost invariably fail at what they set out to do, generally through no fault or flaw of their own."[14] As James Agee recognized early on, Huston was "swiftly stirred by anything which appeals to his sense of justice, magnanimity, or courage."[15] Thus, while he was shooting *Red Badge*, Huston felt the film was to be the hallmark of his career and later told some friends that "this has got to be a masterpiece . . . or it is nothing."[16] In fact, when a Hollywood psychologist read the screenplay, he claimed that with a few alterations in the psychological apparatus, "the picture could be the outstanding one of the year."[17]

Undoubtedly, Huston's adaptation of *The Red Badge of Courage* gave him an opportunity to demythologize the American soldier. As the originator of the notoriously unchivalrous Sam Spade in *The Maltese Falcon* (1941) and of the ineffectual Dix Handley in *The Asphalt Jungle* (1950), Huston was never much impressed with what he called the "warrior myth," which was at an all-time high in the late 1940s. By the time of the release of *Red Badge* in 1951, there were no less than thirteen combat films in circulation—only a few shy of those made each year between 7 December 1941 and 1945.[18]

In a certain sense, the myth of the returning soldier and his therapeutic healing became an icon of the postwar years in Hollywood, which itself was beginning more and more to appropriate vulgarized forms of pop-Freudian narratives. In *The Pride of the Marines* (Delmer Daves, 1945), for example, Al Schmid (John Garfield) undergoes extensive psychological treatment in order to deal with his blindness. Schmid gradually accepts his disability and his place in American culture and is rewarded for his domestication with Ruth Hartley (Eleanor Parker) and the Navy Cross. Even *The Best Years of Our Lives* (William Wyler, 1946), certainly one of the best and most popular of Hollywood's films about the return of soldiers to America, manages to recapitulate the issue of the warrior myth. The soldier may no longer be active, but he is still a man. He may no longer have hands, but he can still get married. As Dr. Golden, the sympathetic psychiatrist, says concerning his work with wounded soldiers in *Since You Went Away* (John Cromwell, 1944), "There's a whole wide broken world to mend."

Some of Dore Schary's most important productions had concerned soldiering and its psychological ramifications. In *Till the End of Time* (Edward Dmytryk, 1946), a lonely soldier (Guy Madison) returns to his parents' house after the war only to find his mother shopping and his father playing golf. Like an abandoned child, the ex-Marine says that "it was kind of spooky coming home and finding no one around"; paradoxically, he finds it difficult to adjust to a world in which his parents still tuck him into bed at night. Like *The Best Years of Our Lives*, *Till the End of Time* barely hints at the loss of virility suffered by many

American servicemen. On the screen, the wounded soldier recovers, usually through a heterosexual union. In the process, the vet is often reassembled either physically or psychologically. The task of psychological integration having to do specifically with war injuries is the subject of *The Enchanted Cottage* (John Cromwell, 1945) and *I'll Be Seeing You* (William Dieterle, 1945), both produced by Dore Schary.

By contrast, Huston's controversial war documentary *Let There Be Light* (1946) did little to negotiate the cultural anxieties of what Dana Polan calls "the problem of placement" of returning veterans in postwar America.[19] I agree with David Desser who says that "returning home, or finding a home once one has returned," is the crucial feature of Huston's theatrical and documentary films.[20] But those pictures tended to defamiliarize, rather than negotiate, American sensibilities.

The War Department sent an armed guard to New York City after the initial screening of *Let There Be Light* in the spring of 1946 and pulled the film from its public exhibition at the Museum of Modern Art in New York City; it was suppressed for thirty-five years.[21] The official response by the War Department was that the soldiers who were photographed during psychiatric interviews needed to sign releases. But *New York Post* critic Archer Winston wrote that the film was hastily withdrawn, that there was no release question because a commercial distributor offered to get releases from all the soldiers before showing the film.[22] It also seems that some people were deeply interested in reproducing the documentary commercially. According to studio records, a letter to Arthur L. Mayer from Colonel Charles W. McCarthy indicates that the War Department would handle all clearances and if not, "[scenes] would be reproduced by professional actors."[23] Yet, on 9 September 1946, the War Department classified the film "For Official Use Only."[24]

Huston is quite explicit about the incident in his autobiography and says that he believed the film was suppressed because its portrait of broken soldiers could have adversely affected military recruitment: "I think it boils down to the fact that they wanted to maintain the 'warrior' myth, which said that our American soldiers went to war and came back all the stronger for the experience."[25]

Huston dismantled the warrior myth no place more poignantly than in his second documentary for the War Department, *The Battle of San Pietro* (1945). Huston and photographers from the U.S. Army Signal Corps "produced one of the most harrowing visions of modern infantry warfare ever filmed: a documentary that conveys the raw, repetitive grind of battle and the grim vulnerability of the men who fought it with a respect and bitterness unprecedented in the history of film."[26] The film shows a factual record of the Thirty-sixth "Texas" Division during the early winter of 1943.[27] In Huston's account, the hero of the war was not the triumphant warrior but the common man, the foot soldier. According to an unpublished memo from 5 August 1944, Huston discussed alternative titles for what was eventually *The Battle of San Pietro* with Frank Capra, and one of the options was simply "Foot Soldier."[28] Clearly, the film is about the underdog and the lower classes—the ones, as Huston says, who could really use psychoanalysis but could not afford it.

Because of disturbing scenes of "battlefield dead," *The Battle of San Pietro* was not released to the public until 21 May 1945 (and was cut from four to three reels). By that time, the war in Europe was over. Thus, *San Pietro* heralded the troubled production history of *Let There Be Light*—and, indeed, of *The Red Badge of Courage*. Huston comments on the response to *San Pietro* in his autobiography:

> The War Department wanted no part of the film. I was told by one of its spokesmen that it was "anti-war." I pompously replied that if I ever made a picture that was pro-war, I hoped someone would take me out and shoot me. The guy looked at me as if he were considering just that. The film was classified SECRET and filed away, to ensure that it would not be viewed by enlisted men. The Army argued that the film would be demoralizing to men who were going into combat for the first time.[29]

Huston wanted his documentary to include frank voice-over discussions with American soldiers at the same time that we see body bags being taken away. He also wanted to include interviews with survivors about the days to come and then to disclose that they were, in fact, killed in battle. Desser's analysis of the film is worth quoting at length:

> *San Pietro* relies on a deceptive simplicity in its basic structure, a chronological approach in which voice-over narration and shots of maps provide information. The voice-over situates us in space and time, and relates a little of the history of the small town and the valley in which it rests. The battle scenes are thus framed by images of peace: what the town was like up until the war and what it will return to after the victorious American troops depart. The battle scenes are, on the one hand, curiously dispassionate. Shot on the spot in the midst of actual combat, the film is not able to rely on standard Hollywood techniques to communicate the feel of battle: multiple angles, point-of-view shots, and dynamic montage are almost impossible. . . . On the other-hand, their very documentary nature makes them gripping. Dispassionate single-take long shots of men falling from machine-gun fire or being struck by a burst of artillery show the dispassionate horror of war.[30]

Huston's deliberate dissonance with conventional Hollywood narration in his documentaries seems especially clear in regard to his representations of mythologies of masculinity. That demythologizing embraced his whole career. For Desser, *Let There Be Light* inaugurates Huston's rethinking and revisioning about traditional American modes of masculinity and male behavior, which would reach fruition in such films as *The Red Badge of Courage, Moulin Rouge* (1952), and *Fat City* (1972).[31] Huston himself noted that what he thought was really behind the banning of *Let There Be Light* was that "the authorities considered it to be more shocking, embarrassing perhaps to them, for a man to suffer emotional distress than to lose a leg, or part of his body. Hardly masculine, I suppose they would say."[32]

General Mark Clark's narrative in *The Battle of San Pietro* seems to smooth over the filmic dissonance and, therefore, operates as a signifier of stability in patriarchal culture. In Max Weber's terms, this is "charismatic authority" co-opted into "traditional authority."[33] Reading the film on a psychologically discursive, postwar contextual level, Clark's narrative functions as the voice of a reassuring patriarch attempting to bestow stability and the law on its audience. Clark has a symbolic, paternal function in *The Battle of San Pietro,* insofar as he levels a patriarchal resolution by virtue of his military status—the "figure of the law" in the Oedipal culture—or what Jacques Lacan calls *"le nom de pere."*[34] But Huston's noir stylistics and interest in unglamorized psychological exploration in both *Let There Be Light* and *The Battle of San Pietro* suggest a very uneasy relationship with Clark's conservative order and cultural stability.

Blind Passages and Seeing the Light

Huston's wartime films "can also be extended to include a number of Huston's later efforts, films not simply about war, or wartime . . . but films that grew out of Huston's personal experience of the Second World War, and the culture's experience of it as well."[35] Clearly, the director allowed his experience of documentary filmmaking to inform his production of *The Red Badge of Courage.* He shares this fate with Crane himself, who allowed his journalistic background to inflect his fiction writing. In Huston's case, *Red Badge* faced censorship much as his documentaries did, calling attention to the parallel narrative dynamics operative in the nonfiction and the fiction film. Scott Hammen recalls the ways in which Huston's documentaries informed *Red Badge* when he says that

> the uncertainty and impatience of untried soldiers in the first part of Crane's book correspond to that pictured in *Report from the Aleutians.* The horror of actual combat that Crane describes later is captured by Huston in *San Pietro,* and finally, the inquiry into what happens to a man's spirit after exposure to such combat that is the novel's central subject is likewise that of *Let There Be Light.* It was as if Huston had already made a documentary version of *The Red Badge of Courage.*[36]

In this regard, much of Huston's work bears directly on industry-related issues in the postwar period. Indeed, the interest in the link between the documentary and Hollywood was never greater than in the postwar years, obviously influenced by the trilogy of productions Huston had made for the War Department. There was also a more general, contemporary (and international) drive toward neorealism, location shooting, and deep-focus photography. In fact, immediately following the war, in January 1946, screenwriter Philip Dunne wrote a now-famous article for the *Hollywood Quarterly* entitled "The Documentary and Hollywood." In this respect, Huston was in the company of Orson Welles, whose celebrated send-up of the "News on the March" ten years earlier in *Citizen Kane* asks the viewer to reconsider the boundaries between truth and falsehood and whether "the gap between the two media is not so wide that it cannot be bridged."[37]

Indeed, Huston's original version of *Red Badge* makes us aware of what it might be like not only to see men at war but to be on the front as well. According to Huston's script additions for the "revised opening," dated 3 May 1950, the opening scene was intended to maximize and problematize the dominant metaphor of the "blind passage" for the audience as well as the soldier:

FADE IN:

Med. Long Shot—Embankment across a river-night.

Low fires are seen in the distance, forming the enemy camp. Trees and bushes. A low whistle is heard from across the river.

Med. Long Shot—The other side of the river.

Moonlight reveals some bushes and trees, and a sentry walking into view. Crickets sing in the still of the night. The low whistle is repeated. The sentry puts his rifle to his shoulder, stands staring into the gloom.

Close Shot—sentry—it is the youth.

THE YOUTH: Who goes there?

Med. Long Shot—across the river

THE SOUTHERN VOICE: Me, Yank—jest me . . . Move back into the shadders, Yank, unless you want one of them little red badges! I couldn't miss yeh standin' there in the moonlight.

Close Shot—The Youth

THE YOUTH: Are you a reb?

Med. Long Shot—across the river

THE SOUTHERN VOICE: That's right—but I don't see much point in us sentries shootin' each other, specially when we ain't fightin' no battle.

Close Shot—The Youth

THE SOUTHERN VOICE: So if yeh'll jest get out a' the moonlight I'll be much obliged to yeh.

THE YOUTH (moving back): Thanks, reb.

THE SOUTHERN VOICE: Now, that's mighty polite of yeh, Yank, to thank me.

Med. Long Shot—across the river

THE SOUTHERN VOICE: I take it most kindly. You're a right dum' good feller. So take keer of yerself and don't go gettin' one of them little red badges pinned on yeh. Over the scene fades in:

"The Red Badge of Courage"

Background dissolves to:

Panoramic Shot of the entire Army Camp—over which follow the credits

As the credits FADE—the first light of dawn reveals the tents of an army encamped on hills below which a river slowly circles. The fog is clearing.

A title appears: "Spring 1862 . . . Tales of great movements shook the land, marches, sieges, conflicts—but for the untried army on the Rappahannock war was simply a matter of waiting, of keeping warm, and of endless drilling."

Med. Long Shot—new angle—Ext. Camp

The regiment is seen drilling in the distance. These soldiers do not drill in the modem manner. Their steps are measured and they are not always in step with each other.[38]

Although there is no such "silent prologue" in the novel, the opening sequence and its place at the beginning of the film are crucial to a consideration of Huston's overall, formal design of the film and his insights into Crane. The dominant issue from the start here is seeing the light—or, rather, being kept in the dark. For we do not see the Southern soldier but, like the Youth, only hear his voice. The audience is also kept in the dark (about the title of the film) until several scenes into the movie, when the title is finally announced. Thus, *The Red Badge of Courage* opened with the MGM lion's roar, accompanied by the sound of drums, which dissolved into gunfire. Then there was the silent prologue, showing the Youth on sentry duty, followed by a harmonica playing the familiar folk tune "Kingdom Coming" as the name of the picture and all the credits rolled.[39]

This sequence does indeed set the narrative stage and echoes James Agee's perspicacious observation that a Huston film "honors the audience," continually opening the eye and requiring it to work vigorously; and through the eye "[it] awaken[s] curiosity and intelligence."[40] Like Orson Welles's unproduced version of Joseph Conrad's *Heart of Darkness*, the issue of audience "liberation" arises in the prologue and occurs throughout the film; it surfaces in both directors in the stylized, literary, and neomodernist way in which they handle point of view.[41]

The inventive, subjective platform for *Red Badge* raised the problem of narration among the producers. After the failure at the first preview, Reinhardt told Huston that Spencer Tracy should record a narration and that the river-scene prologue should be cut because it was "puzzling." Reinhardt's motivation was, like the War Department's in adding a narration to *San Pietro*, to assure a properly conservative tone. Reinhardt said that he wanted to tell the audience, "'Here is a master-piece.' You've got to tell it to them. . . . It might make the difference between life and death. . . . The people must know this is a classic."[42]

One of L. B. Mayer's biggest objections to the picture was what he regarded as Huston's inability to show the Youth's *thoughts*. Huston was absolutely against having a conventional voice-over narration. Reinhardt said he preferred one, but he went along with Huston's more inventive strategy because "he loved John." As Reinhardt recalled, "John kept saying 'No narration.' Billy Wilder in *Sunset Boulevard* had the nerve; after the man is dead, he has him do the narration. Joe Mankiewicz uses narration. Narration is good enough for them but not for John."[43]

Eventually, a more omniscient, highly communicative style became good enough for Dore Schary, who, together with the editors, altered the "silent prologue" considerably from what the preview audience at the Pickwood Theater saw opening night. The scene of the Youth on sentry duty does not appear at the beginning of *Red Badge* but after the Youth's tent scene. Needless to say, the change made the film much less challenging for audiences but much more to Schary's liking.

In his dismissal of a less conventional film style, Schary was exhibiting fairly predictable taste, even if he said he admired Huston's first effort in *Red Badge*. In fact, Schary had expressed his concerns with the music well before the preview. "I think all music in pictures has to be cliché to be effective," he said. "In Marine pictures, you play *Halls of Montezuma*. In Navy pictures, you play *Anchors Aweigh*. In this picture, the music that's effective is the sentimental-cliché music. It's a fact. Let's not debate it."[44]

Schary's opinion about musical scoring was not necessarily the opinion of the entire industry, but his notions about music for films as having to be "sentimental-cliché" is useful insofar as his observations suggest that he wanted to reposition the prologue so as to make the film altogether predictable.[45] Indeed, Schary and others hoped that the music—composed over Huston's objections— would help to fill in what seemed to be missing in the first sequence. According to Lillian Ross, the producers hoped that the newly scored music by Bronislau Kaper "says what Crane says in the novel." As Reinhardt told Ross, "What was missing [was] what goes on inside the boy."[46] From the point of view of Roland Barthes, Schary was well within the boundaries of the classical narrative and configured the musical score through semic connotations, which construct the characters and ambience to narrative.[47]

To investigate the formal properties of the revised prologue further is to find even more evidence of Schary's deployment of semic codes that rely on voice-over narration to redeploy Crane as a literary figure who bestows both cultural and masculine capital. The sequence begins with a shot of a novel over which the following is inscribed:

Stephen Crane's Great Novel of the Civil War
The Red Badge of Courage
A John Huston Production

According to Stephen Philip Cooper, this inscription on screen is an invitation "to conflate the novel with the book and figuratively to read the movie we are about to see."[48]

A montage like the one introducing *Red Badge* is certainly not unique to Hollywood adaptive productions, which early on learned to advert to either a picture of a well-worn book or fairly recognizable textual quotations from the source for the adaptation. Nor are the shots that follow, in which the book opens and displays the credits, together with drawings of the Civil War, unique. Illustrations such as these carry significant hermeneutic function, as J. Hillis Miller and others have noted. Artistic codes that evoke the cultural ambience of the period are important, even crucial, to creating cultural authenticity.[49] What is unusual about this particular sequence is the extradiegetic voice-over that follows after the page turns and that thus constructs an "author" for the audience. A drawing of Stephen Crane appears, captioned "Stephen Crane." As read by James Whitmore, the narration begins:

> *The Red Badge of Courage* was written by Stephen Crane in 1894. From the moment it was published, it was accepted by critics and the public alike as a classic story of war and of boys and men who fought war, Stephen Crane wrote this book when he was a boy of twenty-two. Its publication made him a man. His story is of a boy who, frightened, went into a battle and came out of it a man with courage. More than that, it is the story of many frightened boys who went into a great civil war and came out as a nation of united, strong, and free men.

From the very start, Schary saw his purpose in the revision process to bestow both prestige on the studio and to immobilize Huston's reading of the novel. "The big trick," according to Schary, "was setting up an outside voice saying, 'Look, this is a classic.'"[50] Sarah Kozloff has called our attention to the voice-over convention in Hollywood as "a last-minute patchwork" for panic-stricken producers, which in the case of *Red Badge* has inflected a "heavy-handed and schoolmarmish" quality onto the production. Kozloff hints here at the efforts of the producers for didacticism at the expense of a coherent narration. The film goes out of its way to tell us "of quotes from the text of the book itself."[51] In fact, although the film strives mightily to conflate the novel and the film, the introduction of the "author" as prestigious and literary capital ruptures any contour of "novel into film": the "schoolmarmish" turn to "the author" constructs the canonical legibility of "Stephen Crane" as the writer of a "classic" whose publication of his Civil War novel "made him a man."

Canon Fire and the Warrior Myth Restored

Schary and MGM redeployed a "coming-of-age" novel so as to endorse the values of post–World War II patriarchy: Stephen Crane became a man, and so did the

Youth, so we can all become men. By extension, the Civil War operates vicariously for a contemporary audience: if these soldiers returned from their war as "men," so too must World War II and Korea make men—that is, warriors—of U.S. youth. Thus, Schary makes Stephen Crane a kind of patron saint of masculinity, demonstrating what Barbara Herrnstein Smith calls the very nature of the canon: to support the dominant ideology.[52]

From one perspective, it appears as if the socially conscious Dore Schary was bowing to the conservative interests of L. B. Mayer, who turned out to be right about the audience's taste all along. In another way, both Schary and Reinhardt emerge here as representatives of the new liberal in 1950s America, eager to democratize a "classic" for educational (and moral) purposes. These producers echo Seymour Lipset's remarks that the "market for good books, good paintings, and good music ought to be expanded."[53]

Schary's more or less mythological reading of Crane's novel was not without literary precedent. A prevalent interpretation of *Red Badge* that guided Crane criticism in the early 1950s was informed by New Criticism and popular forms of Jungian psychology, which rendered the novel a kind of rite of passage. Critic John E. Hart viewed the book as recounting a mythic process of self-discovery in manhood: "Following the general pattern of myth with peculiar individual variations, Crane has shown how the moral and spiritual strength of the individual springs from the group, and how, through the identification of self with group, the individual can be 'reborn in identity with the whole meaning of the universe.'"[54] Nevertheless, Schary and Huston were at absolute cross-purposes: as Schary's narrator tells us, writing *The Red Badge of Courage* made Stephen Crane a man. On the contrary, it seems that Crane, and Huston's efforts to redeploy him, had in mind the unmaking of a man and, more particularly, what it means to be a war hero.[55]

Besides repositioning the prologue, Schary eliminated several other features of *Red Badge* that had a noirish potential to be antimasculine, and here we are reminded, once again, of Huston's long history with censorship by the War Department for precisely the same reason. One of these episodes is a key moment in the novel and what Huston regarded as a real jewel in the production. According to his script revisions (dated 26 August 1950), Huston had planned an elaborate scene to come after the death of Jim in which the Tattered Man would give a long discourse that questioned the ability of a soldier to endure in the war and would then wobble off and die. The Youth, now a deserter, would abandon the poor man and go off to the edge of the woods. Although it appeared in the original release print, this entire scene was cut (except for some of the Tattered Man's opening observations), so that after the Tattered Man's first few sentences, the Youth suddenly finds himself alone in the woods.[56]

Close Shot—New Angle—Hillside

TATTERED MAN (in an awe-struck voice): Well, he was a reg'lar jim-dandy fer nerve, wa'n't he? A reg'lar jim-dandy. I wonner where he got 'is stren'th from? I never seen a man do like that before—. Well, he was a reg'lar jim-dandy.

He then takes his eyes off the dead man, turns to the stricken youth.

TATTERED MAN (swinging uncertainly on his legs): Look-a-here, pardner. He's up an' gone, ain't he, an' we ought as well begin t'look out fer ol number one. This here thing is all over. He's up an' gon, ain't e? An' he's all right here. Nobody won't bother 'im. An' I must say I ain't enjoyin' any great health m' self these days.

YOUTH (turning slowly to the Tattered Man): You ain't goin' to—not you, too!

TATTERED MAN (waiving his hand): Nary die. All I want is some pea soup an' a good bed. . . . Some pea soup . . .

They turn their backs on [Jim] the Tall Soldier and walk away, marching in the field, CAMERA DOLLYING with them.

TATTERED MAN: I'm commencin' t' feel pretty bad . . . pretty bad.

YOUTH (groaning): Oh, Lord!

TATTERED MAN: Oh, I'm not goin't die yit! There's too much dependin' on me fer me t'die yit. No sir! Nary die; I can't. Ye'd oughta see th' children I've got an' all like that. (He staggers drunkenly.) Besides, if I died, I would't die the' way that feller did. That was the funniest thing. I'd jest flop down. I would. I never seen a feller die th' way that feller did. Yeh know Tom Jamison, he lives next door t' me up home. He's a nice feller he is, an' we was allus good friends. Smart, too. Smart as a steel trap. Well, when we was a-fighten 'this afternoon, all-of-a sudden he bell t' up an cuss an beller at me. 'Yer shot, yeh blamed fool! He ses t'me. I put up m' hand t' m' head an' when I looked at m' fingers, I seen, sure 'nough, I was shot. I give a holler an' started t' run. I run t' beat all. But b'fore I wuld git away, another one hit me in th' arm an' whirl me clean 'round. I cotch it pretty bad. I've an idee I'da 'been fightin'yit, ift' wasn't fer Tom Jamison. . . . There's two of 'em—little ones—but they're beginnin' t'have fun with me now. I don't believe I kin walk much furder. . . .

They go for a moment in silence.

TATTERED MAN: Yeh look pretty piqued yerself. . . . I bet yeh've got a worser one than yeh think. Ye'd better take keer of yer hurt. It don't do 't let sech things go. It might be inside mostly, an' them plays thunder. Where is it located?

YOUTH (turns on the Tattered Man like one at bay): Now, don't you bother me!

TATTERED MAN (a little accent of despair): Well, Lord knows I don't wanta bother any-body. Lord knows I've got a' nogh m' own t' tend to.

YOUTH: Goodbye.

He walks a little faster. The other pursues him unsteadily.

TATTERED MAN (in gaping amazement): Why, pardner, where yeh goin?

He, too, like the Tall Soldier, is beginning to act dumb and animal-like. His thoughts seem to be floundering about his head.

TATTERED MAN: Now-now-look-a-here, Tom Jamison-now—I woun't have this—here won't do—Where—where yeh goin'?

YOUTH (looks about vaguely): Over there.

TATTERED MAN (head hanging forward, words slurred): Well, now look-a-here-now. This won't do, Tom Jamison. It woun't do. Yeh can't go trompin' off with a bad hurt. It ain't right—now Tom Jamison—It ain't—Yeh wanta leave me take keer ofyeh, Tom Jamison. It din't—right—it.

He rambles on in idiot fashion. CAMERA DOLLIES AHEAD of the Youth as he runs, climbs a low fence, leaving the Tattered Man behind. CAMERA STOPS and the Youth disappears OUT OF SHOT.

TATTERED MAN (bleating plaintively): Look-a-here, now, Tom Jamison— You wanta leave me take keer a'yeh. It ain't right—.

The Tattered Man wanders about helplessly in the field.

DISSOLVE TO: Medium Shot—New Angle—Dusk—The Youth

At this point in the revised film, we pick up the Youth, who wanders confused into the woods and sits down at the log. But, according to the script material, there was a more horrific climax planned for when the Youth encounters the Tattered Man.

> Medium Shot—Edge of Woods The Youth runs into the shot, as if chased by furies. He stops by a tree breathlessly. As if haunted by the memory of the Tattered Man, he looks back in the direction from which he came, breathing heavily: Then he turns and gazes around, wiping the beads of perspiration off his forehead. Then, slowly, he sits on a tree-stump, utterly crushed. He is a lost soul. OFF SCENE we hear rifle shots, which attract the Youth's attention and take him out of his daze. Slowly, he rises and walks OUT OF SCENE.[57]

For Huston, the Tattered Man was the most glaring example of the warrior in crisis and came to represent the plight of virile, bellicose America, shown suffering here from psychological exhaustion—a theme repeatedly emphasized in Huston's wartime documentaries through his *Reflections in a Golden Eye* (1967). Not surprisingly, Schary was absolutely insistent on removing this sequence, which he judged to be altogether harmful to the picture. We might recall that, according to Ross, when the preview audience saw Royal Dano play the scene, viewers "laughed and some murmured in horror."[58] Reinhardt, however, thought that the "Tattered Man scene" was "the greatest in the picture." But even though Reinhardt did manage to get Schary to restore the wounded man singing "John Brown's Body"—doubtless convinced, finally, of its potential as a musical "cliché," which he so admired in war films—Schary revised the scene according to his own taste.[59]

Pam Cook reminds us of the tension between Schary and Huston when she writes that the postwar era was filled with deep ambivalence about masculinity and the patriarchal social order that had been sustained during the war.[60] But while Schary might have reflected the views of his contemporaries in offering a more-or-less mythological reading of *The Red Badge of Courage*, Huston appears to have been closer to expressing what Crane would have wanted himself. In his famous description of the death of the Tattered Man in his novel, Crane could be describing the crisis of patriarchy as a World War II soldier faces death:

> As the flap of the blue jacket fell away from the body, he could *see* that the side looked as if it had been chewed by wolves. The youth turned, with sudden, livid rage, toward the battlefield, He shook his fist. He seemed about to deliver a philippic.
> "Hell—"
> The red sun was pasted in the sky like a wafer.

Neither Huston nor Crane idealized war or the human subject who encountered it; in fact, both made careers of subverting the dominant ideology. While mythologizing the soldier was certainly a traditional way to interpret *The Red Badge of Courage* in the 1950s, Huston's was a newer, more radical reading of the novel. For recent literary critics such as Amy Kaplan, for example, Crane's novel is not so much about a mythological journey or the Civil War, or even, as is commonly supposed, a recollection of fear and a reconstitution of manhood. Rather, Kaplan says, "Crane is the master of forgetting. . . . The novel looks back at the Civil War to map a new arena in which modern forms of international warfare can be imaginatively projected." Crane parodies the romantic tradition of the *Bildungsroman* and "subverts [Theodore] Roosevelt's interpretation of the battlefield as a crucible for redeeming primal virility."[61] Thus, the novel always seems to have invited a certain amount of ambiguity, and its final paragraphs continue to invoke a variety of criticism, questioning whether they are ironic or not.[62]

Huston accentuates this radical rereading even further in his production of *Red Badge* by foregrounding masculinity in crisis through the acting style, particularly by casting Bill Mauldin as Tom Wilson, the Loud Soldier, and, of course, Audie Murphy as the Youth, Henry Fleming.[63] Both men were famous World War II heroes. Mauldin was notable for his cartoons, and Murphy was the most decorated soldier of the war, receiving twenty-four medals, including the Congressional Medal of Honor. After the war, Murphy played in a number of westerns, often as daring outlaws—such as Billy the Kid and Jesse James (whom he played twice). Murphy was even cast as himself in *To Hell and Back* (Jesse Hibbs, 1955), based on his exploits on the battlefield and his extraordinary rise from a private from a poor Texas sharecropper's family to a lieutenant in the Army. Hollywood used him in western after western as if to recall his former military heroics as daring and spunky. Hedda Hopper probably spoke for millions of patriotic Americans when she headlined a column in the *Los Angeles Times* by saying that casting Murphy as Fleming was "the happiest and most appropriate casting of the year. . . . For a change we'll have a real soldier playing a real soldier on the screen. It couldn't happen at a better time."[64]

The bulk of Murphy's work confirms his identity as a strong, masculine man, yet that quality appears to be based largely on a paradox: his extraordinary status as a war hero conflicts with his seemingly boyish demeanor. And Huston knew exactly what he was getting. Perhaps Murphy was not a big movie star, but he did have an ambivalence that could be exploited. As John Ellis reminds us, "the star image is an *incoherent* image. It shows the star as an ordinary person and an extraordinary person. . . . The cinematic image (and the film performance) rests on the photo effect, the paradox that the photograph presents an absence that is present."[65] Thus, Huston wanted Murphy not because the ex-soldier was a movie star but because he was a boyish war hero, whom the director referred to as "a gentle killer." *The Red Badge of Courage* continually works to exploit the paradox of stardom, even the performance frame. Ultimately, if Huston was trying to destroy the myths of heroism in war, he undercut the actor's (masculine) image as a hero by casting Murphy.

Our first glimpses of Murphy in *Red Badge* are anything but a validation of the manly man. A bewildered boy falters in the dark and then, soon after, is seen crying in his tent while composing a letter to his parents. That scene is especially moving because it recalls what Agee regards as Huston's style and technique during an unexpected close-up that could "reverberate like a gong."[66] The scene dissolves into a letter written by the Youth to his father explaining that if anything should happen to him, his dad should break the news to "Ma." Then, there is a very effective extreme close-up of the Youth, so that we see mostly his well-lit facial features and tears. There is a cut back to the letter and then a head-and-shoulders shot of the Youth, followed by a shot of a fellow soldier (Jim) coming into the shot in the background. Henry wipes the tears away as he and Jim talk about bravery on the battlefield. The camera momentarily leaves the Youth again, only to return to the same head-and-shoulders shot. But this time Henry's face moves closer into the shot as he says, "Did you ever think that you might run too, Jim?" The camera leaves the Youth as Jim tells him that "I'd stand and fight. By Jiminy I would." The camera returns to a fascinating close-up of the Youth, reacting to Jim, still in the frame but with a third soldier between them. Recalling Agee's general observations about Huston's style, the close-ups that frame Henry again and again throughout the movie suggest not one "gong" but many, not a single bell but the tolling of several.

In uniting form and content, the scene in the tent poignantly and disarmingly shows the pathetic fear of the Youth. These are crucial scenes that will gov-

The Youth (Audie Murphy) talks to the Tall Soldier (John Dierkes) about battle. The Red Badge of Courage. Courtesy: Photofest

ern the ethical movement of the film, even as the camera emphasizes Henry's fear in a series of "gong"-like reverberations. As if to underline the ambivalence surrounding what was supposed to be a tragic story, Huston took Murphy aside during the shooting and told him that there was a humorous aspect to the Youth's fear: "Fear in a man is something tragic or reprehensible . . . but fear in a youth—it's ludicrous."[67]

As we might expect, the preview audience was extremely upset about Huston's characterization of Murphy, who at the age of nineteen and at the height of the worst part of the war had become identified as the most fearless of youth.[68] Interestingly, after pictures of Murphy appeared in *Life* magazine, the Hollywood establishment was quick to recognize that, in the words of one producer, he "could be photographed from any angle . . . with 'poise . . . spiritual overtones.'"[69] And so it is probably not a coincidence either that the studio cut almost three minutes (237 feet) from the potentially embarrassing tent sequence, perhaps to make Murphy more marketable in the future.[70]

There is a lot more to the studio's revision, which the specific alterations of the film only suggest. Let us briefly recall Schatz's insights about the way in which Schary viewed the film—as a happy successor to Wellman's *Battleground*. In the earlier film, Holly (Van Johnson) has the briefest moment of doubt and runs momentarily from action. He is finally encouraged by his fellow soldiers—with no hint of their knowledge of his potential cowardice—at the Battle of Bastogne. Indeed, while Wellman lends some psychological depth to the film, there is nothing very original, save the insights provided by good acting and careful observation about group dynamics during wartime.

In the end, *Battleground* provides an excellent example of Hollywood's efforts at postwar eclecticism: races, classes, and religious groups unite against the other. Huston, however, has complicated the very notion of the wartime film from the start by inserting a prologue in which the other is portrayed as sympathetic: a young Southern Voice from beyond the river with understanding and empathy. Moreover, the depiction of the Tattered Man was a devastating portrait of the result of wartime "heroics" that faced the difficult issue of the largely uneducated infantry now in Korea. And, from what we have seen, it is hard to ignore that the Tattered Man scene appears to be a direct result of Huston's experience with wartime documentary and "footmen," particularly while working on *Let There Be Light.*

Like the Tattered Man and, indeed, all the infantrymen in *Red Badge,* the returning soldiers in *Let There Be Light* are not only psychologically disoriented but also blue-collar, lower-class citizens guided by elite officers who give them no information. The Tattered Man's speech is a masterful construction of lower-class, regional dialect, and, as such, he elicits our sympathy; he makes a point of telling us that he is together with others like him, such as Tom Jamison, who "lives next door t' me up home." In fact, as Murphy plays the Youth, he is a rather uneducated man. All the infantrymen are represented from the open shots at the camp as workers doing their own laundry who are guided by a destiny known only to the commanding officers. In a certain sense, Huston's representation of the Civil War was that it was fought by the lower classes and was a painful, contemporary reminder of the situation in Korea, where the lower classes were deployed to fight a war caused by bourgeois panic over the Red Scare.

Later in his career, Huston once again would redeploy a novel about a previous war to critique a contemporary one. His adaptation of Carson McCuller's 1941 novel about a soldier in World War II, *Reflections in a Golden Eye,* reminds us of the turbulent issues at stake in Vietnam and the class stratification in the military. Both *Red Badge* and *Reflections* share a "dreamlike interrogation of power, delusion, and violence."[71]

Conclusion

Huston's adaptation of *The Red Badge of Courage* shows his interest in linking (masculine) psychology to both class and politics. In a way, the Youth's flight from battle, his encounter with the Tattered Man, and his facing "himself" in the person of another soldier recall the complicated, difficult psychological agenda facing the returning soldier from World War II. Huston refuses to mythologize a returning veteran formed by violence and war; the past is always a haunting specter—a submerged repressed that threatens to return. The uncut version of *Red Badge* reminds us of the best of the film noir tradition, a narrative that continually wants to come "out of the past," a mystery that may or may not lead to resolution. The Falcon surfaces like a curse that, even in the course of centuries, cannot be shaken loose.

After the Youth runs from battle, it is the Tattered Man who confronts him (unknowingly) with the question, "Ware you hit?" That, of course, becomes the question for Henry Fleming and the rest of the film—the question of how to attain the "red badge," of how to return to the moral center of the self. The Tattered Man's question is repressed, and the long scene Huston designed with the Youth and the Tattered Man only adds to the tension and the Youth's irascibility and avoidance of that question. Henry's flight from the Tattered Man, then, becomes a further flight from that question.

In the next sequence, the Youth encounters a man running away from battle and asks him, "What are you running from?" At that point, the Youth struggles with another soldier and is wounded. The wound on Henry's head is thus a psychological scar, earned not from an encounter with the other but through an existential encounter with himself. Furthermore, from the point of view of plot, the Youth has his chance to replay the former battle. However, that battle, which might have signified a therapeutic "remembering and working through" for the Youth of the first battle, was also cut from the final version of the film.[72] Like *Let There Be Light*, the dynamics of psychoanalysis invested the original version of *Red Badge* with a realistic view of human frailty and cultural blindness. Henry's "dark passage," initiated by a failure to recognize that the enemy is "within," becomes potentially illuminated for the audience. In the film's final version, all these narrative explorations have been significantly diminished.

This reconstruction of *The Red Badge of Courage* invites us to further interrogate a lot of historical and cultural issues, not least of which are Hollywood studio politics. Huston and Schary present fascinating contrasts to each other. One was a director formed in the tradition of modernism who worked to unsettle the comforting presence of the American dream—while working tirelessly in the Hollywood Dream Factory. The other was a product of a liberal tradition but attempted to negotiate the cultural contours of his age as a production chief of a studio in a changing movie industry. Nicholas Schenck, the executive chair at MGM, even claimed that although he recognized that *Red Badge* would be a flop, he "knew that the best way to help him [Schary] was to let him make a mistake."[73] Schary left MGM in 1956 for a career in the theater and as an independent producer.

It is ironic, of course, that although the famous clash between Mayer and Schary caused the older man's ouster, it appears that the mogul who built MGM won at least one of the civil wars staged at Culver City. Nevertheless, MGM's revision of *Red Badge* failed to bestow traditional, canonical prestige on the production by stripping it of its psychologically disturbing, documentary texture. Perhaps the audience outrightly dismissed the original release because Huston gave the production not a mythology but a social consciousness. That story, about the failure of a young man in battle, was one American audiences could never have faced in the shadow of the war in Korea and the threat of communism. There may be even more to the film on the level of allegory. Ultimately, we may even want to speculate on the political signification of the "little red badge" of courage, coming as it did on the edge of HUAC's fateful sweep of Hollywood.[74] That was one badge of honor Dore Schary and MGM would have refused very happily.

NOTES

I am grateful to James Naremore of Indiana University for his helpful suggestions while I was writing this essay.

1. The two-part production history in the *New Yorker* was published as a book the same year. See Lillian Ross, *Picture*, rev. ed. (New York: Doubleday, 1993).

2. William Graebner, *The Age of Doubt* (Boston: Twayne, 1991), 17.

3. See Jim Cullen, *The Civil War in Popular Culture: A Reusable Past* (Washington, D.C.: Smithsonian Institution Press, 1995).

4. Ross, *Picture*, 129.

5. Thomas Schatz, *The Genius of the System* (New York: Pantheon, 1988), 455. Also see Dore Schary, *Heyday* (New York: Little, Brown, 1979).

6. Quoted in Lawrence Grobel, *The Hustons* (New York: Scribner, 1989), 39.

7. Ross, *Picture*, 184. Ross says that the private audience unanimously admired these scenes. However, some elderly ladies walked out, while "one masculine voice, obviously in the process of changing, called out, 'Hooray for Red Skelton!'" (184).

8. In 1975, Metro asked Huston if he had a copy of the original print. He said, "It does not exist." See John Huston, *An Open Book* (New York: Da Capo, 1994), 180.

9. Ross, *Picture*, 15.

10. June Howard, *Form and History in American Literary Naturalism* (Chapel Hill: University of North Carolina Press, 1985), 98.

11. Joseph Conrad, "His War Book: A Preface to Stephen Crane's *The Red Badge of Courage*," in *The Red Badge of Courage*, ed. Sculley Bradley et al. (New York: Norton, 1976), 192.

12. Linda H. Davis, *Badge of Courage: The Life of Stephen Crane* (New York: Houghton Mifflin, 1998), 69.

13. Daniel Weiss, "The Red Badge of Courage," *Psychoanalytic Review* 52, no. 2 (Summer 1965): 41.

14. Andrew Sarris, *The American Cinema* (Chicago: University of Chicago Press, 1968), 157.

15. James Agee, *Agee on Film* (Boston: Beacon, 1958), 325.

16. John Huston, quoted in ibid., 331.

17. Quoted in Ross, *Picture*, 68.

18. Jeanine Basinger reckons that thirteen combat films were released in 1941–1942, sixteen in 1943, thirteen in 1944, and sixteen in 1945. *The Red Badge of Courage* would figure here especially because its subject matter, like the themes of the movies above, is *primarily* an instance in battle. See Basinger, *The World War II Combat Film: Anatomy of a Genre* (New York: Columbia University Press, 1986), 281–294. There were, obviously, many more films in which wartime themes but not battle scenes played an important role.

19. See Dana Polan, *Power and Paranoia: History, Narrative, and the American Cinema, 1940–1950* (New York: Columbia University Press, 1986), 193–249.

20. David Desser also suggests a split between the "therapeutic" films and the "noir" films of Huston as mirror images "in competition." I am suggesting something of a blurring of these

distinctions, in that there is a noirish element to therapy that Huston wants to convey. Desser, "The Wartime Films of John Huston: Film Noir and the Emergence of the Therapeutic," in *Reflections in a Male Eye: John Huston and the American Experience*, ed. Gaylyn Studlar and David Desser (Washington, D.C.: Smithsonian Institution Press, 1993), 19–32.

21. *Let There Be Light* was pulled from the program on 3, 4, 5, and 6 June 1946, and replaced with a British film, *Psychiatry in Action*. According to the museum's memorandum to the public, Iris Barry, curator of the Film Library at the Museum of Modern Art, regretted not being able to show "John Huston's profoundly human and valuable psychiatric picture." Other films were also eliminated during the same exhibition.

22. Archer Winston, *"Let There Be Light," New York Post*, 2 June 1946.

23. Letter, Colonel Charles W. McCarthy to Arthur L. Mayer, 12 August 1946, John Huston collection, Margaret Herrick Library, Academy of Motion Pictures Arts and Sciences, Beverly Hills, Calif.

24. Letter, Kenneth C. Royall to Arthur L. Mayer, 9 September 1946, John Huston collection, Margaret Herrick Library.

25. Huston, *An Open Book*, 125.

26. Lance Bertelsen, "San Pietro and the 'Art' of War," *Southwest Review* 74, no. 2 (Spring 1989): 231. Eric Ambler, who would bring his own literary interests to the film, worked on *San Pietro* but is not credited.

27. The National Archives show that Ernie Pyle also interviewed the troops on 16 December 1943, and this was probably when Pyle was inspired to write "The Death of Captain Waskow." Ibid., 231.

28. See interoffice memo, Major John Huston to Colonel Frank Capra, 5 August 1944, John Huston collection, Margaret Herrick Library. Alternative titles discussed were "The Foot Solider and St. Peter" and "Foot Soldier at San Pietro." Capra, who is often associated with the cinema of the "common man," favored "Foot Soldier," but it was finally agreed that "Foot Soldier" would lead an audience to expect something about the life of a foot soldier in battle—his ideas and psychology. Huston's attention to this issue is indicative of the importance he placed on the social and class function of his work. Moreover, *Let There Be Light* and *Red Badge of Courage* both focus almost exclusively on the infantryman.

29. Huston, *An Open Book*, 119.

30. Desser, "The Wartime Films of John Huston," 26.

31. Ibid., 29.

32. Quoted in ibid.

33. Max Weber, *The Theory of Social and Economic Organization*, trans. A. M. Henderson and Talcott Parsons (New York: Free Press, 1947), 328.

34. See Jacques Lacan, *Ecrits* (Paris: Editions du Seuil, 1966), 278.

35. Desser, "The Wartime Films of John Huston," 19. See also the excellent essay by Gary Edgerton, "Revisiting the Recordings of Wars Past: Remembering the Documentary Trilogy of John Huston," in Studlar and Desser, *Reflections in a Male Eye*, 33–61.

36. Scott Hammen, *John Huston* (Boston: Twayne, 1985), 57.

37. Philip Dunne, "The Documentary and Hollywood," in *Nonfiction Film Theory and Criticism*, ed. Richard Meran Barsam (New York: Dutton, 1976), 159.

38. "Revised Opening," 3 May 1950, MGM collection, Doheny Library, University of Southern California, Los Angeles.

39. Ross, *Picture*, 164.

40. Agee, *Agee on Film*, 330.

41. With the emphasis on a prologue that in some sense would have functioned didactically, one is reminded of Welles's prologue to the unproduced screenplay for Conrad's *Heart of Darkness*. See Guerric DeBona, "Into Africa: Orson Welles and *Heart of Darkness*," *Cinema Journal* 33, no. 3 (Spring 1994): 16–34.

42. Ross, *Picture*, 189–190. It was only at this point that Huston agreed to add some narration, but after the second preview, in which only the scene of the veterans jeering at the recruits had been cut, Huston left Hollywood immediately to make *The African Queen*.

43. Ibid., 165. Also see Gottfried Reinhardt, "Sound Track Narration: Its Use Is Not Always a Resort of the Lazy or the Incompetent," *Films in Review* 4 (November 1953): 459–460.

44. Ross, *Picture*, 182.

45. See Caryl Flinn, *Strains of Utopia: Gender, Nostalgia, and Hollywood Film Music* (Princeton, N.J.: Princeton University Press, 1992). Flinn notes, on the one hand, that Nathan Levinson, a recording director at Warner Bros., said that "the score for each picture is written to suit the moods and tempos of the various scenes, and the music found suitable for one picture is seldom, if ever, employed in another" (30). On the other hand, Roy Prendergast says that Hollywood was always "re-cycling" its musical scores (31). For Flinn, who follows Walter Benjamin here, Hollywood depends on an "aura," a "new romanticism," for its musical authorship (13–50).

46. Ross, *Picture*, 162.

47. Roland Barthes, *S/Z*, trans. Richard Miller (New York: Hill and Wang, 1974), secs. 28, 41, and 81.

48. Stephen Philip Cooper, "Toward a Theory of Adaptation: John Huston and the Interlocutive" (Ph.D. diss., University of California, Los Angeles, 1991), 252. See also Gérard Genette, *Paratexts*, trans. Jane E. Lewin (New York: Cambridge University Press, 1997), 16–36.

49. J. Hillis Miller, *Illustration* (Cambridge, Mass.: Harvard University Press, 1992), esp. 9–60. Undoubtedly, it was Mathew Brady, the most famous photographer of the Civil War, who influenced the visual aspect of the film. Huston told Reinhardt that among his heirlooms was "a Brady" of his great-grandfather. See Ross, *Picture*, 66.

50. Ibid., 221.

51. Sarah Kozloff, *Invisible Storytellers: Voice-Over Narration in the American Fiction Film* (Berkeley: University of California Press, 1988), 22. Another example of how narration was supposed to save a picture was Goldwyn's contemporary production of *Edge of Doom* (1950). See A. Scott Berg, *Goldwyn: A Biography* (New York: Ballantine, 1989), 453.

52. Barbara Herrnstein Smith, *Contingencies of Value: Alternative Perspectives for Literary Theory* (Cambridge, Mass.: Harvard University Press, 1988), 51.

53. Quoted in Richard H. Pells, *The Liberal Mind in a Conservative Age: American Intellectuals in the 1940s and 1950s*, 2d ed. (Middletown, Conn.: Wesleyan University Press, 1989), 219. Pells provides an excellent summary of the debates ensuing over "mass culture." See esp. 183–261.

54. John E. Hart, "*The Red Badge of Courage* as Myth and Symbol," *University of Kansas Review* 19 (Summer 1953): 249.

55. From the moment the novel appeared, it was often viewed as a satire of army life. In the April 1896 issue of *The Dial*, for example, Army General A. C. McClurg said that "the hero of the book, if such he can be called, was an ignorant and stupid country lad without a spark of patriotic feeling or soldierly ambition." In addition, "not the thrill of patriotic devotion to cause or country ever moves his breast, and not even an emotion of manly courage." Quoted in Donald Pease, "Fear, Rage, and the Mistrials of Representation," in *Modern Interpretations: Stephen Crane's "The Red Badge of Courage,"* ed. Harold Bloom (New York: Chelsea House, 1987), 75. Pease's account of Crane in the 1890s sounds very much like Huston in the post–World War II years: "By driving a wedge between authorized versions of this war and experiences alien to them, Crane caused a fissure to form in the nation's self-conception, which not even the ideology of union would be sufficient to heal" (97).

56. According to the official document issued by MGM for production # 1512, dated 17 October 1951, "The Red Badge of Courage" eliminations, this cut corresponds to "Ext. Field-Hillside-Woods," Scenes 172–178, with 232 feet eliminated (estimated cost: $5,635). I am indebted to Ned Comstock at the University of Southern California for bringing these script deletions to my attention.

57. There was a retake dated 27 October 1950. Scene 175 was OUT and replaced by 175x1. But a year later, according to the official MGM eliminations dated 17 October 1951, Scene 175x1A was OUT.

58. Ross, *Picture*, 184.

59. Ross says that, along with the removal of the scene with the Tattered Man, the cuts had the effect of making the picture illogical: "The battle sequences added up to an entirely different war from the one that had been fought and photographed at Huston's ranch in the San Fernando Valley. The elimination of scenes accounted for part of the difference. The old man with the lined face who was digging was gone, the ragged veterans gibing at the recruits both before and after a battle were gone. Many small touches—brief glimpses of the men at war—had been trimmed, including a close-up of a wounded man berating an officer for 'small wounds and big

talk.' The last shot in the picture—of the Youth's regiment marching away from the battlefield—which Huston had wanted to run long, had been cut to run short. . . . The revision had some odd results. Audie Murphy, who played the Youth, started to lead a charge with his head wrapped in a bandanna, rushed forward without the bandanna, and then knelt to fire with the bandanna again around his head." Ross, *Picture,* 226–227.

60. Pam Cook, "Duplicity in *Mildred Pierce,"* in *Women in Film Noir,* ed. E. Ann Kaplan (London: BFI, 1978), 69.

61. Amy Kaplan, "Nation, Region, and Empire," in *The Columbia History of the American Novel,* ed. Emory Elliott et al. (New York: Columbia University Press, 1993), 249.

62. See, for example, Robert M. Rechnitz, "Depersonalization and the Dream in *The Red Badge of Courage," Studies in the Novel* 6 (Spring 1974): 76–87.

63. See, for example, James Naremore, "The Performance Frame," in *Star Texts: Image and Performance in Film and Television,* ed. Jeremy G. Butler (Detroit: Wayne State University Press, 1991), 102–124.

64. Quoted in Ross, *Picture,* 34.

65. John Ellis, *Visible Fictions* (London: Routledge and Kegan Paul, 1982), 92. See also Richard Dyer, *Heavenly Bodies: Film Stars and Society* (New York: St. Martin's, 1986), 11ff., and James Naremore, *Acting in the Cinema* (Berkeley: University of California Press, 1988).

66. Agee, *Agee on Film,* 328.

67. Ross, *Picture,* 73.

68. One person commented that "Audie Murphy is too good of an actor to be stuck in such a stinker as this." See Ross, *Picture,* 188, and A. H. Weiler, "By Way of Report: Information on Audie Murphy and His Role in Film," *New York Times,* 14 October 1951.

69. Charles Whiting, *Hero: The Life and Death of Audie Murphy* (Chelsea, Mich.: Scarborough House, 1990), 175. The photos in *Life* were also responsible for calling James Cagney's attention to Murphy and bringing him to Hollywood.

70. According to the script eliminations, Int. Youth's Tent: Scenes 15–23, was the first footage cut. See "Eliminations," MGM collection, Doheny Library.

71. Stephen Cooper, "Political *Reflections in a Golden Eye,"* in Studlar and Desser, *Reflections in a Male Eye,* 98.

72. The Second Battle, scenes 22–344, was by far the longest and most expensive sequence cut from the film. It ran 768 feet and cost $112,335. See "Eliminations," MGM collection, Doheny Library.

73. Quoted in Ross, *Picture,* 270

74. Huston, in fact, revised his script for *Red Badge* after the Hollywood Ten were sentenced to a year in prison.

Susan Jeffords

The Reagan Hero: Rambo

One of the most popular icons of the Reagan era was the film character of Rambo, played by Sylvester Stallone, a man whom audiences watched develop his hard body throughout the *Rocky* films. While those on the left caricatured Reagan's militarism by referring to him in political cartoons as "Ronbo," Reagan himself quipped at a press conference after the release of the hostages in Lebanon, "Boy, I saw *Rambo* last night. Now I know what to do the next time this happens."[1] The films themselves were among the most popular of the decade, suggesting that they had, for whatever reasons, successfully tapped into a strain of American thinking. In three films that span the years of the Reagan presidency, John Rambo, a Vietnam veteran, takes on and defeats a series of enemies—a small-town sheriff and the National Guard in *First Blood* (Ted Kocheff, 1982), Vietnamese and Russian soldiers in *Rambo: First Blood, Part 2* (George P. Cosmatos, 1985), and Soviet military commandos in Afghanistan in *Rambo III* (Peter MacDonald, 1988). Because the films focus on Rambo's physical prowess, and because Stallone himself did extensive bodybuilding for the part, the films can be used to illustrate how the hard-body imagery evolved during the eight years that Ronald Reagan was in office. Taken in order, the *Rambo* films narrate the production of the hard body during the Reagan years.

A CBS News–New York Times Poll taken shortly after the 1980 election showed that although 11 percent of the people voted for Ronald Reagan because he was conservative, 38 percent voted for him because he was *not* Jimmy Carter. John Orman explains in his study of the Reagan and Carter presidencies that "Reagan, by most accounts, won the [1980] election essentially because he was not Jimmy Carter. By 1984, however, Reagan won precisely because he was Ronald Reagan."[2] In the intervening years, Reagan's personal and national body image was enhanced by two significant events—the assassination attempt on his life in 1981, and the invasion of Grenada in October 1983. In both cases, Reagan was able to show that incidents that could have defeated a lesser man—or, more to the point, a lesser body—were unable to overcome him. Indeed, in all of American history, five presidents have been shot at and hit by assassins' bullets, and of those five—Lincoln, Garfield, McKinley, Kennedy, and Reagan—only Reagan survived. And he not only survived, he stayed in character throughout. As Haynes Johnson concluded, Reagan's optimistic and upbeat actions after the shooting "conveyed a sense to the public that Reagan possessed larger-than-life qualities."[3] And as Lou Cannon put it, "The president rattled off one-liners in the face of death and emerged from the ordeal as a hero."[4] Perhaps more important, the assassination was taken not only as a personal triumph for Reagan but as a national one as well: "His survival from a bullet wound lodged an inch from his heart was taken as an augury of a national turn for the better; it signaled the breaking of the skein of bad luck that had plagued the nation and its leaders for nearly twenty years."[5] And when the deaths of more than two hundred U.S. Marines in Beirut threatened to bring back the national trauma and sense of helplessness that had surrounded the Iran hostage crisis during the Carter years, Reagan distracted the public away from Beirut by invading the small island nation of Grenada only two days later, ostensibly to protect U.S. bodies—students at the medical school in St. George's.

In 1982, however, the year in which *First Blood* appeared, the image of the personal and national hard body was not yet culturally solidified. The nation was still reeling under the traumas of the Vietnam War and the Iranian hostage takeover. Stepping out of both scenarios was John Rambo, veteran of the Vietnam War and an escaped POW who had been tortured in captivity. But although the Reagan hard body was not yet fully configured, there is no doubt from this movie that the focus on the body had already begun.

As the film begins, Rambo is shown from a long shot, walking down a tree-lined road. Only after viewers have assessed his full body does the camera turn, as it does with dramatic effect in the trademark opening of each film, to a close-up of Rambo's calm, emotionless, almost peaceful face. Rambo has arrived at the home of the last surviving member of his Special Forces unit from the war, Delmar Berry, only to be told by Berry's mother that he had died the previous summer from cancer, a cancer brought on, she believes, by Agent Orange contamination. When Rambo shows the photograph of Berry, remarking on how he was so much bigger than all of the other men in his unit, the mother graphically describes how the cancer had so deteriorated his body that she was able to carry him in her own arms. The film opens then with an invocation of an absent strong body—the big man who had been taken down to a less than feminine size by a disease brought on by the war itself—and Rambo's isolation as now the only surviving body from that war. The question the film has posed is one that the Reagan presidency soon would answer: Would that body go the way of its companions and deteriorate as well, or would it find a way to survive the onslaughts of captivity, contamination, and public betrayal?

In the opening scenes of the film, it seems that the answer to this question will be in the negative, as Rambo is arrested and beaten by a small-town sheriff's department, essentially because they did not like the *way he looked*, in other words, not for any particular behavior, belief, or expressed attitude but because his body did not conform to the town's expectations of what a citizen's body should look like. As the sheriff (Brian Dennehey) advises him when he first escorts Rambo out of town, "Get a haircut and take a bath. You won't get hassled so much." The sheriff's animosity is focused solely on how Rambo's body looks and smells. And when he arrests Rambo for vagrancy, he immediately instructs his deputies to "clean him up" so that he'll be able to face the judge the next morning.

It is the act of "cleaning him up" that propels the plot forward into the explosive and violent spectacle for which the Rambo films have become famous. For it is only when the deputies physically strip, hose down, and then attempt to shave Rambo that he exhibits his first overtly physical and aggressive acts of the film, as he uses his expert combat techniques to maim the deputies who have trapped him. To ensure that viewers condemn the deputies, the director, Ted Kotcheff, mixes flashbacks to Rambo's torture by the Vietnamese with his treatment by the deputies. When one of the deputies waves a straight razor in Rambo's face in an attempt to shave him, Rambo balks. Deputy Galt then places his nightstick around Rambo's neck in a choke hold. Rambo flashes to a scene in the POW camp where a Vietnamese soldier is slicing at his chest with a long-bladed knife, yielding the multiple scars that viewers saw on Rambo's torso earlier in the scene. His body is presented not as unclean or unshaven but as victimized, as wrongly, harshly mistreated by enemies foreign and domestic who would like to redefine and reshape that body and its presentations.

The opening scenes of *First Blood* then show that, within the United States in 1982, there were reasons for concern about the future status of the masculine body. The town's guardian, Sheriff Teasle, has, for example, a body that contrasts markedly with Rambo's. Brian Dennehey was an excellent choice to play the part of Teasle, making Rambo's judge and opponent the possessor of a corpulent male body, which in its weakness and lack of stamina and self-assured fullness represents all that Rambo sets out to defeat. If, this film argues, the masculine body is to be reclaimed, it will have to be done, not simply by reclaiming some value or usefulness for that body (for example, its serviceability in time of war), but by rejecting the corpulent body altogether, showing its uselessness and destructiveness even in time of peace. Another highly popular 1982 film, *An Officer and a Gentleman* (Taylor Hackford), works out the same tension between the weakened and the strong masculine body, again explicitly in terms of a national military and identity. The very plot of the film—how a no-good, flip, useless, and soft male body is changed into a triumphant, resilient, and determined heterosexual hard body—narrates the transformations promised by the Reagan presidency. The softened, pampered, and ill-trained male body will become, for the Reagan imaginary, the body of the Carter presidency, the body that was unable to defend its country/its town/its values against outsiders. This is the body, the Reagan logic will declare, that cost American citizens a unified national strength, in the same way that Teasle's unwillingness to accept Rambo's presence in his town eventually cost the town many of the bodies of its male citizens and a large portion of the town's property.

First Blood clarifies the consequences of the "weakened" years of the Carter presidency, when strength and preparedness were, according to the Reagan historians, abandoned in favor of negotiation and capitulation. The "waffling" and "wavering" that Nixon believed characterized the Carter years typified the inability of the national body to defend its principles and national values.[6] Consequently, *First Blood* shows audiences that inadequate, unprepared, and weakened masculine bodies simply cannot compete with the forces of a strengthened and prepared body.

After Rambo escapes from the prison and flees to the mountains, his survival skills already activated, the sheriff and his deputies pursue him, joking about the "hunt" they are on and having no clear idea of who Rambo is. Skillfully and methodically, Rambo maims each of the deputies, each time with a different type of assault. Later, Colonel Trautman (Richard Crenna), the man who trained Rambo, comments that he must be slipping up, since he had been trained to kill, not injure. But the film requires that Rambo not kill these deputies: first, because it would be difficult to maintain his characterization as a victim if he became a successful killer; and second, because helpless, screaming men far more effectively portray the consequences of a weakened masculinity than silent corpses do.[7] Each deputy in turn appeals for help to Sheriff Teasle, who cannot help him, and the soundtrack begins to echo with the pitiful and plaintive voices of disabled men, all at the mercy of their own weakness.

But *First Blood* is not satisfied to show the weakened individual masculine body of the small towns of America. It must show the weakened national body as well. When Teasle calls in the National Guard to help him capture Rambo, the focus shifts away from what might be simply a poorly trained sheriff's department to the national military itself. Led by Lieutenant Clinton Morgan (Patrick Stack), the National Guard unit walks right by Rambo, who has concealed himself in the river. Later, when Rambo holes up in an abandoned mine, Morgan orders each of his men in turn to go in after him. Each refuses. When Rambo fires at them, they throw themselves down in fear. As a last resort, and against Teasle's orders not to kill Rambo, Morgan orders one of his troops to fire a rocket launcher into the mineshaft. When the mine explodes, Morgan is certain that Rambo is dead. Later, when Teasle orders him to clean up the mess made by the explosion, Morgan whines, "Aw, Will! I have to be back at the drugstore tomorrow!"

Here is the film's harshest criticism of the country's military preparedness: a veteran who has been out of combat for at least five years easily defeats the backbone of U.S. national security. Admittedly, as, Trautman reminds Teasle, "Rambo was the best." But these soldiers and deputies are clearly the worst. As Trautman figures it: the odds of two hundred such men against one Rambo are "about right." When the body that had been trained for warfare in the 1960s (Rambo joined the Army in 1964) confronts the body trained for warfare in the late 1970s, the outcome is clear: the soft body, even when massed in numbers and equipped with up-to-date technology, will lose. And it is this soft masculine body, *First Blood* declares, that represents the national body as a whole.

The film thus presents a short history of this national deterioration. Rambo's body was not foreign born or trained, but one that the country's military was more than capable of producing through the early 1970s. The absence of more bodies like his is attributed in the film to two sources: the Vietnam War, which brought on the deaths of all of the other members of Baker team; and the United States itself, which has failed to produce more bodies like these to replace the lost ones. In the intervening years, the country has produced men who view battles as weekend jaunts or hunting sprees, rather than, as Rambo does, struggles for individual and national survival. Indeed, the country is so unaccustomed to seeing bodies like Rambo's that Rambo's soft-bodied adversaries repeatedly fail throughout the film to recognize it. When Teasle first sees Rambo on the road, he takes him for a hippie, even though Rambo is wearing an Army jacket decorated with an American flag. When the deputies see the scars on his body, they cannot imagine what caused them. And, when Rambo disarms all of the deputies and escapes from the prison, they cannot explain his skill. Later, when they're tracking him in the woods, the deputies send attack dogs after a piece of plastic draped over some branches or shoot one another by mistake. They simply cannot recognize his body when they see it because, the film implies, they are not used to seeing men like him anymore.

The film's dynamics work on this assumption that the audience, like these deputies, is not used to seeing bodies like Rambo's anymore and that the more they see them, the more they will desire them, not only at an individual but at a national level. The true success of *First Blood*, both symbolically and as a marketing tool, is to have created the desire in citizens/audiences to see more bodies like Rambo's, an achievement to which the blockbuster films of the 1980s can attest.

In *First Blood* Rambo's body was continually contrasted to the soft bodies of the deputies and National Guard soldiers to show audiences its sufficiency; the later films have found such comparisons unnecessary. If, as Orman put it, in 1980 Reagan was elected "because he was not Jimmy Carter" and in 1984 "because he was Ronald Reagan," by 1985, the release date of *Rambo: First Blood, Part 2*, Rambo was now popular because he was Rambo. There are no recognition problems in this film. When Rambo enters a room, heads turn. Nor is there any ambivalence about the status of his body. In the first film it was unclear whether his body was clean or dirty, lawful or unlawful, strong or weak; by 1985 Rambo's body-strength is indisputable. In the opening shots the camera pans across the bodies of men hammering rocks in a prison yard and stops at Rambo's bulging physique. No longer the contemplative figure walking through the woods at the opening of *First Blood*, Rambo's is now an even more active, muscular, and hardened body. The camera is not ambivalent about and needs no narrative justification to display his physical prowess.

One of the reasons for the success of Rambo's body and the ease of its recognition in 1985 lies in Ronald Reagan's own achievement of the hard-body imaginary that would typify his presidency. Through his first term as president,

Reagan was able to establish himself in the mold of what Orman has called the "macho presidential style," which he defines by the following seven qualities:

1. Competitive in politics and life
2. Sports-minded and athletic
3. Decisive, never wavering or uncertain
4. Unemotional, never revealing true emotions or feelings
5. Strong and aggressive, not weak or passive
6. Powerful
7. A "real man," never "feminine"

As Orman goes on to say, "The macho presidential style places the ability to portray strength, aggressiveness, and power at the top of its demands." And though Orman will claim that to some degree "each president more or less embodied the seven components of the macho presidential style," he also concludes that "Ronald Reagan is the quintessential macho president."[8]

Reagan established these qualities as significant in his presentation of the presidency and his embodiment of the national character. Just as the Rambo films provided narrative models of these characteristics in action, the invasion of Grenada and the bombing of Libya provided concrete, historical instances of the same thing. In particular, the plots of the three films enabled the Reagan hard body to lay to rest the anxieties displayed in the opening scenes of *First Blood* about the future of the masculine body. *First Blood*, for example, establishes Rambo's determined competitiveness. When Trautman tries to encourage Rambo to give himself up so that no one else will get hurt, Rambo reminds him that "they drew first blood" and so the fight must go on. Rambo's strength, speed, and endurance underscore his physical agility, and, when combined with his physique, mark his athleticism. His decisiveness is shown at each stage of his narrative, whether in jumping hundreds of feet into a pine tree to escape a pursuing helicopter in *First Blood* or rescuing an American POW in *Rambo*. And though Rambo broke down at the end of *First Blood* and cried on Trautman's shoulder for his lost friends and uncertain status at home, by *Rambo*, he is emotionless. Even when Co Bao (Julia Nickson) asks him to take her to America with him and then kisses him, he shows no response. The most emotion he shows is in his anger toward Marshall Murdock (Charles Napier) when he learns that Murdock aborted the mission that was to pick up Rambo and a rescued POW, leaving them to the Vietnamese and Soviet torturers. Even here, Rambo shows only a curled upper lip, as he tells Murdock, "I'm coming to get you." And because Rambo is consistently depicted as strong, aggressive, and powerful, these films conclude, he can be nothing other than a "real man." The promised presidential pardon offered to Rambo at the beginning of *Rambo* if he completes his mission successfully solidifies early in the movie the connection between Rambo and Reagan. It is as if Ronald Reagan has personally promised to free the hard-bodied man from his confinement in return for

Rambo (Sylvester Stallone) promises Co Boa (Julia Nickson) he will take her to America. Rambo: First Blood Part II. Courtesy: Jerry Ohlinger's Movie Material Store

bringing back more men like him, the survivors from before the decade when masculine bodies were methodically weakened by a "soft" presidential style.

The shift toward the hard body as a *national* emblem takes place in this second film as well. Whereas in *First Blood* Rambo's own body was assaulted by the sheriff and his deputies, which implies that Rambo alone is the victim of Teasle's form of American domestic torture, in *Rambo* the initial focus has shifted away from Rambo's individual body to that of the anonymous and collective body of the men Rambo is sent to rescue. In a similar fashion, Reagan, by this point in his presidency, had managed to redefine the focus on hostages/captives that had so mesmerized the Carter presidency away from the individual captives to the general status of American bodies. Jimmy Carter knew the names of each Iranian hostage, became friends with their families, and prayed for their rescue individually. As he recorded in his memoirs, "The hostages sometimes seemed like part of my own family."[9] Reagan, however, chose to characterize American hostages as collective and representative groups. From the early days of his first term, when he proclaimed a National POW-MIA Day, to the 1983 Grenada invasion staged to "rescue" American medical students, whom Reagan argued could then be taken as hostages, to the crisis over the TWA hostages in 1985, Reagan treated hostage situations as if America itself was held captive rather than individual diplomats, students, or soldiers. As he told the returning TWA passengers during a White House reception for them, "None of you were held prisoner because of any personal wrong you had done anyone; you were held simply because you are Americans. In the minds of your captors, you represented us."[10]

In the filmic logic of *Rambo*, the forgotten POWs were not individual soldiers who might have committed atrocities or participated in the devastation of an entire nation. Audiences never hear any of their individual stories or learn any of their names. They are referred to in the film as simply "American POWs," Americans who have been left behind to suffer and starve because Congress is unwilling to appropriate money for their rescue (and there is no doubt in this film that it is Congress and not the president who is to blame for this failure). In this sense, these hostages come to represent a crisis in the national body, an effort to suppress a part of the national body that had been, presumably, "forgotten" but has in fact, as this film makes clear, actually been actively suppressed by a weakened government. As Colonel Podovsky (Steven Berkoff), a Soviet advisor, observes as he is torturing Rambo, "It seems you were abandoned on direct command." As *Rambo* goes on to say, it is exactly the deliberate suppression of this part of the national body that has led to the production of the kinds of masculine bodies shown as now in charge of U.S. affairs. Marshall Murdock, the key figure here, is weak-bodied and weak-willed, and he surrenders both body and will to Rambo on his return from the mission. He wears a long-sleeved shirt and tie, which contrasts with Rambo's military gear and then exposed muscular torso. Murdock sweats uncomfortably throughout the film, drinking imported Cokes and positioning himself in front of fans as protection against the climate of Vietnam. In this crucible that crystallized the hardened body of a John Rambo, Marshall Murdock's body is shown to be out of place, ineffective, and weak—in other words, soft.

Ronald Reagan's shift from individual to national bodies had, obviously, a number of consequences. He excluded many from the national body by characterizing them as part of the "soft body" that posed an internal threat to the well-being of the United States. From welfare recipients to homosexuals, from Cuban refugees to university professors, Reagan succeeded in establishing a domestic equivalent to the "foreign terrorist." But, as Richard Nixon argues in *The Real War*, the linchpin for the entire Reagan philosophy was the Soviet Union. If Reagan had not been able to "demonize," to use Michael Rogin's term, the Soviet Union, he would have found it impossible to make his parallel accusations of internal weakness.[11] Only a "hard" external opponent justified the call to strengthen U.S. bodies to meet that threat.

Rambo shows American audiences that threat in the bodies of Soviet "advisors" to the Vietnamese prison camp. For the Reagan logic to work, those Soviet bodies are presented as much harder than those of the sheriff or his deputies in *First Blood*. As both Reagan and *Rambo* declare, during all those years when American bodies were getting fat and comfortable, Soviet bodies were hardening themselves for the coming battle. Sergeant Yushin (Vojo Goric), assistant to the colonel interrogating Rambo, is the only man in any of these films whose muscles are actually larger than Rambo's. His firm-jawed indifference to inflicting pain is only the most obvious indication of his preparedness. As the film goes on, it becomes clear that the only body who could stand up to Yushin's is Rambo's, a body that the U.S. government had rejected and sentenced to hard labor. And whereas the Soviet Union has rewarded Yushin for his hard body, the U.S. government has punished Rambo. Where then, this film invites audiences to worry, would they find the bodies needed to defend the United States against Soviet attack? Like *First Blood*, Rambo is geared toward manufacturing a national desire to produce more hard bodies like Rambo's and reject the soft bodies that have come to inhabit the government.

At one point *Rambo* seems to contradict Reagan's enthusiasm for technology, especially military technology. Although Reagan's increased funding of the military was geared largely toward improved weaponry and sophisticated technologies, Rambo not only does not need such weapons, he is hindered by them: he has to cut himself free of all of Murdock's sophisticated equipment in order to parachute into Vietnam. Though Trautman has referred to him as "a pure fighting machine," Rambo prefers to think of his brains and not his body as his most important asset (he may be the only one in Hollywood who believes this). As he tells Murdock, who has just proudly displayed the banks of computers at Rambo's disposal, "I've always believed the mind was the best weapon."

It is not my goal here to show that the *Rambo* films adhere entirely to the Reagan ideology, but I think it important to work through this apparent contradiction between technology and the individual (one that plagued the entire decade, as can be seen in such films as *Alien* [Ridley Scott, 1979] and *Terminator* [James Cameron, 1984]), largely because it was a contradiction inherent in the Reagan philosophy itself, which continued, despite its insistence on technological innovation, to rely on individuality and not technology as the true basis for American superiority over Soviet thinking.[12] Lou Cannon summarized Reagan's feelings on the matter in these words: "Reagan was always easily convinced that American ingenuity could overcome technological obstacles of great magnitude."[13] With the Strategic Defense Initiative (SDI), conceived in the year of *First Blood*'s release, Reagan tried, unsuccessfully, to combine these two visions of American progress, since it would be the individual ingenuity of American scientists and the individual support of a visionary American president that would launch the technology that would, in Reagan's mind, ensure world peace. But the uneasiness of the marriage between technology and individualism is reflected in the rocky rhetoric of Reagan's 1988 Moscow summit speech:

Like a chrysalis, we are emerging from the economy of the Industrial Revolution, an economy confined and limited by the earth's physical resources, into [one] in which there are no bounds on human imagination and the freedom to create is the most precious natural resource. Think of the little computer chip. Its value isn't in the sand from which it is made, but in the microscopic architecture designed into it by ingenious human minds. In the new economy, human invention increasingly makes physical resources obsolete. We are breaking through the material conditions of existence to a world where man creates his own destiny.[14]

As these remarks make clear, one of the key features of the Reagan hard body was mental as well as physical superiority over its enemies. In the contrast between Yushin and Rambo, for instance, Yushin, though strong, does not seem to be very bright. He never speaks, and acts only when commanded by Podovsky. He seems to be *only* a "fighting machine." Rambo, on the other hand, decides when to work with Murdock and when to disobey his orders (in bringing the POWs back, for example). He uses his body not only to defeat the Soviet soldiers but to outsmart them as well. Given that so much of Reagan's characterization of the Soviet Union as an "evil empire" is grounded on communism's ostensible disregard for human individuality, it is imperative that Rambo be more than a fighting machine. In order to be the embodiment of Reagan democratic ideals, he must be both muscular *and* independent of mind. As Reagan went on to conclude at the Moscow summit, "Progress is not foreordained. The key is freedom of thought, freedom of information, freedom of communication." For Ronald Reagan, the best "weapon" to use against the Soviet Union is not then a tank or a nuclear bomb but the "free" American mind inside a hard body. This would be, as Rambo tells Colonel Zaysen in *Rambo III*, the Soviets' "worst nightmare."

> RAMBO: Do you really think you're going to make a difference?
> TRAUTMAN: If I didn't, I wouldn't be going.
> RAMBO: It didn't before.
> TRAUTMAN: That was another time.

These early lines in *Rambo III*, as Trautman tries to explain to Rambo why he is going in to deliver weapons to Afghani fighters rebelling against Soviet occupation, declare the changes that have taken place in Hollywood's representation of the hard body between 1982 and 1988. In *First Blood* Rambo won his battle only at the expense of a prison sentence; in *Rambo* he was told that winning this time was up to him; but in *Rambo III* his only friend tells him that times have changed, that battles such as those they fought in Vietnam are now winnable, not just by individuals like Rambo, but by the country as a whole. And though Rambo is again fighting the evil Soviet empire, he does it this time not on behalf of a handful of POWs but for an entire nation. Whereas the first Rambo films ground their plots in the loss in Vietnam, a war that spanned the administrations of five presidents and has influenced the policies of an additional four, *Rambo III* takes as its narrative target a specific "loss" of the Carter administration, the Soviet takeover in Afghanistan in 1979, an act that Richard Nixon, setting the tone for the Reagan administration, described in these terms:

> What made the fall of Afghanistan so significant a loss to the West was not just the fate of its 18 million people. . . . Not even its strategic location would make its loss so significant, if that loss had occurred in isolation. But it did

not occur in isolation. It was part of a pattern . . . of ceaseless building by the Soviets toward a position of overwhelming military force, while using subversion and proxy troops, and now even its own, to take over one country after another, until they are in a position to conquer or Finlandize the world.[15]

Afghanistan, in Nixon's and then Reagan's logic, was more than simply another country that the Soviet Union had come to control. For these men, Afghanistan was one more stepping stone to eventual Soviet domination of the world. In such terms, Rambo's defeat of the Soviet garrison in Afghanistan is not simply a victory for himself, Trautman, or even the Afghani mujahideen, but for the entire free world. This is what the Reagan hard body has, by 1988, been advertised to achieve.

Here, as in *Rambo*, the national body is in peril of capture and death at the hands of the Soviet Union, as Trautman, on his mission to deliver weapons to the mujahideen, is captured by soldiers commanded by Colonel Zaysen (Marc de Jonge). And though Rambo enters Afghanistan only to rescue Trautman, his eventual support of the Afghanis escalates the battle from one for the national body to one for the Western body, or, more precisely, is staged as a battle in which the U.S. national body is now valued as *the* Western body itself. The numerous shots of Soviet aircraft firing on defenseless women and children, the tales of Soviets hiding bombs in children's toys, the scenes of Afghanis being tortured in the Soviet prison—all arouse not only images of the "evil empire," but imply that the Soviets would commit such atrocities in any country that stood in the way of its intended goals of domination. Because these practices are, according to the film, typical of Soviets and not specific to their fight in Afghanistan, the people of Afghanistan come to stand in here for any people in the world who are struggling to maintain their freedom against the Soviet Union. It is here that Trautman's body is not simply the body of a captured American officer, but the imprisonment of the warrior for freedom, the one who is willing to confront the Soviets before it is too late. The battle that had been domestic in *First Blood* and against Vietnam's communist government in *Rambo* is now a battle for democracy around the world. And the only body who can wage this battle for the beleaguered West, according to *Rambo III* and those who endorse its policies, is the hardened American body. . . .

In each of the *Rambo* films, there is a moment when his body is wounded. In *First Blood*, when Rambo first confronts Teasle's deputies in the wooded mountains to which he has escaped, one rabid deputy intent on killing Rambo begins firing at him from a helicopter as he is perched precariously on the wall of a sheer cliff. As they both hover above the rocky ravine below, Rambo realizes that Galt will kill him if he remains where he is, so he leaps out from the wall to the pine trees below. As he crashes through the pine branches, one catches his right arm and rips it open. After causing Galt to fall from the helicopter to his death below, Rambo takes a needle and thread from his knife handle and proceeds to stitch together the bleeding

The invulnerable Rambo stands up to the torture of the Russian Yushin (Voyo Goric). Rambo: First Blood Part II. Courtesy: Photofest

skin of his wound. In *Rambo,* he is tortured by Sergeant Yushin. Tied to an electrified bed spring, Rambo's body is continually jolted with higher and higher levels of electricity, enough to make the lights in the camp dim and flicker. Finally, after Podovsky has been forced to admit that Rambo is "the strongest so far," Yushin takes Rambo's knife from a brazier where it has been heating. Placing it against Rambo's face, he slowly cuts a line down Rambo's cheek with the glowing knife. Rambo only grimaces. But the best scene is reserved for *Rambo III,* where a piece of flying shrapnel from an explosion during the prison escape is lodged in Rambo's right side. After rescuing Hamid and the boy and sending them away to safety, Rambo works on his wound by firelight. Using his thumb, Rambo forces the piece of wood out through his body. Then, after pouring gunpowder from a bullet into the back of the wound, Rambo lights it with a stick from his fire. The gunpowder explodes out both sides of his body, cauterizing the wound.[16]

In each of the many times that I watched these films in public, these scenes never failed to arouse discomfort, especially among the male members of the audience. From subtle fidgeting to outright disgust, viewers who had been in synch with Rambo's triumphs a minute before seemed suddenly distanced from him. Those who could fantasize easily about replicating Rambo's assaults on tanks, rescues of prisoners, or uses of weapons seemed now to have difficulty imagining suturing or cauterizing gaping wounds in their own bodies. In each film, the wounds of Rambo's body worked against audience identification with him. Although the overall plot continued to invite identifications with his mission, methods, and muscles, these single moments suggested that such identifications could not be complete.

Such scenes are full of ambivalence and potential contradictions for the ideologies of the films. On the one hand, the ability to endure severe pain underscores how truly hard these bodies are. But on the other hand, the wounds indicate that the hard body *can* be wounded, that it isn't invulnerable or invincible, that it is not a machine but human flesh. On the one hand, these scenes suggest that viewers would all want to have bodies like these, bodies that can overcome pain in order to achieve a goal, bodies that recover from damages to go on and fulfill their mission. On the other hand, they can indicate that viewers would not want a body like this if having such a body means having to undergo such hardships, pain, and isolation. Why risk these contradictions? What can be gained from them?

On the most straightforward filmic level, such moments rationalize sustained attention to the exposed male body, scenes that, as Steve Neale pointed out some time ago, are sources of anxiety in a Hollywood film tradition in which the female body is usually the exclusive object of erotic desire.[17] Although all three films are devoted almost exclusively to the portrayal of Rambo's body, these scenes are among the few in which that body is still, in which Rambo is not pursuing enemies, firing weapons, or blending in with trees and mud. Consequently, audiences can examine Rambo here at some leisure and explain any anxieties aroused by that examination as anxieties of plot and not pleasure. But the eroticization of the male body can be achieved in other kinds of portrayals than suturing and cauterizing bleeding body parts. Why the wound?

There are several ways in which these scenes reinforce rather than contradict Reaganism. By arguing, for example, that the national body *can* be wounded—a case that one would think Reagan's image of national strength could not tolerate—Reaganism can insist on providing adequate protection for that body. If the national body were in fact invincible, there would be no need for arms buildups, weapons development, or billion-dollar military budgets. But by voicing concerns about vulnerabilities, Reaganism can argue that more needs to be done to ensure that those vulnerabilities not be exposed. This cautionary logic can work on two levels—the individual and the national. Taking, as it so often did, the Iranian hostage situation as an indication of a vulnerability, the Reagan administration could argue that individual American lives are at risk and made vulnerable because of inadequate protection against terrorists. Reagan was to say exactly this about Grenada, that "American lives are at stake."[18] Reagan's response to this projected fear was to train Special Forces units as hostage rescue teams, to target Mu'ammar Qaddafi and the PLO as leaders of international terrorist organizations, to subsequently bomb Libya and ban the PLO from any U.S. dealings, and to invade Grenada to ensure that more U.S. hostages would not be taken. Reagan's

"Star Wars" proposal promised to protect the national body from any vulnerabilities it might have in relation to a Soviet nuclear attack, since the country no longer possessed the numerical superiority in nuclear weapons that it had in earlier decades. The need for such a space-based weapons system is contingent on the insistence that the national body *can* be wounded. So although the Reagan military and foreign policy philosophies worked to construct a successful image of the national hard body, they could do so only within the context of acknowledging that that body was vulnerable.

Reagan's own vulnerability becomes an important correlative here, as his hard body was the object of an assassin's bullet. On the one hand, John Hinkley's shot proved the president vulnerable; on the other hand, Reagan's recovery proved him strong and resilient. This is a second reason for the portrayal of vulnerability—that the national body can be shown capable of recovering from a past wound. This is one of the necessary premises of Reagan's attacks on the Carter administration. If the "wounds" suffered by the national body during the Carter years— Iran, hostages, inflation, Afghanistan, Nicaragua, and so on—were irreparable, Reagan would lose the force of one of his most frequent claims, that his leadership would make a difference to the nation ("Are you better off now than you were four years ago?"). Like Rambo, the nation can repair itself. Without the need of outside assistance—from NATO, Japan, China, or other allies—the United States will be able to suture and cauterize its own gaping wounds. Relying only on its own ability to repair itself, the nation can return, like Rambo, to the fight against the Soviet Union.

But by far the most important function of these scenes is to simultaneously offer and deny the promise of Reagan prosperity to the viewers of Rambo's films. Rambo's painful self-surgery insists that the national body can both heal itself and remain strong and combat-ready despite its wounds, offering a reassuring form of "national pleasure" as audience members can identify with the hard national body that survives and defeats its enemies. But these scenes also declare that, at the level of the individual body, there are differences between Rambo and most of the viewers of his films, ensuring that the feelings of sameness and unification that inspire such national pleasures do not "trickle down" to the level of the individual, where sameness and unification would be antithetical to the very mechanisms of prosperity Reaganism holds out. Most viewers, especially male viewers, are invited to recognize through these scenes that their bodies and Rambo's are not the same. Specifically, although viewers' bodies could be as vulnerable as his, suffering wounds and pain, their bodies, many men sense, could not survive those wounds as Rambo has done, because they could not perform the self-repair that enables Rambo to go on. This can only be perceived as a failing, a weakness brought out by the comparison to Rambo's hard body, which places such viewers in a position of inferiority to Rambo and the bodies like his that emblematize the Reagan social and economic system. As a result of such individualized de-identification, viewers are asked to explain discrepancies between themselves and

Rambo as personal failings rather than systemic flaws. In keeping with the logic of the Reagan hierarchy, any differences between relative successes within the Reagan system must be attributed, not to preexisting racism, disproportionate allocations of social resources, or economic and class inequalities, but to personal inadequacies considered as internal *bodily* failures. In such a system, some men have earned their survival and others have not. And whereas weak men may not be actual enemies, they are nonetheless not entitled to the profits due to those whose strength ensures the survival of the nation as a whole.

NOTES

1. Quoted in Michael Rogin, *Ronald Reagan, the Movie and Other Episodes in American Demonology* (Berkeley: University of California Press, 1987), 7.

2. John Ormond, *Comparing Presidential Behavior: Carter, Reagan, and the Macho Presidential Style* (New York: Green, 1987), 110.

3. Haynes Johnson, *Sleepwalking Through History: America in the Reagan Years* (New York: Norton, 1991), 161.

4. Lou Cannon, *President Reagan: The Role of a Lifetime* (New York: Simon & Schuster, 1991), 115.

5. Johnson, *Sleepwalking Through History*, 153.

6. Richard Nixon, *The Real War* (New York: Simon & Schuster, 1980), 3.

7. In David Morrell's original novel, Rambo does kill these men and more, requiring Rambo's own sacrifice at the end, as he is killed by Trautman himself (*First Blood*, [New York: Ballantine, 1982]).

8. Orman, *Comparing Presidential Behavior*, 7–8, 66, 7, and 18.

9. Jimmy Carter, *Keeping Faith* (New York: Bantam, 1982), 4.

10. Ronald Reagan, "The Trans World Airlines Hijacking Incident," *Weekly Compilation of Presidential Documents*, 2 July 1985, 869.

11. Rogin, *Ronald Reagan*, n.p.

12. There are in fact several places where the *Rambo* films critique the government, particularly in its failure to retrieve U.S. POWS from Vietnam, to have properly received returning U.S. veterans and offered them training or jobs, or to have investigated Agent Orange contamination. Pointedly, Rambo refuses to return "home" at the end of *Rambo*, feeling that "[his] country does not love him as much as [he] loves it." But most of these critiques can be leveled at previous administrations and not at Reagan himself. Even where Rambo criticizes current government policies, the charges seem more to be laid at the door of an inactive Congress than an indifferent president.

13. Cannon, *President Reagan*, 321.

14. Quoted in Richard Crawford, *In the Era of Human Capital* (New York: HarperBusiness, 1991), 74.

15. Nixon, *The Real War*, 11–12.

16. Clint Eastwood used this same gimmick in *Two Mules for Sister Sara* (Don Siegel, 1970), but he needed assistance to perform the operation, and his shoulder gave him great pain afterward.

17. Steve Neale, "Masculinity as Spectacle: Reflections on Men and Mainstream Cinema," *Screen* 24, no. 6 (1983): 2–17.

18. John Tower, Edmund Muskie, and Brent Scowcroft, *Report of the President's Special Review Board*, 26 February 1987, B-1.

Tania Modleski

Do We Get to Lose This Time?
Revising the Vietnam War Film

If there ever was a purely masculine genre, it is surely the war film. That women in the genre represent a threat to the male warrior is revealed in a time-worn convention: whenever a soldier displays a photograph of his girlfriend, wife, or family, he is doomed to die by the end of the film. The convention is so well known that it is parodied in *Hot Shots!* (Jim Abrahams, 1991), a spoof of the very popular film *Top Gun* (Tony Scott, 1986). Playing off the nicknaming of fighter pilots, one of the early scenes in *Hot Shots* shows the hero's side-kick slamming a locker door on which is taped a family photo. He then introduces himself to the hero as "Dead Meat."

Feminist critics of the war film, most notably Susan Jeffords, have convincingly argued that the genre is not only *for* men but plays a crucial role in the masculinizing process so necessary to the creation of warriors. Through spectacle (bombs bursting in air) and sound (usually heavy rock music), pro-war fantasies like *Top Gun* mobilize the kind of aggression essential to the functioning of men as killing machines. So too, problematically enough, do many antiwar films. Indeed, it is frequently noted that films like *Platoon* (Oliver Stone, 1986) not only do not effectively protest the war but actually participate in and, in a way, extend it, to the point where the spectator himself or herself becomes the target of the warrior-filmmaker's assault. As Gilbert Adair, in a thoughtful critique of *Platoon*, puts it: "It is surely time that film-makers learned that the meticulously detailed aping of an atrocity *is* an atrocity; that the hyper-realistic depiction of an obscenity cannot avoid being contaminated with that obscenity; and that the unmediated representation of violence constitutes in itself an act of violence against the spectator."[1] Moreover, just as it is the goal of war to crush opposing viewpoints and violently secure the opposing side's assent to the conqueror's truth, films like *Platoon* "bully" us into "craven submission," as Adair puts it, by pointing "an accusatory finger" and asking, "How do you know what it was like unless you've been there?"[2] Such questions are often literally addressed to women in the Vietnam films: "Who the hell are you to judge him?" the uncle, a vet (Bruce Willis), rebukes his niece (Emily Lloyd) in Norman Jewison's *In Country* (1989) when she expresses dismay at the racist remarks she finds in the diary her father kept before being killed in the war. Thus, since "being there" has so far been out of the question for women, who are prohibited from combat, their authority on any issue related to war is discredited from the outset and insofar as they may be inclined to question or oppose war (except in and on the terms granted them by men), they find themselves consigned to the ranks of the always-already defeated.[3]

Given the extent to which war has been an exclusive masculine preserve it is not surprising to find the critics themselves desiring generic purity, expressing discomfort when bits of "feminine discourse," for example, elements of melodrama or the love story, invade and "contaminate" the war film. One of the earliest films about the Vietnam War, *Coming Home* (Hal Ashby, 1978), which David James criticizes because it "rewrite[s] the invasion of Vietnam as erotic melodrama," is a case in point.[4] While commentators like John Hellman have found much to praise in films that rewrite the invasion in terms of *male* genres—the western (*The Deer Hunter* [Michael Cimino, 1978]) and the detective genre *(Apocalypse Now* [Frances Ford Coppola, 1979])—*Coming Home*'s incorporation of female genres has often provoked derision. Of course, *Coming Home* is not really about the war, but about its aftermath, and thus it is situated in a tradition of films about veterans' adjustment to civilian life. Nevertheless, critics have faulted it for focusing less on the problems of returning veterans than on the clichéd love story.

Coming Home is about a disabled veteran, Luke (Jon Voight), returning to civilian life and meeting Sally (Jane Fonda) who is married to a Marine serving in Vietnam and whose consciousness about the war is raised when she serves as a volunteer in a VA hospital. This consciousness receives a gigantic boost when Sally makes love with Luke, who brings her to climax orally, giving her her first orgasm. Critics have struggled to understand this scene in symbolic terms. Jason Katzman writes, "[*Coming Home*] uses the love story as a metaphor for the impotence of an entire country in understanding Vietnam. . . . Sally's ability to reach an orgasm with Luke where she could never before with her husband Bob (Bruce Dern), is one of the more widely discussed symbols."[5]

It is not clear to me what exactly the woman's orgasm is a symbol *of;* but it is clear that the event was less satisfying to some male critics than it was to *her.* Albert Auster and Leonard Quart, for example, express uneasiness about this plot element although they do not really specify the source of their discomfort: "unfortunately," they write, "Sally's transformation seems unconvincing and mechanical, especially in the emphasis it places on her achieving orgasm . . . while making love to Luke."[6]

Suppose, however, we take the orgasm to be an end in itself, rather than a symbol or a metaphor for something else. Suppose, in fact, that one of the problems with Vietnam War films in particular is their relentless exploitation of experiences and events for the significance they have solely to the soldiers who fought in the war rather than to the men's loved ones, allies, or enemies. I suspect that the critics' discomfort stems from the vividness with which the film demonstrates the point that men's losses may be a gain for women. Kaja Silverman has identified a similar theme in *The Best Years of Our Lives*, William Wyler's 1946 film about men returning from World War II and attempting to adjust to civilian life. Silverman heralds the film as a kind of feminist milestone in the history of what she calls "libidinal politics," since at this moment of "historical trauma" in which men came back from war mutilated both psychically and physically, non-phallic forms of male sexuality emerged.[7]

One might argue that from the point of view of women on the home front, *Coming Home* is even more important in this regard: unlike *The Best Years of Our Lives*, in which the women must find satisfaction in an eroticized maternal relation to their men, *Coming Home*, based on a story written by a woman, was made at a time when feminists were vociferously proclaiming the myth of the vaginal orgasm and agitating for the requisite attention to be paid to the clitoris. Women were hardly passive beneficiaries of the historical vicissitudes of male sexuality (and male warmongering) but were actively demanding and sometimes winning their sexual rights. However attenuated the film's politics are in other respects, it is important not to overlook the film's significant place in the ongoing struggles over sexual politics.[8]

To see how far women have been forced to retreat from this position of sexual advantage, we need only briefly compare *Coming Home* to a film on the same subject made a dozen years later. In Oliver Stone's *Born on the Fourth of July* (1989), a fictionalized version of the story of Ron Kovic—a war hero obsessed about his dysfunctional penis—the protagonist (Tom Cruise) reaches a low point when he goes down to Mexico and spends days and nights whoring, gambling, and boozing it up with other disabled vets. In one scene Ron appears to bring a whore to climax through manual stimulation; but in contrast to *Coming Home*, which focuses on the woman's tears of joy and passion, in this film we see *the man* crying out of self-pity for his lost potency. (In *In Country* there is also a scene in which a vet is impotent with the young heroine, who is kind and understanding. Nowhere is there a hint that his hard-on might not be the sine qua non of *her* sexual pleasure, for the question of her sexual pleasure is not even on the horizon.) In a brief subsequent scene, the camera assumes the hero's point of view as he wheels himself around a whorehouse in which various Mexican women beckon him with lewd remarks. Racism and misogyny combine in a scene meant to demonstrate the depths of degradation to which the hero has sunk. This scene constitutes a typical example of the commonplace phenomenon in Vietnam films in which exploited people (in this instance, the Mexican prostitutes) are further exploited by the films themselves for the symbolic value they hold for the hero. Thus do the films perpetuate the social and cultural insensitivity that led to America's involvement in the war and the atrocities committed there.

The film *Casualties of War* (Brian De Palma, 1989) presents another example of this phenomenon. In this film, as Pat Aufderheide argues, the rape and murder of a Vietnamese peasant girl by American soldiers signify "the collapse of a moral framework for the men who killed her. The spectacular agony of her death is intended to stir not the audience's righteous anger at the grunts . . . but empathy for the ordinary fighting men who have been turned into beasts by their tour of duty."[9] Equally extreme and still more bizarre is a scene in *Born on the Fourth of July* in which Kovic and another vet quarrel over which of them has killed more babies. The implication is that the superior person is the one who has killed the most babies since he has to carry a greater burden of guilt![10]

It is eminently clear from *Born on the Fourth of July* that historical trauma does not necessarily result in a progressive politics—libidinal or otherwise. Nor is the phallus necessarily relinquished by men who have suffered from such trauma. As Tony Williams has shrewdly observed in his discussion of the film, the trip to Mexico allows Ron to "confront his dark side . . . , confess his sins to the family of the man he shot, and gain the phallus (if not the penis) by speaking at the 1984 Democratic convention before an audience mainly composed of silent . . . and admiring, autograph seeking women."[11] Previously in the film, when Ron is released from the hospital he goes to see his girlfriend from high school. She, however, is so caught up in antiwar activities that she is unable to connect with him. As Ron wheels through her college campus, he declares his love for her, and the camera focuses on her walking beside him but looking in the direction of a group of activists about to hold a meeting. The proper role for a woman, the film makes clear, is that of silent supporter of male protestors, not independent actor, in the antiwar movement. The feminism that grew up partly in response to this attitude is, needless to say, nowhere evident in the film.

In addition to *Coming Home,* one other film is noteworthy not only for its incorporation of a love story, but most important, for the emphasis it places on the effects of the war and the war's aftermath on women.[12] In the film *Jacknife* (David Jones, 1989) Ed Harris plays Dave, a pent-up, alcoholic vet whose antisocial attitudes and behavior are ruining the life of his schoolteacher sister (Kathy Baker) with whom he resides. A friend called Megs, played by Robert DeNiro, comes to visit Dave and attempts to break him out of his shell; in the process Megs falls in love with Dave's sister. Dave violently opposes the relationship and works to sabotage it, although not entirely aware of what he is doing. One night when his sister and Megs are at the prom (she chaperones, but clearly they are both attempting to capture something lost in their youth), Dave comes to the high school, sees old trophies and an old picture of himself, and smashes the glass cases. After he runs off, his sister attempts to go on with the evening as if nothing had happened, while Megs is understandably distracted and distraught. Astonishingly, the film does not demonize the woman for resenting the way her brother's trauma has circumscribed her life. Indeed, it shows that the brother needs to accept a certain amount of responsibility for casting a pall on her existence. At the end we see him in group therapy coming to terms with the fact that he betrayed Megs one time in battle and coming to terms as well with what he sees as his own cowardice.

Rick Berg, a combat veteran, has written in an influential essay, "Losing Vietnam," that "the vet can begin to overcome his alienation" only when he recognizes that Vietnam's "consequences range throughout a community."[13] While for the most part Berg's concern is with issues of class, *Jacknife* has the merit of focusing on the vet's recognition of the way the war affects the relations between the sexes. The film is certainly not without many of the problems characteristic of films about post-Vietnam life. For instance it never, of course, even alludes to the feminism that arose from antiwar activity; on the contrary, the sister is cast in stereotypically spinsterish terms ("I know what I am," she says, not, however, voicing the dreaded term), and to her the goal of a life of her own is having a husband and family. The ending of the film is especially problematic in simplistically suggesting that somehow the union of Megs and Dave's sister will allow the couple to capture the lost innocence of their high school days. Nevertheless, if the film accomplished nothing more than granting Baker the line, "Don't you want a point of view?" when her brother says he won't take her, a woman, fishing with his friend, it would have done more than almost any other Vietnam film in granting woman an independent subjectivity and hinting at the possibility that she can be the maker and not just the bearer of meaning.[14]

The ending of *Jacknife,* with its nostalgic promise of a return to innocence, is characteristic of the genre. "Return" is a constant motif in Vietnam films, as many critics have noted. In the Rambo-type films, there is one heroic man's return to Vietnam so he can "win the war this time." For all its apparent liberalism, the same concern is detectable in *Born on the Fourth of July*. Ron's activism at the end of the film is *explicitly* associated with warfare: turned out of the Republican convention the veterans have stormed, Ron uses militarist language in instructing his men to return and "take the hall." Not only is Kovic thus positioned as a victorious warrior, a man who wins the war against the war, but in taking the hall he reverses another ignominious defeat, a wrestling match he lost in high school, to the tremendous disappointment of his mother and girlfriend sitting in the bleachers.

The notion of return is also present in the constant process of "metaphorization" that occurs in these films, which as we have seen make everything and everyone (raped women, murdered babies, etc.) refer back to and stand in for the American soldier (or veteran) and his plight. Difference and otherness are recognized only to the extent that they are seen to signify something about the American male. Some feminists have identified metaphor, which reduces differences to versions of sameness, as basic to Western "phallocentric" thought; in making this point they draw on the paradigmatic Freudian scenario whereby the male reads the female body in terms of his own standard—the penis, which the female body is judged to be lacking.[15] Now, given the crisis in America's "phallic" authority that opened up with the loss of the war and given the occasionally literal severing of the penis from the phallus which symbolizes it, it is not surprising to see metaphorical operations such as those I have described move into high gear in representations of Vietnam. Thinking again of the coming in *Coming Home,* we can see why a feminist would appreciate the sex scene in that film, might prize its

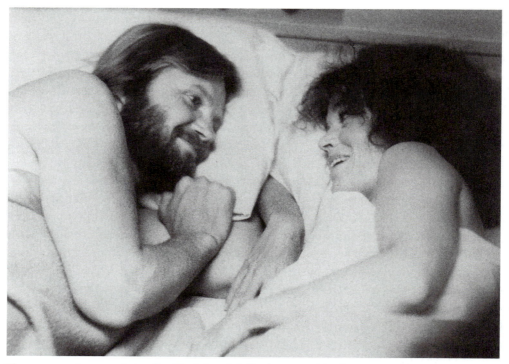

The sex scene between Luke (Jon Voight) and Sally (Jane Fonda) offers a "brief acknowledgment of feminine difference." Coming Home. Courtesy: Photofest

brief acknowledgment of feminine difference, and want to insist that sometimes a clitoris is just a clitoris, and a woman's orgasm simply that.

This rather lengthy preamble is designed to put in relief the achievement of Nancy Savoca's understated little film *Dogfight* (1991), since it is easily lost in the midst of the loud, frantic, spectacular representations with which we have been bombarded by so many male directors of Vietnam films. *Dogfight* is a film about a group of Marines about to be shipped overseas (they don't know it but they are destined for Vietnam). The group of men set up a "dogfight," which turns out to be a dance, to which each of the Marines is supposed to bring an ugly date. The man who finds the ugliest woman will be the winner and receive a cash prize. One of the four men, Eddie (River Phoenix), is unsuccessful at convincing the women he encounters to go out with him; more or less giving up on the attempt he goes into a diner and meets Rose (Lili Taylor, padded up a bit for the role), a waitress whose mother owns the diner and who, when he first sees her, is picking out a folk tune on her guitar. He invites her to the dance, and after some hesitation she accepts. One of the interesting aspects of the way the film sets up the initial sequence is that the spectator is not sure whether or not Eddie really considers Rose to be "dogfight" material, a question that the film in fact never clears up.

At the end of the evening Rose discovers the purpose of the dogfight, slugs Eddie, and leaves in a rage. Remorseful, Eddie goes to the apartment over the diner where Rose lives and gets Rose to agree to go out with him for the night. Scenes of their evening out, which is sweetly romantic despite periodic arguments (Rose is a budding peacenik), are intercut with scenes of Eddie's three friends, who spend their last night in the States brawling with sailors and watching pornography in a theater as a prostitute fellates them, chewing gum in between bouts. At the end of the evening they go to a tattoo parlor and get tattoos of bees on their arms (each has a last name beginning with "B") to mark their loyalty to one another. Eddie and Rose sleep together and in the morning he goes off to meet his bus. After a very brief battle scene set in Vietnam, Eddie returns, wounded, to San Francisco, and the film very movingly presents us with the point of view of a man who sees an entirely different world from the one he left. Flower children fill the street: one of them walks past Eddie and softly asks, "Hey, man, did you kill any babies over there?" For all the preoccupation of films like *Born on the Fourth of July* with the soldier's readjustment to civilian life, in my view no other movie captures as vividly as this scene the estrangement and confusion of the returning vet. Eddie goes into the diner that Rose now runs and encounters a more mature woman; as they look at each other, they are at a loss for words, and in a mournful ending the two embrace.

I want to argue against the grain of the voluminous criticism written about Vietnam War movies and to propose that precisely *because Dogfight* is a love story and gives us a woman's perspective on war and the warrior mentality, it is less compromising in its opposition to war than any other film in that most paradoxical of genres, the antiwar war movie. The antiwar sentiment is not only present in *Dogfight's* narrative but is conveyed at the level of style: much of the film's subversiveness lies in the peacefulness and restraint of its pacing, rhythms, and soundtrack. There is a sweetness in the encounter between boy and girl that is genuinely moving. At the same time it must be said that this film is less sentimental than most Vietnam films, which Andrew Martin has convincingly shown to be for the most part male melodrama. To measure the gap between the sentimentality of some of these films and *Dogfight's* uncompromising view of the cruelties of which people are capable and which, after all, have some bearing on our desire or at least our willingness to make war, we need only compare one event, the prom that is featured prominently in Vietnam films, with a very different one in Savoca's film—the dogfight. The latter is, to say the least, an event for which it is difficult to muster up the same sort of nostalgia inspired by the former.

The eponymous event of the dogfight may be seen as the antithesis of the prom scenes in *Jacknife* and *Born on the Fourth of July*, both of which nourish us in the dangerous illusion of a prewar era of lost innocence and unimpaired relations between the sexes. In *Born on the Fourth of July* Ron Kovic, on the eve of his departure for military service, runs through a storm in his old clothes and arrives soaked at the prom to dance with his starry-eyed girlfriend. In *Dogfight*, of course, the "dance" is the cruel event of the dogfight itself (staged, like the prom in *Born on the Fourth of July*, on the eve of the men's departure for Vietnam). Rose finds out about the point of the dance, the dogfight, in a scene that takes place in the ladies room. One of the girls, Marcy, who has gone toothless to the affair and earned the prize for the man who brought her, stands in front of the bathroom mirror putting her teeth back in and tells Rose about the rules of the contest. "The thing that gets me," Marcy concludes, "is how great they think they are. Did you ever see such a pack of pukes in your life?" Rose is, naturally, appalled and marches out to Eddie and punches him, confronting him directly with his cruelty and lack of feelings for others. The script, written by ex-Marine Bob Comfort, has the infinite merit of focusing here on the anger and humiliation of the object, rather than the sad plight of the subject, of the cruelty.

Yet in creating Rose, who in the original script was supposed to be excessively overweight, Comfort intended to make the woman serve as a "metaphor" for the Marine, her unacceptable looks symbolizing his "outsider status." Comfort has publicly expressed his unhappiness with Savoca's changes in his script, and one can only speculate that his feeling of dispossession, his sense of discomfort, as it were, stemmed from director Savoca's resistance to turning the heroine into a metaphor, a reflection of the hero. According to Savoca, in the original script Rose "was more of a catalyst for change," and, she says, "this bored me and Lili to tears." They resolved to make the character someone in her own right. Importantly, however, the transformation in the female character does not occur at the *expense* of the male character (almost a primal fear of men when women make art); on the contrary, Savoca maintains, "as her IQ comes up, so does his. Because rather than reacting to a thing, he's reacting to a complicated person. Something happens between two people and not just between this guy and his revelation." Savoca continues: "We decided that the first thing to do was give her a passion—so that regardless of what she looks like there's something going on within herself. And that something is music. . . . He becomes attracted to her because she has a love in her that goes beyond their small world and the rigid narrow existence he's used to living—and not because one day she takes out the ribbon in her hair and, oh my god, she's stunning."[16]

In view of the narcissistic self-referentiality of many male-directed Vietnam films, which repeatedly and utterly disqualify women as authorities in matters of war and peace (we recall Ron Kovic's girlfriend being judged harshly by the film *Born on the Fourth of July* for turning away from Kovic and toward the antiwar demonstrators), we can perhaps appreciate Savoca's audacity in having her heroine's aspirations and values point a way out of the trap in which the soldier finds himself. Indeed, we might say that, by extension, just as Eddie is required to treat Rose as a person with an independent subjectivity who has the potential for giving him a glimpse of more expansive horizons, so too does Savoca's encounter with Comfort's text strengthen it while respecting and underscoring its powerful indictment of a society that devours young working-class men and spits them out.

Rose is a young girl who dreams of changing the world, of possibly joining the civil rights movement in the South or engaging in some other form of social activism; she also aspires to be a folk singer and during their date she argues with Eddie throughout the evening about the most effective means of changing the world: he, of course, has opted for guns; she for guitars. That the aspirations and values of the heroine are expressed in her love of folk music is particularly appropriate. Vietnam was, as more than one critic has noted, America's rock-and-roll war, and many of the films about the war are edited to supercharged rhythms of the Rolling Stones and similar groups. Even if the lyrics of many of these songs are intended to make an ironic or critical comment on the war, the music itself often serves to pump up the testosterone level, working viscerally against the antiwar sentiments supposedly being promoted. Such music, as David James has argued, is always at least ambivalent.[17] In this regard, then, we might compare the nihilistic song by the Stones, "Paint It Black," that ends Stanley Kubrick's antiwar, antimilitary film *Full Metal Jacket* (1987) with the Malvina Reynolds song that Rose haltingly sings sitting at a piano in a nearly deserted café as Eddie looks on: "The grass is gone / the boy disappears / and rain keeps falling like helpless tears."

Eddie and his friends do disappear, and only Eddie returns. When he comes back to San Francisco, the world has changed drastically, and he is viewed with disdain and suspicion by the flower children milling around in the street. Eddie limps into a bar across the street from Rose's café wearing his uniform. When the bartender sees Eddie's tattoo he shows him his: a girl who jiggles and performs a "belly dance" on his protruding gut. Eddie asks about Rose, describing her to the bartender as kind of chubby; the bartender responds, "She ain't no prize," and one of the men chimes in, "Yeah, like you're really something, eh Carl?" At one point the bartender asks Eddie if he served in Vietnam. When Eddie responds in the affirmative, the bartender, at a loss for words, says, "Yeah, bummer," and walks away. "No charge on that," says the owner of the bar when Eddie gets a second drink. "Thank you," Eddie replies. "Thank *you*," says the man quietly, but he can't look Eddie in the eye.

Such moments convey the pathos and isolation of the returning veteran more eloquently than a thousand bombastic moments in an Oliver Stone movie. They strike a note of pure loss, prolonged through the final shots when Eddie goes across the street to see Rose and she too seems not to know what to say or do. They embrace, though this is clearly not the embrace of two people destined to live happily ever after; it is an act of mutual consolation over all the sorrow and loss that has occurred in the intervening years, including the severing of their slender connection, which of course cannot ever be reforged. Warner Brothers Studio, encouraged by a preview audience's positive response to the first part of the movie (some of the crowd found the dogfight idea hilarious), exerted intense pressure on Savoca to change the ending to make it more upbeat. Finally, an exasperated Savoca asked sardonically, "Do you want us to change the ending so we win the war?"—apparently not realizing that that was *exactly* what Hollywood wanted and what movie directors for the last decade or so have been all too happy to provide.

   Dogfight, in a certain sense, may be seen as the second in a two-part series Savoca filmed on relations between the sexes. Her brilliant film debut was a movie, *True Love* (1989), that gained a certain cult following among women. Drawing on some techniques of documentary, *True Love* is a dystopian "wedding comedy" that focuses on the rituals leading up to the big day. Donna (Annabella Sciorra) and Mikey (Ron Eldard), the engaged couple, battle over whether or not Donna will get to go out with Mikey after his bachelor party. Throughout the film, Savoca cuts between the group of guys (Mikey and his friends) and the group of girls (Donna and hers), showing us two worlds that are so separate, their inhabitants might as well live on separate planets. "Sometimes she says things to me and I don't understand what the fuck she's talkin' about," says Mikey at one point. As the boys party on throughout the night, getting drunker and drunker (while the camera angles and positions get wilder and wilder), the girls just hang out waiting, talking of marriage, home decorating, and the like. At one point they go to watch a male stripper, but it is clear they do so defiantly, in order to prove their ability to have the same kind of fun as the boys—thereby, of course, proving the opposite. The climax of the movie occurs during the wedding itself when Mikey proposes to his friends that they go out for a while on the wedding night. He begs Donna to let him go just for an hour or two with the boys, and she runs crying into the ladies room, where she is followed first by her friends and then by Mikey. The film ends inconclusively, although one senses the two will go on with married life, living it as happily or rather as unhappily as most.

   True Love documents better than almost any film I have ever seen the asymmetries of life as it is generally lived by the two sexes in modern America. It submits to a trenchant analysis the relations between men that are glorified and idealized by the overwhelming majority of Hollywood films. *Dogfight* continues in this vein, alternating scenes of the developing relation between Eddie and Rose with scenes of Eddie's friends out on the town boozing and whoring. From wedding to war and home again, Savoca's first two films, taken together, cover the same territory as Michael Cimino's lengthy and controversial Vietnam film *The Deer Hunter* and may be read as a rewriting of that film in feminist terms.

   Roughly the first third of *The Deer Hunter* depicts a wedding that takes place in a highly sex-segregated working-class community of Russian Americans, just as *True Love* is situated in a working-class Italian American section of the Bronx. In an excellent analysis of *The Deer Hunter*, Susan Jeffords argues that the wedding sets up the basic conflict of the film, which is most clearly played out in relation to the character of Nicky (Christopher Walken) who is killed off by the film, precisely because his loyalties are divided between the world associated with women (sex, marriage, domesticity) and his affiliation with men—specifically Michael, played by Robert DeNiro. Jeffords writes, "One must either live all of the points of the code ('discipline, endurance, purity') or not attempt it at all; . . . one must fulfill either the masculine or the feminine, but not both."[18] Of course, these two options are not equally valued by the film, for the character who chooses the feminine comes home a paraplegic; rather, its primary emotional investment is in the relations between men, in particular, between Nick and Michael, whose friendship is highly idealized by Cimino. Jeffords goes so far as to claim that "Vietnam is . . . not the subject of *The Deer Hunter* but merely the occasion for announcing the primacy of the bonds between men."[19]

While many Vietnam films, most notably perhaps *Full Metal Jacket*, have exposed the misogynistic aspects of military life, none of them focuses as unwaveringly as *Dogfight* on the more unappealing aspects of the male bonding that is part and parcel of the misogyny—the dirty jokes, the lies about sexual prowess, the animal behavior and brawling, the humiliation of those farther down the pecking order, and so on. Soldiers who fought in Vietnam were, after all, just boys out of high school (a fact we're inclined to forget when a thirty-something Robert DeNiro is the star). *Dogfight* goes very far indeed in contravening one of the most basic assumptions of Hollywood war films in regard to women and male bonding, suggesting *not* that men must give up ties to women and families in order to survive, but that the unthinking loyalty to the all-male group, an ideal promoted by military life and by much of our civilian culture as well, is what threatens their survival. The point may seem obvious, but it is never made in Hollywood films.

To emphasize the irrationality of these bonds the film includes a discussion at the dogfight in which the boys explain to the girls how it is their surnames all begin with the same initial. One of the four explains that they had to line up by alphabetical order when they were in infantry training. Rose conversationally concludes, "So you got to be friends by standing in line?" There is an awkward pause, and then Marcy, the toothless girl, guffaws loudly. The guys call themselves the four B's, and the film makes much of the ritual in which they get themselves tattooed with bees on their arms—all except Eddie who is with Rose. When Eddie rejoins the group the morning after sleeping with Rose, he tells one of his friends, Berzin (Richard Panebianco), that he has learned from Rose that Berzin had fixed the dogfight. Berzin in turn tells Eddie that when he was getting his tattoo he saw him with Rose—not with the gorgeous officer's wife Eddie has lied about having spent his last night with. In a rare moment of honesty between men Eddie asks his friend Berzin, "How'd we get to be so full of shit like this . . . such idiots?" All these lies are "bullshit," Eddie says. Berzin replies:

> Let me tell you something about bullshit. It's everywhere. You hit me with a little, and I buy it. I hit you with a little, you buy it. That doesn't make us idiots. It's what makes us buddies. We buy what the Corps hands out, and that's what makes us Marines. And the Corps's buying all the bullshit from President Kennedy and President Kennedy's buying all the bullshit from everybody in the U.S. of Fuckin' A and that's what makes us Americans.

"It's still bullshit," Eddie insists. "Right, and we're in it up to our goddam lips, Buddy. . . . I don't know if I'm making sense, but [here he rolls up his sleeve to show the bee tattoos], this makes a hell of a lot of sense to me. There's no bullshit in this." At this point, one of the four "bees" farts loudly; the guys all start laughing and joking again about the officer's wife. In a chilling gesture Eddie tears up the address Rose has given him and throws the pieces out the window of the bus, where they are scattered to the wind. The act of renouncing association with women would in the logic of most war films help to secure the man's safety, which as I noted at the outset, is endangered whenever men keep mementos of their attachments at home.

In *Dogfight* the outcome is very different. The film devotes about one minute of screen time to depicting the men in combat (thereby avoiding the contradictions involved when films rely on combat sequences for their antiwar message). In this brief scene we see the four young men sitting around playing cards, and one of them brings up a joke: "What did the ghost say to the bee? 'Boo, bee.'" As two of the four "bees" laugh at a dumb pun that condenses various themes of the film—male bonding (the four bees), the degradation of women (the crude reference to a part of female anatomy), and death (the ghost)—mortar falls into their midst and apparently kills Eddie's friends. It might be said that, at the fantasmatic level, Eddie is allowed to survive *because* his loyalties were at least temporarily divided between the male group and a woman—the very reason, in Jeffords's argument, that Nick in *The Deer Hunter* must be killed off.

In Savoca's previous film, *True Love*, the heroine Donna resents the all-male group but recognizes its primacy. The night before the wedding Donna takes Mikey aside and cuts both their hands to intermingle their blood, like "blood brothers," she explains. The acknowledgment of the primacy of male bonds, along with the yearning to become a member of the privileged male group, is something that is also expressed in representations of Vietnam created by women. In her discussion of Bobbie Ann Mason's *In Country*, for instance, Jeffords shows how the heroine longs to have the same kind of understanding of war that men have and how finally the novel confirms "collectivity as a function of the masculine bond."[20] When Sam/Samantha, who is named after her father, goes to the Vietnam War Memorial, she is able to touch her own name and symbolically become part of the collectivity from which she has felt excluded. In *Dogfight*, however, the woman stands for a higher form of collectivity than the military group exemplified by the four bees—and her vision of a better world achievable through artistic endeavor and political activism (*not* through any essentialized categories such as feminine nurturance) is presented by the film as admirable, if vague and a bit naively idealistic.

On the film's horizon is a faint glimpse, barely discernible, of another kind of collectivity. Taking place on the eve of a feminist revolt that would gain momentum in the 1970s, *Dogfight* reminds us, most particularly in the casting of folksinger Holly Near as the mother of a heroine who believes in the power of music to change the world, of a time when *women* would bond together in lesbian separatist spaces, preeminent of which was the woman's music festival. Additionally, in locating Rose and her mother in a place called "Rose's Coffee Shop," which is handed down from mother to daughter, beginning with Rose's grandmother, the film privileges matrilineality and presages the alternative economies that feminists would be attempting to devise.

The fullness of that story, though, is left to another time, another film. For Savoca and her husband, screenwriter Richard Guay with whom she works closely, the principal concern is the relation, or more accurately nonrelation, between the sexes. One finds a fairly persistent pessimism in Savoca's work about the possibilities for meaningful union between male and female. But the connection between Rose and Eddie when it does occur is luminescent. The physical part of the relationship begins after Rose has sung for Eddie in the café. He takes her to a musical arcade where they put money in all the machines and dance to a cacophony of music box tunes. Then as the music winds down, it is as if the raucous soundtrack of every Vietnam film ever made were being stilled, the rhythm cranked down and a temporary truce called in the hostilities between men and women. The noisy soundtrack is replaced by the sound of two people awkwardly embracing, fumbling to get their arms right, breathing unevenly in excitement and surprise at the intense pleasures of newly awakening sexuality.

When Eddie goes to Rose's bedroom, they begin kissing to the tune of a Malvina Reynolds song playing on Rose's phonograph machine; then Rose goes into her closet "to change." Eddie whisks out of his clothes and stops when he remembers to go through his wallet to find a condom. He slips it under the bib of a teddy bear on Rose's bed and quickly gets into the bed. Rose comes out wearing a long flannel nightgown, and Eddie is dazzled: "You look good, you look real good." The process in which Rose goes from being perceived as possible dogfight material to being looked upon as a vision of loveliness is complete and entirely believable, without the film's ever stopping to make a point of it. As if responding to the commentators who have criticized Vietnam representations for seldom acknowledging that warriors are just boys, the film in this scene touchingly evokes precisely the liminal space between childhood and adulthood so crucial to the future of humanity (its end—in war; its beginning—in sex).

Because the movie is about teenagers, Warner Brothers thought it should be marketed as a teen comedy—the ghetto to which so many women directors are relegated in Hollywood. Such a confusion might seem laughable on the face of it, but the fact that the movie is as much about a teenage *girl* as it is about boys makes it especially vulnerable to being judged trivial. Nor is *Dogfight* alone in being patronized because of its protagonist. In an article entitled "Men, Women and Vietnam," Milton J. Bates writes of Bobbie Ann Mason's novel *In Country*: "Mason, having elected to tell her story from a teenage girl's point of view, cannot realistically venture a more mature critique of the War or sexual roles. Why inflict such a handicap on one's narrative?"[21] One might as well say that *Huckleberry Finn* is handicapped

Rose (Lili Taylor) with Eddie (River Phoenix). Her character is used "to advance an important critique of the war mentality and especially of war narratives." Dogfight. Courtesy: Photofest

by having a young boy as its protagonist and that consequently Mark Twain cannot venture a mature critique of American society or slavery! I am arguing, however, that having a teenage girl as (co)protagonist provides Savoca with a unique vantage point from which to advance an important critique of the war mentality and especially of war narratives—a critique, in part, of their exclusive emphasis *on the white male soldier's point of view.*

Discussing the sex scene in class, one of my students remarked that this was the first time in the movies she had seen a man ask a woman if it was okay to proceed in his sexual "advances." It is in such small details that the subversive nature of women's popular cinema often lies. This detail might be dismissed as another instance in which "the invasion is rewritten as erotic melodrama." But I would counter that in being anti-invasion on a very minute scale, the film points to the existence of other subjectivities and other desires besides those of the white male hero. In so saying, I do not, I hope, commit the same error I lamented in mainstream representations of Vietnam and implicitly offer Rose as a metaphor for Asia. I do, however, mean to suggest that in the film one man is shown to take a crucial *step* toward recognizing otherness in the variety of forms it takes; the movie thus prepares the ground for the emergence of an antiwar sensibility, even though it doesn't go the entire distance.

The film itself respects the integrity and independence of its viewers as well and never bludgeons them with the moral. Rather than beginning by condemning the men for their barbarous treatment of women, for example, the film depicts the staging of the dogfight in such a way that the point of the men's search for ugly women, which may initially strike us as somewhat amusing, only gradually becomes clear. We tend to identify with Eddie until Rose learns about the dogfight, and then we find ourselves implicated in his lack of sensitivity and his propensity for cruelty. This development, along with the film's somber finale, angered preview audiences who wanted the comfort of a happy and predictable ending: boy loses war but at least wins girl (the boo-bee prize).

The anger is certainly understandable. The war itself seemed to many Americans to have had the wrong ending, and rather than mourning its loss, they have fallen victim to a widespread melancholia, in which they cling to the lost object rather than letting it go.[22] According to Sigmund Freud, when people are unable to mourn a loss and put it behind them, they internalize it, preserving it within themselves, and become inconsolable. Turning inward, they appear narcissistic. This malady is what Freud calls "melancholia" ("Mourning and Melancholia"). Having denied loss, denied the fact of having lost the war, America internalized the war and cannot seem to move beyond the question of what this loss has meant to itself, rather than to others who were also affected by it. *Dogfight* points to the necessity of moving beyond narcissism and coming to terms with the losses we incurred in being vanquished—the necessity, then, of mourning.

And in mourning who better than women to lead the way? In her important study, *The Gendering of Melancholia*, Juliana Schiesari, following and reassessing Freud, discusses mourning as a social ritual that has generally been performed by women. Melancholia, in contrast to mourning, is a category by which a solitary male elevates and glorifies his losses (a comrade; a lover; a war) into "signifiers of cultural superiority."[23] A literary critic, Schiesari is speaking primarily of poets and other creative writers who through masterful elegiac displays put their own exquisite sensibilities forward for us to admire, offering themselves as objects to be pitied for the losses they have sustained, and—in some cases—hoping to acquire immortality, paradoxically, through creating for posterity a work that supposedly acknowledges death. For our purposes, Oliver Stone, who cannot seem to stop making movies about Vietnam, might be seen as an example of the inconsolable melancholic. A quintessentially melancholic scene would be the one in *Born on the Fourth of July* in which we're asked to focus on *Kovic*'s pain and guilt when he has to talk to the parents of a dead buddy. Schiesari concludes that mourning is a social ritual that "accommodates the imagination to reality" while melancholia accommodates reality to the imagination. In her capacity as mourner, too, then, woman stands for the collectivity over male individualism.

Doing the work of mourning, accommodating the imagination to reality, the film confronts us both with the reality of our losses and, concomitantly, with the real—as opposed to figural-status of woman. The struggle to establish this reality by asserting a female vision and female authority was waged at several levels of the text's production and reception. First, in order to make the female character of equal importance to the male, Savoca had to take on scriptwriter Comfort, who was displeased at some of her revisions. Second, many of the changes were decided on during the filming and were worked out collectively between cast and crew, most particularly between Savoca and Taylor. Finally, after preview audiences responded unfavorably to the film's ending, Savoca refused to comply with Warner Brothers' attempts to get her to change the ending. She conceded that Warner Brothers had the authority to do what they liked with the film, but she demanded that her name be taken off the project if the ending was reshot. Warner Brothers executives called River Phoenix and Lili Taylor, but both refused to reshoot the ending without Savoca. Savoca believes that neither she nor Taylor counted for much with the studio but thinks that Phoenix's refusal to reshoot forced Warner Brothers' decision to stop pursuing the issue (whereupon, according to Savoca, the project was dumped "into the toilet"). I like to think that Phoenix's role taught him something *about* resisting the orders of a male power structure and the desirability of sometimes deferring to the vision of a woman—in this case, Nancy Savoca, who elicited from him one of the finest performances of his tragically short life. Fittingly, Phoenix ended up being eloquently memorialized in a work that asserts the legitimacy of female authority.

NOTES

1. Gilbert Adair, *Hollywood's Vietnam: From "The Green Berets" to "Full Metal Jacket"* (London: Heinemann, 1989), 159.

2. Adair, *Hollywood's Vietnam*, 169.

3. See the chapter, "A Father Is Being Beaten" in my *Feminism without Women: Culture and Criticism in a "Postfeminist" Age* (New York: Routledge, 1991).

4. David James, "Rock and Roll in Representations of the Museum of Vietnam," *Representations* 29 (Winter 1990): 91.

5. Jason Katzman, "Outcast to Cliché: How Family Shaped, Warped and Developed the Image of the Vietnam Veterans, 1967–90," *Journal of American Culture* 16, no. 1 (Spring 1993): 12.

6. Albert Auster and Leonard Quart, *How the War Was Remembered: Hollywood and Vietnam* (New York: Praeger, 1988), 50.

7. Kaja Silverman, *Male Subjectivity at the Margins* (New York: Routledge, 1992), 52–121.

8. As David James reminds us, though, *Coming Home*'s "unequivocal assertion that the invasion is *wrong* distinguishes it from all other films made in Hollywood" (James, "Rock and Roll," 90).

9. Pat Aufderheide, "Good Soldiers," in *Seeing Through the Movies*, ed. Mark Crispin Miller (New York: Pantheon, 1990), 88.

10. One might be tempted to read the scene as satiric; yet the entire film presents its hero and its subject with such hysterical immediacy and apparent overidentification that it lacks the distance necessary for a satiric commentary.

11. Tony Williams, "Narrative Patterns and Mythic Trajectories in Mid-1980s Vietnam Movies," in *Inventing Vietnam*, ed. Michael Anderegg (Philadelphia: Temple University Press, 1991), 129.

12. This film too has been criticized for involving a "love story" which, writes Katzman, "digressed from the film's more interesting element, which was Dave's healing process" (21).

13. Rick Berg, "Losing Vietnam: Covering the War in an Age of Technology," in *From Hanoi to Hollywood: The Vietnam War in American Film*, ed. Linda Dittmar and Gene Michaud (New Brunswick: Rutgers University Press, 1996), 65.

14. These are Laura Mulvey's terms in "Visual Pleasure and Narrative Cinema," *Visual and Other Pleasures* (Bloomington: Indiana University Press, 1989), 14–26.

15. See ibid.

16. All quotations are from an interview I conducted with Nancy Savoca on 30 November 1994.

17. In addition to James, "Rock and Roll," see Douglas Reitinger, "Paint it Black: Rock Music and Vietnam War Films," *Journal of American Culture* 15, no. 3 (1992): 1913–1956.

18. Susan Jeffords, *The Remasculinization of America: Gender and the Vietnam War* (Bloomington: Indiana University Press, 1989), 95.

19. Ibid., 99.

20. Ibid., 62.

21. Milton J. Bates, "Men, Women and Vietnam," in *America Rediscovered: Cultural Essays on International Film of the Vietnam Era*, ed. Owen W. Gilman Jr. and Lorrie Smith (New York: Garland, 1990), 29.

22. J. Hoberman speaks of the war's "bummer of a finale that's left us with a compulsion to remake, if not history, then at least the movie." "America Dearest," *American Film* 13, no. 7 (May 1988), 41.

23. Juliana Schiesari, *The Gendering of Melancholia: Feminism, Psychoanalysis, and the Symbolics of Loss in Renaissance Literature* (Ithaca: Cornell University Press, 1992), 62.

Yvonne Tasker

Soldiers' Stories:
Women and Military Masculinities in
Courage Under Fire

Masculinity . . . becomes legible as masculinity where and when it leaves the white male middle-class body.

—Judith Halberstam

Sometimes masculinity has nothing to do with . . . men.

—Eve Sedgwick

Both images and narratives focused on military women disrupt very directly assumptions that behaviors or qualities designated masculine are reserved only for men. Obviously they are also framed by ongoing, hard-fought arguments concerning the proper role of women in the U.S. military, arguments that involve factors including combat and noncombat roles, new technologies, and (in Hollywood films at least) shifting political ideas about the role of U.S. intervention. I don't want to argue here that cinematic images of military women should be understood in any straightforward way as "transgressive." After all, a respect for rules and order as well as fantasies of inclusion and belonging are so central and so powerful in the films I'll be discussing. Indeed, what strikes me most forcibly about the two most high-profile American films of the 1990s to focus on military women in combat, *Courage Under Fire* (Edward Zwick, 1996), a melodramatic war movie that provides the main focus for this essay, and the Ridley Scott-directed *G. I. Jane* (1997), is that while the central female characters are tough and masculine-coded, they are also both normalized and revered. To the extent that such images are transgressive at all then, I would argue that this lies not only in the act of proposing a viable female masculinity, but in their construction of heroic female protagonists whose very desire to be part of a masculine conformity troubles both the cinematic world in which they operate and many assumptions that have come to be conventional within feminist film criticism.

I want to suggest here that masculinity is important for understanding contemporary cinematic representations of women, and not only when the female protagonist appears explicitly in male guise. As such this essay is part of an ongoing

Quarterly Review of Film and Video 19 (2002): 209–222. © 2002 Routledge. Reprinted with permission of Taylor & Francis Ltd. http://www.tandf.co.uk/journals.

attempt to untangle gendered concepts, terms, and images that are regularly used in both feminist-informed (typically psychoanalytic) film studies, and more sociological explorations of masculinities, not to mention popular discourses about gender. In effect I'm trying to think through a critical slippage that occurs between talking about gender as a set of qualities or characteristics culturally aligned with men or women, and the ways in which both images and identities regularly transgress these borders or boundaries. The essay argues for a more flexible model of gender in thinking about popular cinema (or indeed art cinema). Most important, I'd like to suggest that contemporary cinema makes use of images of "men" and "women" that articulate a complex relationship between sex and gender: a complexity that, even in fantasy genres (I'm thinking of 1990s movies such as *Strange Days* [Kathryn Bigelow, 1995] or *The Long Kiss Goodnight* [Renny Harlin, 1996]) may speak to lived experiences of gender in which, "post-feminism," women are constituted in terms of gendered discourses not simply in terms of femininity.

Before moving to a broader discussion of the perspectives that film studies had developed on masculinity, it is worth saying a little more about *Courage Under Fire* and the generic context that helps to frame the film and my reading of it. A more or less explicit reworking of Akira Kurosawa's *Rashomon* (1950), *Courage Under Fire* uses a complex series of flashbacks to explore themes of guilt, courage, and heroism through the investigation of events leading to the death during the Gulf War of Captain Karen Walden, a medevac pilot played by Meg Ryan. Although Ryan and Denzel Washington co-star they don't share a single scene (despite the suggestion of promotional images). Instead, the film works to construct a fairly sophisticated set of parallels between them, interweaving their stories. Colonel Nat Serling's (Washington) task is to establish whether or not Walden should be posthumously awarded the Medal of Honor. He visits her family and her crew, building up a fragmented and contradictory picture of her character, and gradually piecing together the circumstances of her death. The investigation culminates in Serling's discovery of a mutiny. Worse, fearful of the court-martial that awaits him, Monfriez (Lou Diamond Phillips) reports that the injured Walden is already dead, leaving her on the ground to be engulfed in the flames of an air strike. Running alongside this story of betrayal, we follow Serling's attempts to come to terms with his own failure in combat: in the opening scene his mistaken order results in the death of Lieutenant Boylar, a close friend under his command. In its elaboration of bravery and cowardice, of judgment, authority, and failure within the context of combat and its aftermath, the film thus maps masculinity across several soldiers' stories.

Military Masculinities

Military movies and war movies typically feature a carefully managed tension between conformity and individualism, the uniformity and sublimation of personal desires suggested by service against the award of medals for distinction. Thus Robert Ashley's *Sight and Sound* review of *G.I. Jane* suggested that the film was about the individual rather than the team, its insistent message, despite the recuperative ending, that women can never really be incorporated into the male group. *Courage Under Fire* can equally be read as a narrative that demonstrates the problem posed by women in combat. Walden's men fail to respect her authority at the crucial moment. At the same time, however, these films both offer powerful fantasies of incorporation, fantasies central to the war movie at least since films of and about World War II, with their emphasis on the development of allegiances across differences of race, religion, ethnicity, and class. The boot camp subgenre within which *G.I. Jane* is situated, for example, emphasizes the need for exceptional individual strength on the one hand and self-effacement in the interests of the group (and by extension the nation) on the other.

The cynical, world-weary soldier is another stalwart of the genre. Though the Gulf War has shifted this somewhat, the prevailing stereotype of the veteran has long been that of an alienated, violent male soldier whose physical and mental scars nonetheless operate as marks of (masculine) character. Military women cannot be coded quite so easily in terms of dutiful but melancholy heroism, since whether or not they get to do the job at all remains such a contested issue. Can a privilege that has been fought for so hard be presented as a burden reluctantly shouldered? The terms in which male masculinity is constructed in the war film are in many ways quite at odds with the emerging stereotype of the determined, somewhat idealized military career woman showcased in television movies such as *Serving in Silence: The Margarethe Cammermeyer Story* (Jeff Bleckner, 1995) and *She Stood Alone: The Tailhook Scandal* (Larry Shaw, 1995). It is interesting in this context to look back to the TV series *M*A*S*H* (1972–1983) in which Major Margaret Houlihan (Loretta Swit) functioned as the sexualized butt ("Hotlips") of the show's oddly macho pacifism. As a career army nurse, Houlihan stands in for an extreme of military conformity in a particularly invidious way. She is ridiculed for being simultaneously too evidently female (read sexually demanding) and too masculine (read ambitious). Although a figure of fun, Houlihan's female masculinity nonetheless underlines the extent to which bodies and behaviors do not always conform to type, even as they are reinscribed within a stereotypical frame.

Although it inevitably frames the film, *Courage Under Fire* focuses resolutely on individual dramas, only implicitly acknowledging the wider questions around the combat role of military women. Similarly, Serling's self-searching and antagonistic yet respectful relationship to the military suggests that he also struggles with the normative masculinity that a white political establishment represents, without ever explicitly addressing the racial politics of the U.S. military. A kick-ass woman's picture, *G.I. Jane* is much more direct on both counts: O'Neil's acceptance by her male colleagues is approvingly developed through the course of the narrative. The role of military women is explicitly discussed, with a black soldier comparing the bar on women in combat roles to the racial exclusions of the

Jordan O'Neil (Demi Moore) enduring the same rigors in boot camp as her male counterparts. G.I. Jane. Courtesy: Photofest

past. The script quite explicitly presents the case for (exceptional/masculine) women in combat, which is not to say that it simply endorses it. *Courage Under Fire* offers a rather different elaboration of these discourses around the body of a (dead) white female captain through the point of view of a vulnerable black male colonel, constructing a narrative in which masculinity is understood in both raced and gendered terms.

Media coverage of military actions has a double significance in relation to military women whose exploits, achievements, and failures are subject to commentary by both journalists and politicians. Like the more recent *Three Kings* (David O. Russell, 1999), *Courage Under Fire* acknowledges the intensely mediated character of U.S. military involvement in the Persian Gulf, insistently juxtaposing television images with the physical, material experience of war. Thus the film opens with a montage of familiar images, the U.S. military defined starkly against the Iraqi people (military and civilian). Ghostly images of attacks at night, of George Bush and Saddam Hussein, and, briefly, of Colin Powell lead us from the discredited precision of the tactical air strikes to the messiness of the ground war that provides the setting to which the film will repeatedly return. Although here President Bush speaks of clear goals and defined objectives, elsewhere in the film the White House is treated with cynicism.

Courage Under Fire commences in the tension and confusion of battle at night, with Serling and his men about to move into combat at al-Bathra.

Inadvertently ordering an attack on another U.S. tank, he causes the death of his friend Boylar (of whom he later says "he was like a brother to me"). The following day Walden is killed at al-Kufan in the uncertain circumstances that Serling must investigate. Since caught up in controversy over *The Siege* (1996), here Zwick casts the Iraqi forces as stereotypical movie villains—Ilario (Matt Damon) nervously recalls hearing enemy laughter as they dig in. Serling begins his investigation by interviewing the Black Hawk crew saved by Walden. Images and sounds from the incident itself and the conversation in the interview room overlay each other, blurring the distinction between remembrance and event. The bonding over shared memories of combat is reinforced by the following brief exchange:

> LIEUTENANT CHELLI: . . . now the fuckers are letting . . . (silence. awkward pause). I'm sorry Sir, the Iraqis are letting loose with everything they've got.
> SERLING: You were right the first time (group laughter).

Putting the men at their ease, this moment of bonding against the enemy recalls Serling's opening gung-ho attitude ("let's kill 'em all"), though moderated to some extent by Washington's trademark understated style and undercut by the subsequent death of Boylar. These shared memories of fear and exhilaration are only partly triumphal, their function being to emphasize the shared experiences of combat in a film that is concerned to test the integrity of U.S. military masculinity.

Courage Under Fire juxtaposes Scott Glenn's earnest *Washington Post* reporter (a determined ex-military man), with the feminized political world of public relations. Crucially, Glenn/Gardner is involved in investigating Serling's war record and not the circumstances surrounding Walden's death or the broader issue of military women. In this way although an intense media scrutiny is acknowledged, this focuses on Serling while a military scrutiny—conducted via the figure of Serling—of Walden's performance is a more private in-house affair. Whether male or female, military masculinity is defined in *Courage Under Fire* not only, or even primarily, in relation to the enemy but against the insubstantial world of politicians and the domestic media. An opposition between male soldiers and female soldiers is thus framed by the wider generic discourses of the war movie, discourses in which soldiers' stories are valorized even when particular conflicts are questioned.

Mapping Masculinities

Over the past twenty years, feminist film criticism has worked and reworked the analysis of those relatively few high-profile Hollywood movies in which female protagonists are more or less explicitly coded in terms of masculinity. While this coding has most centrally to do with agency and self-determination, these women are also variously decisive, self-possessed, tough, resourceful, capable with vehicles, weaponry, and machinery: in short, it is a distinctly military masculinity (or at least one associated with war and action movies) that has entranced critics and audiences. The titles make familiar reading by now: dating more or less from Ridley Scott's original *Alien* (1979) through the reference points of *Terminator 2* and *Thelma and Louise* (both 1991) with recent entrants *Strange Days* and *The Long Kiss Goodnight* now receiving attention. For Ros Jennings, Weaver's Ripley represents the possibility of an autonomy "in desire and action" that doesn't involve "masculinization."[1] For others Ripley is "tough," a "warrior," while Linda Hamilton's muscular Sarah Connor is described as "tough-minded, fearless and strong."[2] Or [she is] cast, along with Thelma and Louise as figurations of a "literally empowered womanhood."[3] Neither the term *masculine* nor discourses of masculinity are regularly foregrounded in the discussion of these iconic figures; Connor and Ripley are more often understood in terms of a re-vision of femininity. Lesbian criticism has shown less reluctance to framing cinematic women in terms of masculinity: Paula Graham sees Weaver, Hamilton, and Jodie Foster (in her role as Clarice Starling) as "masculinized,"[4] while Sonya Andermahr reads Weaver and Hamilton in terms of an invitation to identify with/desire "masculine beauty in female form."[5] Although in her discussion of *Aliens* (James Cameron, 1986), Jennings sees discourses of masculinity as displaced onto the more evidently butch figure of Vasquez, the term is nonetheless introduced. More typically Sharon Willis situates her discussion of Ripley/Connor in terms of "a form of drag based on a masculinity that aggressively displays its difference from an anatomical base" within a chapter indicatively titled "Combative Femininity."[6]

Perhaps a reluctance around terminology represents little more than a desire to keep hold of femininity, while appropriating for women many of the qualities conventionally associated with men and masculinity (purpose, independence, even aggression). Broadly speaking though, and despite the inadequacies of "femininity" as a discourse within which to exclusively situate women in Hollywood movies, let alone the cinema's pattern of ambivalence toward male masculinities, it is striking that most feminist writers don't even come near putting into play masculinity as a term that has some relationship to women until confronted, say, by the spectacle of a female movie star engaged in some serious macho posturing. I'm thinking here of Demi Moore as Jordan O'Neil in *G.I. Jane,* single-handedly reviving the workout montage so beloved of 1980s cinema, although the cross-dressing protagonist of Maggie Greenwald's western *The Ballad of Little Jo* (1993), hunched over her food, picking up the defensive-aggressive body language of a prospector, serves just as well. It might be argued that military women represent one such extreme—a sort of limit case for gendered representation. Perhaps. But I would argue that a discussion of such images of female masculinity does more than illuminate these few examples, posing larger questions for the analysis of other less obviously (i.e., less embodied) masculine images of women.

My own use of *musculinity* in relation to the action movies of the 1980s and early 1990s both alludes to and to some extent sidelines biology, implying that a muscular physique can function as a signifier of strength for both male and female protagonists.[7] Musculinity proposes a sense in which masculinity is both culturally constructed and physically embodied. In this way Moore's muscular physique and shaven head in *G.I. Jane* signal her commitment to a masculinized military identity. Yet it seems to me that masculinity is more complex, more nuanced, than this kind of reduction to an impersonation or physical performance might suggest. While the suggestion that Meg Ryan's Walden was "butch" was reportedly one of the reasons the U.S. military refused to cooperate with Zwick's production, her butchness is actually relatively understated within the film. (Just as significantly, officials apparently objected to the portrayal of Serling's drinking and the suggestion of a military cover-up.) And although, as Clare Whatling has noted, a Hollywood butch is "virtually a femme anywhere else," it is precisely the understated mobilization of discourses of masculinity, indeed the insistence on the co-existence of her military masculinity and her status as a military woman that makes *Courage Under Fire* such an intriguing movie.[8] If butchness is associated with masculine clothing and appearance it is thus once more linked if not to the physical then to the visual as much as to narrative agency. We should be aware then of the fact that Ryan/Walden's "butch" wears the uniform of a military woman, not a passing woman or even necessarily a physically masculine woman. Her clothes are neither illicit nor borrowed. She has earned her uniform and its decorations, even as the narrative revolves around the question of whether she should really have the right to wear them.

Feminism's fundamental critique of essentialism notwithstanding, it is no surprise that criticism finds it tricky to keep apart terms that Western culture so continually and consistently conflates (men/masculinity/activity) and can end up replicating the very terms it wishes to redefine or to challenge. To some extent the messy ways in which a term like *masculinity* or even *masculinities* gets used has to do with its position within (at least) two distinct, if mutually informing, intellectual traditions. First, analyses that take as their reference point a psychoanalytic terminology and the framing concept of the male gaze, a critical trajectory firmly rooted in the modernist paradigm of psychosemiotics. Second, perspectives that emerge from the distinct context of cultural studies, exploring constructions of masculinity in relation to the diverse lived experiences of distinct groups of men. Both trajectories might use similar terms and phrases but with very different objects in view. Thus, although the interaction between a psychoanalytic feminist film studies and an ethnographic cultural studies has undoubtedly produced a situation in which masculinities have been increasingly explored within a social/political context, there nonetheless remains some confusion as to what is actually being discussed when critics or theorists talk about masculinities and movies. The value of psychoanalysis lies partly in its insistence on the instability of identities, on the permeability of categories as they are experienced rather than in the abstract. And yet, as Dimitris Eleftheriotis notes, all too often a normative model of heterosexual masculinity remains in place within psychoanalytic film theory, continuing to operate as a kind of structuring norm in relation to all the "other" masculinities it defines, "the logical outcome of a methodology that theorizes dominant masculinity as universal."[9]

The conflation of men and masculinity tends to obscure differences between men, differences that are frequently foregrounded in the war movie and have arguably preoccupied other action genres in recent years. Since discourses of gender are quite evidently linked to economies of class, race, and sexuality in Western political ideology, it is not only women, but "other" kinds of men who are excluded from the masculinity that film theory typically analyzes. As Robyn Wiegman suggests in her discussion of *Boyz N the Hood* (John Singleton, 1991), it is in part the critical reduction of gender "to the specular embodiment of woman" that has so often erased both African American men and the complexities of gendered discourse from contemporary film theory.[10] Leaving aside for one moment the importance of masculinities for images of women, Weigman's comments underline the importance of questioning both "which men" and "which movies" provide film theory's object. There was good reason for the title of an early 1990s anthology to suggest that film theory might "go to the movies" more often. It is precisely by talking about noncanonical films that critics have argued for a historical and cultural specificity lacking in the homogenizing application of a "film theory" model to the subject of masculinities. Many of the contributors to Cohan and Hark's *Screening the Male* attempt to redefine monolithic assumptions about "dominant masculinity" through the analysis of genres (the epic, the musical) or stars (Valentino, Astaire) that underline the heterogeneity of popular representations. The diversity of gendered discourse in the popular cinema is too easily erased within a film theory that confines itself to the work of a few filmmakers and stars.

In relation to action genres the biracial buddy movie—within which race and gender are mapped onto but exceed each other—has been one site for a more detailed critical reflection on the intersection of these discourses. To some extent this subgenre frames *Courage Under Fire* as well, although the construction of the narrative in terms of a thematic parallel between Walden and Serling is quite unusual. As I'll suggest in more detail below, it is the film's construction of masculinity across a range of characters (a staple of the military movie) that underlines the need to understand gender as experienced in relational rather than individual terms. Such a discursive construction of military masculinity across male and female protagonists contrasts with a marked critical tendency to emphasize an Oedipal model of narrative centered primarily on the hero's goals.

Since *masculinity* is commonly reserved as a term to describe men and their relationships to each other, female characters in the movies are often, by default, left with a femininity constructed in opposition, pieced together out of remnants and discarded values. Of course, to some extent the work that discourses of masculinity most obviously perform is to delimit ways of "being a man." There is even some agreement on what normative or dominant masculinity might consist of—qualities such as strength, control, restraint (possibly heroism, possibly violence). So it seems to make perfect sense to understand masculinities in terms of different and distinct ways of "being a man," negotiations around the demands of a patriarchal culture and its divisions and hierarchies of class, race, and sexuality. Within a cultural studies frame, then, discussion of constructed masculinities leads to concerns of diverse male identities and, within film, to an analysis of images of men (whether as fantasy response, anxious negotiation, or ideological reflection of wider gender relations). There is an obviousness and an inevitability to this chain of association. And yet neither paradigm seems to immediately offer a way to think about a small but growing number of cinematic images of women which are codified as "masculine" but are not rendered as perverse. This isn't to say that there aren't plenty of images of masculine-codified women that are rendered perverse, implicitly or explicitly, through sexuality, violence, or other signs of a transgression taken "too far." Yet, as I've noted already, one of the most suggestive aspects of *Courage Under Fire,* and of the more recent *G.I. Jane,* is that these images of military women are normalized precisely through, and not despite or against, discourses of masculinity. Is it too much to wish for a film criticism that is alive to such images, rather than discounting them as exceptions that once more prove the rules of gendered hierarchies?

Becoming Butch: The Mobility of Gendered Discourse

Gender can be best understood as a set of discourses that are contested, accepted, and resisted within networks, rather than binaries. Instead of proposing an analysis of movies in which female characters tell us about femininity and male characters about masculinity, an analysis of gendered discourse opens up these qualities operating across characters, scenarios, and narratives as well as interacting with other discourses. Thus, I'm not suggesting that a movie like *Courage Under Fire* simply offers its central female protagonist as masculine, though the film raises a question as to whether a self-reliant woman inevitably becomes coded as butch in the Hollywood cinema. The film maps the acquisition of Walden's status through naming and questioning the plausibility of her heroism. Thus, she is variously described as "a soldier," as "tough," as "afraid," a "wreck," a "fucking coward," a "real good mom": different versions to try on for size. And of course, ultimately a "truthful" one, shaped by all the other renditions we have seen and heard. This is also, inevitably, a sort of testing of Meg Ryan as a star/performer—can she carry a dramatic role?—just as *G.I. Jane* was widely discussed in terms of Demi Moore's physical transformation and commitment to her performance as aspiring Navy SEAL (her shorn head, her muscles). As one review had it, *Courage Under Fire* asks both

"Can a woman be a real soldier?" and "Can America's sweetheart, Meg Ryan yell motherfucker with conviction?"[11] It might seem that these questions pull the film in different directions. But it is their superimposition, whereby Ryan's "ordinariness" secures the generic heroism she is called on to perform, that is ultimately crucial to the military masculinity the movie enacts around her.

There is an exchange early on in *Courage Under Fire*, which rehearses something of this complexity. Serling makes the first of his visits to the members of Walden's crew, asking each in turn what they remember of the incident at al-Kufan. Rady, her former co-pilot, injured during the crash (and unconscious through the key part of the action) is now a civilian. Serling and Rady sit outdoors with Rady's girlfriend Annie, a pretty blonde woman. Here the perspectives of the soldier and the former soldier, rooted in loyalty to the (implicitly masculine, if not, in this context, male) group, are juxtaposed with those of a (femme) female civilian:

> RADY: I remember the earth . . . (shots of al-Kufan) . . . I remember Ilario's
> face . . . (distressed) . . . I wish . . .
> ANNIE: If she hadn't needed to be a hero so bad . . .
> RADY: That's not fair—we were just doing our job. It's not 'Ren's fault I got
> hit. . . she sure as hell saved the lives of those guys on that Black Hawk.
> ANNIE: You always defend her . . .
> SERLING: (to Annie) Why didn't you like her?
> ANNIE: She was so butch . . .
> RADY: Honey—shut up. (to Serling, smiling) She was, you know . . .
> ANNIE: These women who want to be officers . . .
> RADY: Annie, shut up! She gave her life up for those men! (turning to Ser-
> ling) She was a soldier.

Petite, serving coffee, relegated to the background, and excluded from the soldiers' exchange of significant looks, Annie is the outsider here. The camera-work underlines her position, pulling away slightly as she speaks—just enough to being Serling into the frame and to emphasize her marginality. It's perfectly acceptable for the *soldiers*—Rady and Serling—to talk about Walden as butch. The disagreement is not about being "butch" but the value attributed to Walden's toughness, an evaluation that mirrors the film's central narrative question (is she a hero?). A rejection of the butch/military woman as inappropriate comes here from a marginalized female character, defined primarily as a civilian, and then from Monfriez, who defines himself as a good soldier, a combat veteran, and Walden as a "cunt," a term of abuse that explicitly seeks to recode her in terms of the (female) body. While for Rady *butch* is an affectionate term, he recognizes that for Annie it means something different. He rejects the implicit devaluing of masculinity by appealing to a shared understanding with Serling—masculine bonding we might say—simultaneously silencing her.

Later in the film, when Serling is falling apart (drinking too much, living in a motel, unable to speak to his wife) and is convinced that he is being lied to, flashback images of Walden graduating as an officer are introduced. These images of ritual and celebration are introduced and overlaid by the taped words of Ilario (one of the crew who, we later learn, has betrayed her) speaking of her courage and decisiveness: "Karen—the captain—she had this quality: the heavier the pressure, the calmer she got. She, y' know, she put up with a lot of shit to become an Officer. Y'know—had to work twice as hard as everybody else, be twice as good. She never let her guard down—show any sign of weakness. But she was tough. She could handle it." In the original interview we hear only the first line of the speech—followed immediately by a discussion of the besieged crew's fearful anticipation of the attack that is to come at first light ("I don't know why people think only good things happen when the sun comes up"). Replayed on Serling's recorder over dreamlike images of Walden and her peers, the film presents us with an elegiac sense of her toughness, her capacity to "handle it," and, crucially, underlines the labor she has put into her military identity, to becoming an officer.

The insistence on Walden's struggle to become an officer underlines that, far from being a coward, Walden possesses the very qualities Serling is losing—he can't handle it, showing his weakness through his drinking. Later when Serling is "out of the loop," pursuing the investigation unofficially with the help of sympathetic journalist Gardner, we see another such montage sequence. As he looks at a photo of Walden, Serling imagines her singing softly, with her daughter and with her crew. At a moment when Serling is waiting for events beyond his control to work themselves out, Walden's image functions as a moral anchor, signifying the good soldier whose toughness helps her overcome the odds in training, if not in combat. These imaginings prefigure the elaboration of a revised, heroic narrative around the "friendly fire" incident that opens the movie in which a tape of communications between U.S. tanks reveals Serling's rapid response to and recovery from his mistake, his own courage under fire.

Tough, a soldier, a good mother: Walden's records describe her as an "officer of exceptional moral courage." Of course, many action movies cast strong female protagonists as iconic mothers, though this doesn't mean that the image somehow inevitably returns us simply to femininity. At a superficial level it might seem that *Courage Under Fire* operates a sort of separation of the martial and the maternal or familial. Accounts of Walden as a good mother are given by her parents (who now care for their granddaughter) while praise for her as a soldier comes from her male colleagues. And yet the two are hard to keep apart. Her father also speaks of the importance of duty to his daughter. And, crucially, Walden has a strongly paternalistic role in relation to her crew—her fear of letting them down is expressed when her final letter is read on the soundtrack at the close of the film: "these people depend on me. They put their lives in my hands. I just can't fail them." Moreover, the film evokes maternal toughness in physical terms quite explicitly in Walden's contemptuous comment to the mutinous Monfriez (who has shot her), "I gave birth to a nine-pound baby, asshole—I think I can handle it." While centrally concerned with power and status, then, becoming butch is insistently not about becoming male.

Masculinity and Medals

As the crisis in his personal life mounts, we see Serling absorbed in the details of appearance, carefully pressing the creases in his uniform, insisting on the decorative details as a way of holding together his faith in the military. We might recall here Marjorie Garber's astute comments on the different connotations of "making" men and women, together with the anxiety she pinpoints that it might not, after all, be that difficult to literally—surgically—make a man. Garber also, although briefly, turns her attention to medals, uniforms, and the dressing-up involved in the military. Discussing the story of Dr. Mary Walker (who wore the Medal of Honor) she notes that "the wearing of military orders by women has been regarded as a curious reversion to 'feminine' taste, a kind of jewelry. Does the sight of women wearing medals or 'Orders' attached to their lapels suggest that such 'orders' can be unpinned, detached, from men? The spectacle of women in men's clothes, or at least men's uniforms, both military and lay, seems to lead back to the question of male cross-dressing and its relationship to structures of hierarchy and power."[12] It is interesting to note that for Garber this leads us back to cross-dressing and to men. But when women wear the medals and uniforms on their own account, a rather different articulation of female masculinity is foregrounded.

Both *Courage Under Fire* and *G.I. Jane* end with an indicative contrast between a public ceremony in which gallantry is rewarded and a private one in which a courageous man passes his own medal to a woman who has proved herself in combat. After confessing his mistake to Boylar's parents, Serling lays a medal on Walden's grave. Following her public admittance to the SEALS, Jordan finds in her locker a medal tucked into a volume of D. H. Lawrence poems (no less), a discovery followed by a silent exchange of looks between Moore and her erstwhile tormentor Urgayle. Crucially these ceremonies are moments of recognition and incorporation, testament that while official recognition has its place, it is just as, if not more important, to be recognized by one's peers. Thus, although Urgayle is Jordan's commanding officer, his gesture of approval is distinguished from the machinations of politicians that structure the film, inscribing her within a revised "us and them."

The ambivalent elaboration of discourses of masculinity in action movies is nowhere more evident than in the melodrama of the soldier, a heroic figure who is respected and decorated, yet simultaneously a commodified body (cannon fodder in the most extreme instance). Both heroism and decoration (medals, uniform) mask an awareness that permeates war movies of the disposability of soldiers' bodies. Such an awareness is evident in quite distinct ways in the spectacular opening scenes of carnage on the beaches of Normandy and the death of the highly individuated Captain Miller (Tom Hanks) in Spielberg's *Saving Private Ryan* (1998). Within war movies female bodies, defined primarily in terms of sexuality, have typically been disposable in rather different ways. Ironically, it is in part an American anxiety about female bodies that, officially at least, so long kept women out of combat. In *G.I. Jane* both soldiers ("her presence makes us all vulnerable") and politicians ("no politician can afford to let women come home in body bags") argue the case in these terms. This anxiety is foregrounded in *Courage Under Fire* through the construction of a parallel between the two protagonists. Walden's status as modern military woman who strays into combat and is killed is evidently over-determined. She provides the locus for Serling's self-doubt and for his quest to have the truth made public, while her story is explicitly appropriated by a cynical political establishment, personified in the White House aide who is pushing for her to be awarded the medal of honor. While the public recognition of her heroism is revealed to be a superficial public relations opportunity, for Serling Walden is primarily a soldier to whom he wishes to do justice. The fact that there is a political motivation in giving him the case—a "way back," as his mentor General Hershberg puts it—only serves to underline Serling's desire to know the real story, his refusal to rubber-stamp this, or any, file.

Although the comparisons between *Courage Under Fire* and *Rashomon* were deemed rather superficial by some, they repay further attention. Zwick's movie doesn't end on quite the same ambiguous note; after all, Serling's desire for something to be clear, for "somebody to be a hero," is ultimately fulfilled. We might say, if so inclined, that the film offers an Oedipal story—the spectacle of a male soldier, Serling, growing up (accepting his limits, coming to terms with failure) through the investigation of a female soldier/body. Ultimately he is reconciled to his life, able to return to domesticity. Similarly, *Rashomon* concludes with an image of the woodcutter quite literally holding the baby, accepting responsibility within an uncertain context (however cynical we might be by this stage). Writers have tended to regard the ending of both films as too pat, overly sentimental; yet in neither case is it particularly helpful to reduce the movie to that one narrative moment, collapsing the complex orchestration of images and moments to the supposed resolution found in the ending. It may be the case that Walden/Ryan (unlike *Rashomon*'s Machiko Kyo) offers no account of herself and her actions, other than via her final letter or the fantasized gesture of approval she bestows on Washington's Serling in the film's final moments. Yet if finding the truth enables Serling to resolve his own personal turmoil, this doesn't mean automatically that the figure is somehow negated, subordinated to a narrative dynamic concerned with Serling's story alone.

Both *Courage Under Fire* and *Rashomon* explore the public face of bravery and heroism, terms central to discourses of masculinity. They underline the posturing at stake in narrating bravery—and the suspicion of imposture that

Karen Walden (Meg Ryan). The film "explores the public face of bravery and heroism, terms central to the discourse of femininity." Courage Under Fire. Courtesy: Photofest

accompanies such narration. The physical chaos of combat, as well as the intensity of shame, cowardice, and fear, are set against the public performance made of military success, whether in the award of medals or simply in personal bragging, inordinate boasting of individual strength. In *Rashomon* both the murdered nobleman (speaking through a medium) and the bandit, Tajomaru, offer heroic accounts of their performance in battle. The woodcutter's recollections from a spectator's point of view, by contrast, emphasize the awkward physicality of the fight (sweating, breathless stumbles) and the evident fear of death displayed by both men. Despite their differences, a shared social code—of which the woman is a sign—compels them reluctantly into combat. Thus while *Courage Under Fire* is centered on a crew's betrayal of their officer, *Rashomon* is concerned with a rape and murder, with a woman's body as the object of sexual exchange, with the physical expression of a rivalry between men of different classes, and not least with the stories men and women tell and the rather messier version of events that these stories aim to make intelligible. Crudely put, the narrative question—which revolves around the impossibility of all these stories being true—is whether or not the woman "deserved it." Did she kill her husband when he rejected her following her rape, or did she incite the bandit to kill him? Either way she comes out pretty badly—as does everyone else of course. More important, across all of the versions that the film recounts, even when she is the most "spirited," she is constituted primarily in terms of an hysterical femininity.

In the martial setting of *Courage Under Fire*, the narrative question of arthouse rape-revenge is supplanted by a testing of moral courage and physical resilience: was she really butch or, perhaps, "was she butch enough?" "She was a fucking coward," spits Monfriez in his first interview; "She was a soldier" (Rady); "She was tough" (Ilario); "If she hadn't needed to be a hero so bad . . ." (Annie). These questions revolve around the relative significance of Walden's tears ("just tension") and an M-16 (who was firing it during the rescue?). Serling's investigation looks past the tears to focus on the action, the M-16, Of course, war movies constitute one of the few genres in which men get to shed tears, typically over each other's corpses. Sure enough, one of Serling's closing gestures is to don all his medals before finally shedding tears as he confesses to Boylar's parents that it was he who gave the order to fire.

If power was self-evident, medals wouldn't have the resonance that they do. Suggesting a tension between display and embodiment, the role of the medal in naming and constructing masculinity is nicely—and of course comically—acknowledged in *The Wizard of Oz* (Victor Fleming, 1939) when Bert Lahr's camp cowardly lion is given a badge of courage as both the solution to his fears and a sign of having overcome them. Chris Holmlund has linked a notion of masculinity as display with Stephen Heath's contention that "male masquerade is more intimately tied to power structures than female masquerade," citing his observation that "the trappings of authority, hierarchy, order, position make the man."[13] Here again we are back to male and female. However, within the current historical and cultural context, the significance of the military woman for the codes of Hollywood cinema is that her masculinity is tied to such power structures. By constructing its narrative around an exploration of whether a butch woman should be awarded the Medal of Honor, *Courage Under Fire* works to complexly repudiate the feminizing/superficial world of media and public relations, and to achieve the incorporation (albeit posthumously) of a female soldier into the community of military honor.

Courage Under Fire stages a careful balancing act in relation to the symbols around which its narrative revolves. To the extent that medals honor bravery in combat they are valuable tokens. Yet, their use as political symbols is understood with cynicism. Serling must decide whether Walden should be awarded the Medal of Honor, having been awarded a medal himself in the military's cover-up of events at al-Bathra, events of which he is ashamed. Meanwhile the White House demands results, for the investigation to be completed so that the planned ceremony in the rose garden can take place (tears again: "'there is not going to be a dry eye from Nashua to Sacramento"). Serling's disgust with all this is generic, rendered in terms of a soldier's suspicion of the superficiality of politicians. That the military codes Serling falls back on have been broken becomes, in the film's terms, particularly shocking.

Women and Military Masculinity: A Longing for Belonging

The played for straight performance of masculinity articulated around the military women in both *G.I. Jane* and *Courage Under Fire* can be situated within the context of a wider discursive presentation of military women in terms of a threatening sexualization of a single-sex workplace. As war movie meets the woman's film, military women pose the issues raised by women's entry to supposedly male workplaces in a distinctive, polarized fashion. And it's not just the military who find this disturbing or who resort to a sexualized language in response: consider the following from the *Guardian*'s "Women" section on 22 December 1998: "Equality rarely leaves a bad taste in a woman's mouth, but the missile raids [on Iraq] have done just that. American women pilots made military history by flying combat missions for the first time during Operation Desert Fox, according to a report in yesterday's *Times*. Now it's not just Monica who's reaching for the mouthwash." The U.S./U.K. raids were widely referred to "Operation Monica," the attacks seen as an attempt to divert public attention from a sexual scandal surrounding a president who, we might recall, became so publicly embroiled over lesbians and gays in the military in the opening months of his first term of office.

Media discourses about military women express the "incursion" of women into Western armies, navies, and air forces in terms of a discursive disruption of masculinity. It is in this context that Amy Taubin praises *G.I. Jane* as an exhilarating gender-fuck, taking the opportunity to dismiss *Courage Under Fire* out of hand as "thoroughly reactionary" for using "its female hero to whitewash militarism and the stranglehold of the Pentagon on the post–Cold War economy."[14] I began by posing a question: how to make sense of images of women codified as masculine but not as perverse? Moore/Jordan's notorious challenge to Urgayle to "suck my dick" is richly redolent, yet if either of these films can be read as transgressive it is not in any particularly grand fashion. Jordan has the shit kicked out of her and appropriates it into a sign of equality. Her desire to be treated just as badly as everybody else (and thence to participate in the action movie's masculine narcissism) while she is still effectively marked as different—whether as an officer, a woman, as smart (her background in intelligence)—enacts a tension between individual and team that is central to the war movie. Demi Moore's star status, together with her involvement as co-producer, simply allows (or requires) a more spectacular packaging of Meg Ryan's (extra)ordinary butchness.

What Taubin seems to miss is that the pitch of both films is for women to be included in the sentimental brotherhood extolled in movies like *Saving Private Ryan*. Of course, it doesn't work out quite like that: both films feature key scenes in which male soldiers disobey their female officers' orders in combat situations (actual in *Courage Under Fire*, simulated in *G.I. Jane*). Monfriez's mutiny leads to Walden's death in *Courage Under Fire*, while in *G.I. Jane*, Sergeant Cortez (whose individualism marks him as a problem early on) gets the whole team captured during a training mission by ignoring Jordan's orders. Monfriez is shown screaming at a recruit: "you never leave a man behind." The film works to argue that, in effect, this is exactly what he has done. In this way, of course, the films both rehearse one of the standard arguments against involving women in combat situations (military women lack the right stuff; military men get disoriented around them). Indeed, *Courage Under Fire*'s artful structure allows it to condemn Monfriez's neurotic (and racially othered) masculinity while ultimately avoiding taking sides on a contentious issue. Instead, the argument is rehearsed and resolved through a discursive masculinity that renders Walden tough enough just as Moore's Jordan proves herself by triumphing over and then rescuing her commanding officer.

If these debates seem bound to the context of both contemporary fiction and warfare, we might consider Judith Halberstam's comments on how World War I provided "some masculine women" with "the opportunity to live out the kinds of active lives that in peacetime they could only fantasize about. Although [Toupie] Lowther's ambulance unit was constantly hampered by conventional notions of female activity, they also did see active combat, and many of these women were applauded for the first time in their lives for behaving more like men than women."[15] It is important to note that fantasy and applause (public recognition) are as significant here as the notions of female activity, combat, and masculinity that Halberstam brings together. That is, a militarized female masculinity here embodies both the transgression of gendered codes and a longing for belonging.

Accepted by some into the military group and rejected by others, there is no doubt that Karen Walden signifies disruption for a conservative institution in transition. To this extent she figures a problem of representation, of gendered discourse. But within this, her ordinariness (so central to Meg Ryan's star image) and her butchness are both central. It is not even the case, as we might expect, that her ordinariness (or her death) somehow mitigates her butchness and the perversity that this might suggest. Rather, her status as a good soldier is constituted in terms of a discursive masculinity, which purports to value star performer and extras, officers and crew. That is, her butchness normalizes her at the same time as it renders her exceptional.

There is a thoroughgoing perversity within popular culture that provides images and narratives that disrupt the gendered and other binaries through which we seek to make sense of them (voyeurism/fetishism, sadistic/masochistic, active/passive). Such images suggest a need to extend to women the implications of Michael Uebel's comment that masculinity be understood not as "the defining quality of men, of their fantasies and real experiences of self and other, but one coordinate of their identity that exists in a constant dialectical relation with other coordinates."[16] Movies are sophisticated forms of representation, sets of images with the power to articulate complex sets of relations, investments (erotic, emotional) and ambivalent, even contradictory desires. The articulation of martial masculine prowess—courage under fire—around a female soldier/officer works both to underline qualities of self-sufficiency or leadership as learned, while simultaneously clinging to a romantically redemptive concept of honor. The coexistence of public and private award ceremonies recognizes that symbols of success are both compromised and valued. In the search for grander transgressions, we run the risk of missing the significance of just what is being offered up as "mainstream" these days.

NOTES

1. Ros Jennings, "Desire and Design—Ripley Undressed," in *Immortal, Invisible: Lesbians and the Moving Image,* ed. Tamsin Wilton (London: Routledge, 1995), 204.

2. Susan Jefford, "Can Masculinity Be Terminated?" in *Screening the Male: Exploring Masculinities in Hollywood Cinema,* ed. Steven Cohan and Ina Rae Hark (London: Routledge, 1993), 240.

3. Fred Pfeil, *White Guys: Studies in Postmodern Domination and Difference* (London: Verso, 1995), 53.

4. Paula Graham, "Girl's Camp? The Politics of Parody," in *Immortal, Invisible: Lesbians and the Moving Image,* ed. Tamsen Wilton (London: Routledge, 1995), 195.

5. Sonya Andermahr, "A Queer Love Affair? Madonna and Lesbian and Gay Culture," in *The Good, the Bad and the Gorgeous: Popular Cinema's Romance with Lesbianism,* ed. Diana Hamer and Belinda Budge (London: Pandora, 1994), 34.

6. Sharon Willis, *High Contrast: Race and Gender in Contemporary Hollywood* (Durham: Duke University Press, 1997), 113.

7. Yvonne Tasker, *Spectacular Bodies: Gender, Genre and the Action Cinema* (London: Routledge, 1993), 146.

8. Clare Watling, *Screen Dreams: Fantasizing Lesbians in Film* (Manchester: Manchester University Press, 1997), 77.

9. Dimitris Eleftheriotis, "Questioning Totalities: Construction of Masculinity in the Popular Greek Cinema of the 1960s," *Screen* 36, no. 3 (1995): 236.

10. Robyn Wiegman, "Feminism, 'The Boyz,' and Other Matters Regarding the Male," in *Screening the Male: Exploring Masculinities in Hollywood Cinema,* ed. Steven Cohan and Ina Rae Hark (London: Routledge, 1993), 180.

11. Georgia Brown, "Battle Cry," *Village Voice,* 16 July 1994, 57.

12. Marjorie Garber, *Vested Interests: Cross-Dressing and Cultural Anxiety* (London: Routledge: 1992), 55.

13. Chris Holmlund, "Masculinity as Multiple Masquerade," in *Screening the Male: Exploring Masculinities in Hollywood Cinema,* ed. Steven Cohan and Ina Rae Hark (London: Routledge, 1993), 213.

14. Amy Taubin, "Dicks and Jane," *Village Voice,* 26 September 1997, 73.

15. Judith Halberstam, *Female Masculinity* (Durham: Duke University Press, 1998), 85.

16. In *Race and the Subject of Masculinities,* ed. Harry Stecopoulos and Michael Uebel (Durham: Duke University Press, 1997), 4.

History

Mimi White

Rehearsing Feminism:
Women/History in *The Life and Times*
of Rosie the Riveter and *Swing Shift*

The Life and Times of Rosie the Riveter (Connie Field, 1980) and *Swing Shift* (Jonathan Demme, 1983) both deal with women's experience during World War II, a period that saw an unprecedented number of women entering the workforce and a temporary change in the sexual division of labor as women were recruited for work in a wide range of industries. One of the films is an independently produced documentary, the other a Hollywood fictional narrative. In light of their respective modes of production one might expect the films to be quite different. However, while they are by no means identical, they significantly adopt a similar perspective on the events they treat.

The films share a common reference period, focusing on the "unusual" positions and opportunities available to women during the war, and are hardly singular in turning attention to women working in World War II. On the contrary, there exists a vast body of material dealing with the same events in the same period, constituting an emergent historical tradition.[1] In this context the films extend a body of discourse, elaborating on the investigation of a specific aspect of women's past in a popular medium. Both films evince an awareness of the preoccupations of this "tradition," signaling their own status as historical narratives in a number of ways.

The signs of history—marker dates, period documents, and so forth—are incorporated in both films to authenticate the narratives of working women. Stylistically and narrationally this material identifies the narrativized events as "past" and as "having really happened." The radio broadcast announcing the Japanese attack on Pearl Harbor and the official entry of the United States into World War II is replayed in both films. *Rosie the Riveter* uses a variety of archival footage, newspaper headlines, and popular songs from the period. *Swing Shift* offers glimpses of period film clips and restages/rewrites material from the newsreels as dramatic scenes. The inclusion of this sort of archival material does not simply serve as a neutral sign of authenticity and pastness. Rather, in both films

White, Mimi. "Rehearsing Feminism: Women/History in 'The Life and Times of Rosie the Riveter' and 'Swing Shift.'" *Wide Angle* 7:3 (1985): 34–43. © Ohio University School of Film. Reprinted with permission of the Johns Hopkins University Press.

it is seen to construct and address a representation of "woman," a representation subsequently confirmed and/or belied by the films' respective heroines.

With their connections to an extrafilmic body of historical discourse and use of period media documents as constructions of a specific historical (narrative) setting, the films cannot escape the function of meta-texts: they construct their own images and meanings in and for a present of production as they incorporate and comment on images and meanings cited from the past. The narratives they construct and positions they make possible (for viewers and for understanding events of the past) are inevitably caught up in preexisting networks of discourse. And while their narrative strategies are very different, the narrational perspectives engaged in the confrontation between past and present in both films—a historical perspective and the founding terms of narrativization—are remarkably similar.

In this context an examination of these particular contemporary texts (contemporary with us, with the production of this essay) may help clarify issues of historical writing and rewriting specifically with regard to questions of women's history and feminist history (not always, or necessarily, the same thing). The analysis proceeds from the assumption that a closer look at *Rosie the Riveter* and *Swing Shift* will help focus on issues that arise from the conjunction of history, cinema, and feminism.

The Life and Times of Rosie the Riveter alternates between period documents and interviews conducted in the film's "present" with five women (three black, two white) who worked in various branches of the war industry between 1942 and 1945.[2] The period footage is compiled from an array of sources; this is apparent in the editing and confirmed by the film's end titles with its long list of archival sources. But only a few of the clips are specifically identified in the film. Otherwise, in the absence of differentiation, the film suggests that the sources are equivalent, conveying in concert the unified self-image of a culture entreating women to enter the "silent army" of defense plant workers; offering a rosy view of the nature and conditions of this work; and finally urging women to cede their jobs to returning veterans and to resume more appropriate feminine roles as wives and mothers.

The interviews supplement this "official" representation of women's work and working women as it is compiled in the film from period sources. Embedded in the traditions of oral history and women's documentary filmmaking, they give a voice to individuals and views repressed in the more conventional channels of information dissemination.[3] Through the representation of individuals of the silent army we get an alternative account of the period, one that undermines the authority, truth, and unity carried by the period footage. For example, a newsreel offers a picture of middle-class housewives sacrificing afternoon card games to enter the workforce out of a sense of patriotic duty. But all five of the women in the interviews speak of working before and after the war, needing the income to support their families, of work as economic necessity. In another period documentary a factory official, the (female) Supervisor of Women Employees, describes

Archival footage shows African American women working during World War II. The Life and Times of Rosie the Riveter. Courtesy: Photofest

the workplace as safer than the home. We then hear stories from the women in the interviews of dangerous working conditions and accidents in the factories. A newsreel clip on day-care facilities that allow mothers to work without worrying about their children is followed by tales of women regretfully leaving their children with parents in another state or sending them to boarding school.

Two discourses thus confront each other, an array of period documents and an array of contemporary narratives about the past. They speak of the same period and the same events in an asymmetrical opposition. The period documents come to be seen as a cultural mythology, manipulative fantasy, when filtered through the individual experiences recounted by the women in the interviews. And each range of discourse, although plural in sources (a variety of archival footage, a variety of individual stories), is seen as basically unified in its diversity. The film's "multiple" discourse is a function of this confrontation between two relatively unified bodies of discourse. If no "one" can speak/represent the truth of history, or represent the whole picture, the film's power comes from its ability to compile or assemble an adequate series of representations to construct two discrete poles of coherence and unity.

We are given, on the one hand, the past's version of its own truth or, more appropriately, a contemporary version of the past's self-representation in the film's compilation of archival footage. On the other hand, the interviews give us a presumably superior truth in the "real working women" who tell us their stories. But these individual narratives are all retrospective accounts, conveying attitudes toward and memories of the period from a distance of thirty-odd years. And they are offered as a counter to the traditional historical documentation without questioning that the perspectives in the present of recounting may only be available as a present truth about the past. Indeed, the very possibility of expressibility may be a function of this temporal distance.

For example, near the end of the film one of the women describes the postwar shift in women's status. The society, she says, wanted babies and women who were psychologically prepared to assume this reproductive function. "We all wanted babies, and that's okay. But we gave up everything for that. We gave up everything." This expression of loss stands in stark contrast to the previous discussion of wartime work as providing expanded personal and economic opportunities for women. But the clear terms of a trade-off—babies or everything, domestic roles or the new woman, reproduction or production—are recognized from the perspective of the 1970s. This expression of a decisive either/or situation, confronting women individually and collectively, caps off the film's examination of women's experience during the war with an air of nostalgia: lost opportunity, crushed hopes, wrong choices. But such a perception is definitive only from the vantage of retrospection; a decisive choice or final loss can be identified only in relation to a closed sequence of events.

This is not to challenge the sincerity of the stories we hear or the genuineness of the women's lived/remembered experience. Rather, the key issue is how the film implements these stories in contrast to the period documents without questioning or examining their disparate determinations. The film requires temporal distance as the founding condition of its own discourse. Indeed, the differentiation of past from present, the assertion of temporal demarcation to define this gap, is the a priori and effectivity of historical discourse. As Michel de Certeau explains, in the very process of addressing the past, history signals a differential relation between past and present that in turn functions to constitute a social-historical identity:

> If on the one hand history functions by expressing the position of one gener-ation in relation to previous ones by saying: "I am not that," it always affects this affirmation with a no less dangerous complement which makes a society avow: "I am other than I want and determined by that which I deny." It attests to an autonomy and a dependence whose proportions vary according to the social milieux and political situations where it is elaborated.[4]

The identity constructed through the operations of history is necessarily contradictory; it emerges and is defined on the basis of a past that is simultane-ously excluded and preserved. This act of demarcation/affiliation is carried out on the basis of representations that mediate past and present. (The representations are *in* the present but not *of* the present.) In the case of *Rosie the Riveter* it is pre-cisely this distance that enables the compilation of archival source footage and that determines that the women speak as they do. But the film also represses this distance as an active principle informing its structure.

More precisely, the implication of a break, a boundary, of terms of demar-cation, is figured in the opposition between two temporally discrete bodies of dis-course (past/present) while the specification of the division is absent. A change has occurred: the present has incorporated and surpassed the past. But the histor-ical "moments" of the filmic discourse are presented as an abstract before and after, implying that the break—the transformation allowing recognition of and regret over decisive loss and passed opportunities—must be somewhere between 1946 and the mid-1970s, a "somewhere" that remains unrepresented and unex-plored in the film. The differential determinations of its two arenas of discourse—past/present, male-generated discourse/female-generated discourse—are through alternation construed as an absolute value difference: patriarchal myth/feminist truth. Women's history and the feminist perspective on women's past experience are thereby seen as the rewriting of a previous discourse—a relatively unified set of representations—from the vantage of a relatively unified set of current beliefs/positions in the spirit of progress.

In many ways *Swing Shift* stands as the complementary inverse of *Rosie the Riveter*. Kay Walsh (Goldie Hawn), the protagonist of *Swing Shift*, is not the "real working woman" ignored by the dominant media of the war era, but is instead the ideal subject addressed therein, the fictional spectator (and fictional character) constructed by the documentary discourse. We are first introduced to Kay and her husband, Jack, on the eve of the United States' entry into World War II. Their marriage is presented in terms of emphatic, conventional domesticity. Kay's clothing and her behavior with Jack code her as an infantilized housewife; he returns home from a hard day of work to shower as she, in her white anklets and little-girl dress, fetches his beer and cuddles in his lap.

A hostile co-worker has just slapped the "heat treatable" sign on the slacks of Kay Walsh (Goldie Hawn). Swing Shift. Courtesy: Photofest

When the United States declares war on Japan, Jack immediately enlists in the Navy. We see Kay, left to fend for herself, alone in a movie theater watching a newsreel about the need for women in defense work. Soon thereafter she applies for a job at a local aircraft plant, conceding to another woman applicant, "My husband would kill me if he knew what I was doing." Initially bumbling and insecure on the job, Kay learns to stand up to the male bullies in the factory who think that women do not belong there, masters mechanical skills so well that she can repair home appliances, and finally averts a fatal accident in the factory, leading to her promotion to leadman.

As Kay undergoes this transformation, narrative attention is focused on her relationship with Lucky (Kurt Russell), her supervisor in the factory. He persistently asks her out and she refuses at first but finally succumbs to his advances/charms and embarks on a full-scale affair. In this way the film suggests that Kay's growth and independence is manifested in both the public and private spheres. But in concentrating on the latter, it clearly circumscribes the terms of this independence. The key to Kay's success as a "new woman" lies in replacing the support of one male with that of another. The affair ends when Jack comes home on an unannounced leave and discovers his wife's involvement with Lucky. His unease with her job success is exponentially compounded by the affair. Indeed his acknowledgment/recognition of the affair is initiated through the agency of her success in the workplace. He finds her factory uniform and asks who the "leadman" is. She feebly explains that *she* is the leadman, which is in fact the case. Yet the shirt, emblazoned with her job title, is clearly the condensed locus of the dual transformation—professional and personal—effected by her wartime experience. Still, Kay does not actively or consciously choose one man over the other. In love with both of them, she decides (as much out of guilt as anything) to reinstate behavior in line with her marriage vows, and Lucky leaves town with a group of musicians.

With the end of the war Kay and her women friends lose their jobs as the normative order of postwar domesticity is reinstated. However, the final scene indicates that the reassertion of aggressive patriarchal dominance, a force that is always present but loosened during the war, is not totally or simply embraced. At a party with her former co-workers, Kay and her husband circulate. The women, all married, enthuse over the different hors d'oeuvres being served and the wonderful new household appliances; the men discuss new housing developments. Kay seems surprisingly uninvolved in the proceedings. As most of the couples dance contentedly, Kay signals to her closest friend, Hazel, to meet her outside. They tearfully embrace as Kay asks, "Well, we showed them. Didn't we?" The film ends with a freeze-frame on an overwhelming note of loss, nostalgia.

Kay Walsh may not be an ideal of feminist independence, but she is singled out in her feeling/knowledge that the impending postwar order of things will deny the sense of achievement afforded by the war. Whatever limitations are imposed on Kay as a narrative character, the film traces her path from ordinariness to extraordinariness embodied in her singular moment of nostalgic despair. If at the start of the film she ideally responds to the media appeal for housewives to enter the workforce, at the end she is unwilling to assume the role of ideal subject of a similar but reversed media campaign and to return to the home graciously or happily.

This conclusion is in one sense typical of the constitutive ambiguity at work in a number of recent films; it is simultaneously conservative and progressive.[5] The film can unproblematically return its case of working women characters to the household *and* suggest that the terms of its own narrative stability are not unequivocally acceptable or untroubling. This narrational position, and the specific nature of the film's equivocal resolution, are made possible because it is *historical* narrative. What begins to emerge here is the same structure of history that was seen in *Rosie the Riveter*, history as founding narrational perspective and repressed distance.

This appropriation and disavowal of historical distance is clear from the outset as the film's first narrative scene opens with a superimposed title: Dec. 6, 1941. A few scenes later a second similar title appears: Sunday, Dec. 7, 1941. These titles generate narrative suspense as (and only if) the viewer recognizes the meaning of these dates. This is not anytime, anywhere, or even a generalized past, but the day before and the day of the Japanese attack on Pearl Harbor. But this is a prospective narrative device that can be reconstructed only as recognized retrospectively, even as it is used to engage an audience in the otherwise unknown and unfamiliar fates of the film's fictional characters. The truth of history as it is known in the present is thus the founding alibi of narrative involvement in *Swing Shift*.

A similar but more elaborate structure informs the film's concluding scene. The return to domesticity as the impending state of affairs (in the terms of the fiction) can be justified as the dominant historical truth, but only when the period is reviewed from a distance of nearly forty years. In 1983 the postwar introduction of suburban housing projects and new consumer appliances does not merely signify a change of address or some abstract conception of a "higher standard of living," but connotes a whole social and cultural regime with specific implications for women. Once again we confront the problem of the temporal break constituting historical perspective and allowing a retrospective reevaluation of events defined as past, closed. The film assumes that a viewer will grasp the implications of the fiction's impending socio-cultural regime, or at least promotes this as one important (if potential) interpretive position, as postwar marriages and consumerism are the prevalent topic of conversation in the final scene. At the same time it does not investigate/specify how or when this perception takes hold. The truth of the past is held up in the light of current terms of understanding as an abstract before and after; postwar life was understood (indeed misunderstood) one way "then," but we understand it (correctly) another way "now."

This distance is redoubled and conflated with the representation of at least one character, Kay, who is dissatisfied with the state of things at the end of the film. Her attitude suggests—perhaps even requires—a clear image of the fiction's imaginary future, "The Fifties," and it implies more crucially that she shares values that come from somewhere even beyond the 1950s. She not only "knows" what is coming, but also knows that this future (imaginary, implied) is undesirable. (If the dominant mentality/ideology of the film's narrational perspective matched that of the 1950s, or matched the terms in which we currently understand "The Fifties," one would not expect such a clear expression of dissatisfaction.) Kay embodies a position that is retrospectively projected onto her by the film so that she can prospectively anticipate our present. Thus the film can offer a conservative resolution for its construction of the past, relying on "truth to history" as an alibi, and can simultaneously hint at a way out that leads directly to the present and to liberal feminist ideology. In doing so, however, the film does not allow Kay to project the rise of feminism in the 1960s, but instead expresses this "out" in the narrative form of her immediate nostalgia.

It is in light of this process of construction that it is possible to identify a common structure of history at work in both *Swing Shift* and *Rosie the Riveter*. The past is construed as a closed sequence of events with a clear beginning, middle, and end. In the case of these two films the narrative sequence is clearly focused, 1941–1945. This period is seen from a later point in time that narrationally asserts its teleological superiority. A contemporary feminist consciousness is an a priori condition of the films' respective narrational postures, and the opportunity lost in the past is expressed from the perspective or opportunity regained. However, this split perspective—a distance repressed—is manifested differently according to the conventions of documentary film on the one hand and narrative film on the other.

The clear delineation of two discourses in *Rosie the Riveter*—period footage and interviews—is displaced but reproduced in *Swing Shift*, where it is manifested in the interaction between narrative development (the construction of imaginary characters and events of their lives) and the narrational perspectives that can only be a function of retrospective projection. This includes not only the opening and closing sequences described above, but encompasses also the film's restaging of sequences from period newsreels, sometimes duplicating scenes included in the compilation footage of *Rosie the Riveter*.

For example, *Rosie the Riveter* presents footage of training films and promotional documentaries comparing various factory jobs to more traditional household tasks. This material is dramatized in *Swing Shift* as the factory boss describes specific jobs to new women employees with similar kinds of metaphors; riveting is like sewing. In fact, in relation to conventional filmic coding, *Swing Shift*'s opening title sequence literally enacts the move from "documentary" to "fiction," as it opens with a series of black-and-white photographs representing the period and dissolves into color footage only with the first dramatic scene. This does not authenticate the film's events in relation to a "real" past, but in relation to a familiar body of filmic and photographic material from the past, including the film *Rosie the Riveter* and its archival footage.

In terms of the two filmic narratives, the past offered a series of irreconcilable choices. In general, the choice was between new possibilities and more conventional, restrictive lifestyles for the various female protagonists. More specifically, this is defined as jobs/families, work/nonwork, "men's" work/"women's" work, production/reproduction, independence/dependence, and, in *Swing Shift*, lover/husband. But the loss entailed in this structure of absolute choice is projected into the past with the implication that the options, as real and compatible, are recoverable and recovered in the present. The way in which the choices are (re)activated in the interim remains absent. "Before" the choices are incompatible; "after," or now, they are reclaimed. But before and after what?

The synchronic structure embodied by the films' logic of choice is projected as diachronic progression: then/now, before/after, past/present. Through this temporal-historical sleight of hand the past can be closed and can become the basis for representing the present as a terrain of unlimited opportunity. The past is thus a nonidentical mirror for the present: "we" have reenacted the struggle and have succeeded where "they" have failed. The narrational logic in both cases hinges on a tacit scheme of progress and hierarchical development in the face of an absent break, absent because it may indeed be impossible to finally articulate the boundary that constitutes our difference from that which is represented as past in the films.

In both films, then, the historical perspective is the alibi for including certain materials from the past that are in turn the pretext for asserting mastery and superiority over the past as that which can be contained by the present. Historical perspective confers authority on the instance of production in the present: the narrated events of the past are not only true, but also inferior. This is not simply a conclusion achieved through the "work" of the films as textual systems, but also the stance that determines their use of history, documents, and events from the start—the meeting of prospective and retrospective strategies of narration and the joining of the supposedly antithetical positions of historicism and antihistoricism. History is at once a determined sequence of past events that really happened and a discursive practice that serves knowledge in and for the present as a function of specific social and political ideologies.

The investment in the study of women's status during World War II makes sense from the perspective of contemporary feminism, as something on the order of a rehearsal for the present. But to engage or activate this period as a closed sequence of events is to diffuse the political force of this representation. The attention per se suggests a degree of self-recognition within the past, but the terms of its representation refuse to push the implications of this self-recognition. The possibility of a call to struggle and self-examination is muted by the narrative and narrational containment offered by both films, and this in spite of the meta-textual substructures and split discursive perspectives they offer.

World War II becomes a dream scenario for feminist theory and history, the deficient mirror of the present, a past that can now and only now be written with a different ending. However, as wish fulfillment this scenario elides the contradictions within both the past and present. Contradiction, a process, is rewritten as a set of irreconcilable choices in the past and as the superior achievement of the present over the past. The question that emerges is whether and how a feminist historical understanding can embrace a model of complex, heterogeneous determinations and sustain political effectivity. At a minimum it must be possible to conceive of a history that negotiates the relation between past and present in terms that address and activate the constitutive contradictions of the various temporal sites that compose the particular history being narrated. The very conception of historical process and temporal relations may also be reconstrued. For example, nonhierarchical models of causality would shift the focus of attention to intersecting discursive and temporal schemes that inflect one another and exert interdependent pressures. From this perspective, the contemporary understanding of World War II as a period of new opportunities for women in the labor force might be seen as the effect of unresolved issues and contradictions in women's current status rather than as an unfulfilled but closed sequence, merely a stage en route to a fulfilled present. Concomitantly, more supple and subtle notions of textual ideology and social ideology must be developed.[6]

Swing Shift and *The Life and Times of Rosie the Riveter* bring these issues into focus in a particularly pointed way. To acknowledge the embedded meta-textual substructures and double temporality at work in both films is to allow the possibility of a (presumably progressive) split in identification. And there is clearly something to be gained in giving a voice to women and turning attention to a period of women's achievement, however provisional. At the same time, to trace the constitutive limits of the films' historical conception is to imply conservative containment. The point is not to conclude by identifying the films in an ideological typology, but to initiate a consideration of the constitutive contradictions that inform present feminist historical perspectives.

In part this involves a reexamination of reigning conceptions of textual ideology. But it is also necessary to question more aggressively how and why we appropriate particular histories. The 1940s as a site of overdetermined historical investigation is an obvious case in point, expressed as feminist fascination with World War II as a lost possibility on the one hand and with film noir as the simultaneous displacement of and retribution for the provisional independence afforded by the wartime economy on the other.[7] In this context, and with this emphasis, the rest of cinema is reduced to pale ordinariness, though echoes of contradictory and ambiguously progressive practices remain in the work of select, privileged genres and directors (e.g., the 1950s melodramas of Douglas Sirk or Vincente Minnelli). Otherwise, the 1930s and the 1950s as periods of social activity and cultural signification are by and large represented as "merely" the normative reign of dominant patriarchal ideology.

This fascination is not strictly scholarly but is becoming progressively institutionalized and generalized, embodied, for example, in the revival of "Rosie the Riveter" as a feminist popular cultural icon and in the revival/rewriting of film noir in contemporary cinema (e.g., *Against All Odds* [Taylor Hackford, 1984], *Body Heat* [Lawrence Kasdan, 1981], *Blood Simple* [Joel Coen, 1984]). The developing historical tradition focused on the 1940s both contributes to this revival and curiously ignores its own contradictory and complex extrication in the events presented as distant and closed. In the face of *this* strategy and use of history, what is needed is a reconceptualization of historical process and historical writing that can simultaneously confront this extrication and grant to the past its otherness. This seemingly paradoxical proposal is necessary if past Rosies are to function as more than our disadvantaged if heroic predecessors to confirm/position us as the inheritors of a determined and rosier future—only to become the ground of another closed sequence of past events.

NOTES

1. A very partial listing of work in this vein includes Karen Anderson, *Wartime Women* (Westport, Conn.: Greenwood, 1981); Susan M. Hartman, *The Home Front and Beyond* (Boston: Twayne, 1982); idem, "Prescriptions for Penelope: Literature on Women's Obligations to Returning World War II Veterans," *Women's Studies* 5 (1978): 223–239; Paddy Quick, "Rosie the Riveter: Myths and Realities," *Radical America* 9 (July–October 1975): 115–131; Leila J. Rupp, *Mobilizing Women for War* (Princeton, N.J.: Princeton University Press, 1978).

2. It should be noted that the film's "present" is in fact relatively dispersed and unstable, both in theoretical terms and more specifically in terms of its actual production; research, filming, and postproduction were carried out over a number of years.

3. Discussions of these traditions in feminist documentary filmmaking are found in Julia Lesage, "The Political Aesthetics of the Feminist Documentary Film," *Quarterly Review of Film Studies* 3 (Fall 1978): 507–523; Sonya Michel, "Feminism, Film, and Public History," *Radical History Review*, no. 25 (1981): 47–61; and Bill Nichols, "The Voice of Documentary," *Film Quarterly* 34 (Spring 1983): 17–30.

4. Michel de Certeau, *L'Ecriture de l'Histoire* (Paris: Gallimard, 1975), 59 (my translation).

5. Julia Lesage discusses the ending of *An Unmarried Woman* (Paul Mazursky, 1978) in terms that are relevant here in "The Hegemonic Female Fantasy in *An Unmarried Woman* and *Craig's Wife*," *Film Reader* 5 (1982): 83–94. *Romancing the Stone* (Robert Zemeckis, 1984) is another film, released at about the same time as *Swing Shift*, that resolves itself in terms of constitutive ambiguity, though in this case the equivocation is whether one takes the end as "really" fulfilling in terms of the same old "ideology of true love" or as blatantly and self-consciously fictional.

6. On this latter point, similar arguments are advanced in relation to readings of genre texts in a number of articles in *Screen* 25 (January–February 1984). In particular, see Jane Feuer, "Melodrama, Serial Form, and Television Today," 4–16; Annette Kuhn, "Women's Genres," 18–28; and Barbara Klinger, " 'Cinema/Ideology/Criticism' Revisited: The Progressive Text," 30–44.

7. While there is an extensive body of critical work on film noir, an exemplary collection of essays is available in E. Ann Kaplan, ed., *Women in Film Noir* (London: British Film Institute, 1978).

Albert Auster

Saving Private Ryan and American Triumphalism

The war is now away back in the past, and you can tell what books cannot.
—General William T. Sherman, 1880

One notable cultural theme that emerged in American society as it entered the twenty-first century was the glorification of the generation that had endured the Great Depression and heroically sacrificed to win World War II. That sanctification occurred in best-selling books, such as television news anchorman Tom Brokaw's *The Greatest Generation* and *The Greatest Generation Speaks*; James Bradley's story of his father, John Bradley, one of the celebrated Marine flag raisers on Iwo Jima, in *Flag of our Fathers*; and historian Stephen E. Ambrose's World War II historical series *D-Day, Citizen Soldiers, Band of Brothers,* and *The Victors*. It was also seen in the controversial decision to build a $100 million World War II memorial on the Mall in Washington, D.C., to honor the 400,000 men and women who died in that war as well as the 16 million Americans who served in uniform.

This glorification comes as a complete reversal from the 1980s and even the late 1990s when no war, not even World War II, was safe from revisionists, who, like the literary-critics-turned-war-memoirists Paul Fussell (*Wartime*) and Samuel Hynes (*A Soldier's Tale*), emphasized the war's absurdities and atrocities. These World War II revisionists were undoubtedly influenced by America's involvement and defeat in Vietnam and by the need to deflate the orthodoxy that World War II was the "Good War."

Fascination with the Depression and World War II generations was coincident with a number of epochal events in the 1990s—the American victory in the Cold War against the Soviet Union and the American-led military triumphs in the Gulf War against Iraq and the wars of the Yugoslav secession. Ironically, although these triumphs confirmed America's status as the sole remaining superpower, none came with the kind of victorious endings that were the hallmarks of other wars or diplomatic successes, such as V-E and V-J celebrations. In fact, the highest governing circles in the West made a conscious effort not to rub the Russians'

Journal of Popular Film and Television 30:2 (Summer 2002): 98–104. Reprinted with permission of the Helen Dwight Reid Educational Foundation. Published by Heldref Publications, 1319 Eighteenth St., NW, Washington, DC 20036-1802. © 2002.

noses in the disintegration of their former empire.[1] The Gulf War and the conflict in the Balkans ended in an equally anticlimactic fashion because they lacked any real resolution, with Saddam Hussein still in power in Iraq and the Balkans dealing with struggles for lasting peace.

Those victories lifted the burden of the Vietnam War from the American military and permitted a much more positive representation of the U.S. armed forces in film. But the films never allowed any sense of American triumph to emerge. For example, in one of the few films made about the Gulf War, David O. Russell's *Three Kings* (1999), renegade American GIs steal the gold bullion that Iraqi troops stole from Kuwait. Jettisoning their avarice, the GIs help a group of beleaguered Shiites flee Iraq to the protection of Iran, thus allowing the American military to don the mantle of "good guys" it hadn't had in war films in decades. Except for allowing the military a moral victory, *Three Kings* provides no real sense of triumph in the Gulf War.

Indeed, there did not seem to be much glory in a victory over Iraq, a country with the gross national product of Kentucky, or over a people like the Serbs, who wore Nike sneakers and sported Grateful Dead T-shirts at anti-U.S. bombing rallies. As a result, Hollywood, as it had done with *M*A*S*H* (Robert Altman, 1970) and *The Wild Bunch* (Sam Peckinpah, 1969) during the Vietnam War, sought a surrogate for American triumph in the Cold War and subsequent victories. Perhaps the defining moment of that quest was the release and box-office and Academy Award-winning success of Steven Spielberg's *Saving Private Ryan* (1998).

To some degree Spielberg was the perfect person to direct an epic of World War II and a landmark of fin de siècle American triumphalism. In fact, it is somewhat surprising that he hadn't made a World War II combat film prior to *Saving Private Ryan* because the war has figured so prominently in many of his films. Even before *Schindler's List* (1993), Nazis were featured as villains in *Raiders of the Lost Ark* (1981) and *Indiana Jones and the Last Crusade* (1989, in which Hitler even makes a brief appearance). *Always* (1989) was Spielberg's rather self-indulgent remake of the 1943 war melodrama *A Guy Named Joe* (Victor Fleming, 1943). *Empire of the Sun* (1987) deals with a World War II Japanese internment camp, and *1941* (1979), Spielberg's sole and rather feeble attempt at slapstick comedy, was about the aftermath of the attack on Pearl Harbor. The teenage Spielberg's first film was an 8 mm version of a World War II film called *Escape to Nowhere* (1960).

Even more significant is the fact that Spielberg, who has directed six of the highest-grossing films of all time, has added to his already glossy reputation as Hollywood's most successful entertainer the aura of *gravitas* that came from his critically acclaimed and prize-winning Holocaust film *Schindler's List*. Although Spielberg still makes crowd-pleasing box-office films, such as *Jurassic Park* (1993), more and more his work has attempted to bear witness to great events and enduring issues, such as American racism in *Amistad* (1997) and World War II in *Saving Private Ryan*.

Captain Miller (Tom Hanks) heroically leads his men on to Omaha Beach. Saving Private Ryan.
Courtesy: Photofest

Both the consummate entertainer and the *homme serieux* are on hand
from the first frames of *Saving Private Ryan* when Spielberg establishes a somber
mood with images of a screen-filling American flag, mournful John Williams
music, and an elderly American man and his family passing by the graves of the
honored Normandy dead. With a few broad strokes Spielberg touches the collective memory, evoking feelings both elegiac and patriotic. It is collective memory
that Spielberg relies on in the film's first twenty-five Goyaesque minutes of war
horrors rather than the actual mind and experience of the aged veteran we see in
the cemetery. Military historian Sir John Keegan called the scenes "the most ter-
rifying, realistic thing ever done in the cinema."[2]

Some critics contend that Spielberg's depiction of war as bloody abattoir
was influenced by decades of antiwar films inspired by the Vietnam War. But it is
more realistic to see the scenes as antideath than as antiwar. Spielberg shows the
murderous, random nature of death in battle with such images as an infantryman,
who in one moment marvels at how his helmet has saved his life only to die in
the next with a bullet through the head, and when Captain Miller (Tom Hanks)
drags ashore a GI to find that the bottom half of the soldier has been blown away.

Despite the originality of the ground-level shots, drained colors, camera
lenses spotted with water and blood, and the hellish scenes of GIs screaming and

searching for severed limbs, the images still rely for their inspiration on those old, grainy combat photos and newsreels that have become the iconic symbol of the D-Day invasion since the end of the war.

It is the collective memory of the terror, pain, and sacrifice of the men who swept ashore on that first day at Omaha Beach that sets the tone of *Saving Private Ryan* and stamps it from the start with the seal of heroism and of America's ultimate triumph in World War II. It reminds us, as President Ronald Reagan did, quoting General Omar Bradley, at the fortieth-anniversary celebration of the D-Day landings, "every man who set foot on Omaha Beach that day was a hero."[3]

Spielberg does not let the matter rest with mere heroism, however. With the unparalleled realism of the film's opening sequences barely moments behind, the scene shifts to one of patriotic transcendence. First, we follow the news that three Ryan brothers have died that day (two on Omaha Beach and one in New Guinea) and that a fourth brother is missing in France after parachuting in on D-Day. All of this is depicted in solemn scenes of War Department secretaries diligently typing official letters of condolence. The scene next shifts to the tragic image of the Ryan brothers' mother collapsing on hearing the news of her sons' fates.

This latter encounter with Americana, with its images drawn from Grant Wood and Andrew Wyeth, is followed by a war room assemblage in the office of Army Chief of Staff General George C. Marshall (Herve Presnell). The officials are there to discuss the potential public relations calamity of an Army version of the Navy's Sullivan brothers tragedy in which five brothers all died when their ship was sunk. The debate over military necessity versus battlefield humanitarianism takes a patriotic turn, however, when General Marshall reads a letter written by President Lincoln to Mrs. Lydia Bixby during the Civil War. In the letter, the president consoles Mrs. Bixby on the battlefield deaths of her five sons. Invoking Lincoln's words takes the film out of the realm of mere realism and bathes it in the more luminous power of a sublime nationalism that has come to be associated with Lincoln. As Edmund Wilson notes in *Patriotic Gore*, "he [Lincoln] had indeed his heroic role, in which he was eventually to seem to tower . . . as the prophet of the cause of righteousness."[4]

This connection with the Bixby letter injects an almost spiritual element into the upcoming mission to find the remaining Ryan brother and bring him home. (Lincoln biographer Carl Sandburg referred to the letter as a "piece of the American Bible" and, because the actual letter has never been recovered, it has become something akin to the "Holy Grail" of Civil War memorabilia.)[5] It is also a connection fraught with some degree of irony, since it was later discovered that Mrs. Bixby had only two sons, not five, and historians have long debated over the question of whether or not Lincoln actually wrote the letter.[6]

The question of the Bixby letter's authenticity aside, its presence in *Saving Private Ryan* represents the first bit of triumph in the film—the triumph of the American spirit. We see that our leaders from Lincoln to Marshall, whatever the harsh historical burdens imposed on them by wartime, still have the compassion to comfort the war's victims and the strength to act justly.

General Marshall's decision to find Private Ryan sets in motion what Captain John Miller, the squad's leader, refers to as a "public relations" mission. The group he assembles is that old keepsake of World War II films: the ethnically, religiously, regionally, and socially diverse platoon (the only missing piece is racial diversity because American armed forces were not integrated in World War II). As a result, the squad comprises a working-class Italian, Private Carpozo (Vin Diesel); the Nazi-hating Jew, Private Mellish (Adam Goldberg); the Brooklyn loner, Private Reiban (Edward Burns); the southern, Bible-quoting sharpshooter, Private Jackson (Barry Pepper); the compassionate medic, Private Wade (Giovanni Ribisi); the nononsense Sergeant Horvath (Tom Sizemore); and the bookish, untested Corporal Upham (Jeremy Davies).

The important thing to remember about this platoon and the others that preceded it in such World War II films such as *Guadalcanal Diary* (Lewis Seiler, 1943), *A Walk in the Sun* (Lewis Milestone, 1945), and *The Story of G.I. Joe* (William Wellman, 1945) is that they are not just a metaphor for American diversity and tolerance and a walking-talking example of the melting pot; they are the very essence of American civilization and its values. Similarly, Captain Miller, whose pre-military life is a mystery to his men (they even have a betting pool about it) and whom they refer to as being "assembled from the spare body parts of dead GIs," is that generic of all Hollywood heroes, "the uncommon common man."

A high school English teacher and part-time baseball coach, Miller does not fight out of blood lust or a desire for glory, promotion, or conquest; he fights, instead, because of the time-tested wish of the average American GI to return home to his wife and family, a goal that Miller says recedes with every man he kills. Miller, whose hand trembles from the stress of too many battles and the torment of seeing men die, is as much a casualty of the war as the ninety-four men who, by his own count, have been killed under his command. Despite this, Miller never wavers in his devotion to duty because, in the ultimate sense, the real "mission" of all World War platoons is nothing less than the defeat of barbarism.[7]

In *Saving Private Ryan*, American triumphalism is seemingly won without allies. In contrast, Darryl Zanuck's epic of the Normandy Invasion *The Longest Day* (Ken Annakin, Andrew Marton, Bernhard Wicki, 1962) acknowledged the contribution of our British, French, and Canadian allies with dozens of cameos of characters both celebrated and obscure who played a role in the landings. Zanuck even paid tribute to the enemy with sympathetic portraits of Rommel, von Runstedt, and ordinary German soldiers. In Spielberg's film, there is no mention of the Russians, and the only mention of the British is a brief reference to General Montgomery as "overrated." Although the French do make an appearance in the film, it is only in the symbolic form of the tricolor that waves above the Normandy cemetery visited by the Ryan family in the opening scene and when a terrified French family hides in a shell of an apartment as a firefight between American and German sharpshooters rages around them.

The only positive references to allies in the film are indirect, such as the Edith Piaf record that the GIs listen to curiously during a moment of battlefield repose and the starring of Kathleen Byron as the aged Private Ryan's wife (in no small part due to Spielberg's admiration for and as a bit of homage to Michael Powell who directed her in *Stairway to Heaven* [*A Matter of Life and Death*, 1946], and *Black Narcissus* [1947]).[8]

Not content to merely diminish the significant contribution of the Allies and to trumpet America's own in the Normandy invasion, Spielberg and screenwriter Robert Rodat go a step further, invoking the worldwide consciousness of American popular culture even among denizens of the master race. Thus, a terrified German soldier captured by the squad tries to curry favor by hysterically parading his knowledge of Betty Boop, Betty Grable ("Nice gams!"), and, in a last desperate attempt to save his life, finally blurts out the ultimate in American obscenities, "Fuck Hitler!"

The German's capture and Captain Miller's refusal to order his execution after Corporal Upham's protest bring the simmering tension within the squad to a head. Frustrated by a mission that places their lives in jeopardy to rescue only one man and their lust for revenge aroused by "Doc" Wade's death during the assault on the German position, the men want nothing better than to shoot the prisoner. Miller's decision to spare the soldier initiates a near mutiny that is quelled only when the captain finally reveals something about his civilian life, becoming a real person to his men instead of an epigone of orders and chain of command. This moment underscores the difference between the American GI and other armies and is another source of American triumph in *Saving Private Ryan.* Although the Americans fight with ferocity and sometimes do commit atrocities in the fog of war (Spielberg depicts the almost gleeful massacre of a few surrendering Germans on Omaha Beach), this is the exception rather than the rule. In other instances, the American voice of conscience and commitment to the rules of war prevails.

That voice of conscience is Corporal Upham, who occupies a curious role in the squad and the film. A stranger to combat among the battle-hardened rangers, Miller recruits Upham as a translator. An intellectual, Upham can easily quote Emerson's famous 1838 lecture "War." "War educates the senses, calls into action the will. Perfects the physical constitution, brings men into such swift and close collision in critical moments, so man measures man."[9] What Upham cannot do is carry his own weight in battle and, until the last moment in the film, neither can he perform the ultimate soldierly function—kill.

In a real sense, Upham is everything that Emerson denounces in his classic American Scholar: the bookish man who relies on the past. In contrast, Miller, who recognizes the Emerson quote immediately, thus revealing that he is something of an intellectual too, is a person whom Emerson would have understood

Captain Miller talks with Private John Ryan (Matt Damon). Saving Private Ryan. Courtesy: Photofest

and approved of as someone of self-reliance, who, "in the midst of the crowd keeps with perfect sweetness the independence of solitude."[10]

The references to the first great American man of letters only serve to underscore Spielberg and Rodat's commitment to American sources. They might just as easily have found quotes about war from any number of European poets and philosophers. That they chose the poet and philosopher of what critic Irving Howe once referred to as the "American newness" creates in the film another example of American preeminence, this time in intellectual endeavor.

In contrast to Miller and Upham's erudition and the squad's ethnicity and regionalism, Private Ryan (Matt Damon) is the fresh, untouched American farm boy thrown into the horrors of the European war. He is someone whom Ernest Hemingway, John Dos Passos, e. e. cummings, and perhaps F. Scott Fitzgerald might have recognized instantly: the American who existentially creates himself in war. Thus, Ryan's comment on hearing of his brothers' deaths and the orders for him to go home is, "I'm with the only brothers I have left, and I won't desert them."

Indeed, Ryan can barely remember his brothers and family. Only after Miller's suggestion that he think of them in a context does Ryan even begin to recall the moment when he and his brothers were last together. Although a silly memory of a practical joke he and two of his brothers played on their oldest sibling, it nonetheless serves as a striking recollection of innocent times and is in vivid contrast to the devastated French village where Miller and Ryan find themselves, awaiting an imminent German attack.

Ryan's refusal to go home and his memory lapse, along with the other sol-diers' alternately salacious and sentimental memories before the German attack, highlight what Spielberg and Rodat find so special about this generation and the ultimate evidence of American triumphalism: otherwise ordinary men became a band of brothers and a lethal fighting machine that would defeat one of the world's mightiest armies. The last twenty minutes of the film prove just how deadly profi-cient the soldiers have become. Using small-unit tactics, Captain Miller's inventive "sticky bombs," Private Jackson's sharpshooting, and the unwavering commitment of most of the men, they stymie a German mechanized unit's advance on a vital bridge until a relief column and air cover arrive.

Predictably, most of the original squad members die in the battle, includ-ing Sergeant Horvath and Captain Miller, whose last words are the injunction to Private Ryan to "Earn this!" His dying epigram is carried by the surviving Ryan over the years so that he demands of his concerned wife at Miller's grave, "Tell me I have led a good life. Tell me I'm a good man." The answer to Ryan's soul-searching plea is made abundantly clear by the adoring family and caring wife by his side.

Although a command directed at Ryan and implicitly his generation that did return from the war, "Earn this" is also a command that resonates far beyond Ryan's generation to the baby boomers and Generations X and Y. Indeed, every generation of Americans must somehow deserve the sacrifices made at Omaha Beach and other battles in World War II.

Captain Miller's dying words make it possible for future generations to turn the Depression/World War II generation into the embodiment of American ideals of self-sacrifice for the twentieth and twenty-first centuries. Just as the Civil War served as the touchstone for those same patriotic values in the last half of the nineteenth century and the early part of the twentieth, World War II has become for Americans that mythic, edenic moment when the entire nation bent itself to victory over evil and barbarism.

The strength of the memory from World War II did not wane, even during the Cold War, the "Forgotten War" in Korea, and the U.S. involvement in Viet-nam.[11] Thus, World War II has become the indispensable symbol of American patriotic virtue and triumph. It can be brought forward to exalt American arms and the American spirit whenever contemporary events require it. *Saving Private Ryan* was a perfect anodyne to the somewhat equivocal glory of the low-key American victories in the Cold War and the Gulf War. *Saving Private Ryan*, except for the shattering realism of its opening sequences, is a brilliant, mythic blend of the religious aura of America's martyred sixteenth president, Hollywood's classic World War II films, the ahistorical refusal to acknowledge the major role that the Allies played in the downfall of fascism, the celebration of the American intel-lectual tradition, and the glorification of American GIs as the world's greatest fighting men. They combine to make *Saving Private Ryan* a serious inspiration and reference point for books and films, such as *Pearl Harbor* (Michael Bay, 2001) and *Thirteen Days*, (Roger Donaldson, 2000) which continue to proclaim American triumphalism into the twenty-first century.

NOTES

1. Michael Bechloss and Strobe Talbott, *At the Highest Levels: The Inside Story of the End of the Cold War* (New York: Simon & Schuster, 1993).

2. Quoted in Mel Gussow, "A Child (and an Adult) of War: A Military Historian Puts a Vivid Cast on World War I," *New York Times*, 3 July 1999, B11.

3. Quoted in Lou Cannon, *President Reagan: The Role of a Lifetime* (New York: Simon & Schuster, 1991), 484.

4. Edmund Wilson, *Patriot Gore: Studies in the Literature of the American Civil War* (New York: Oxford University Press, 1966), 115.

5. Merrill D. Peterson, *Lincoln in American Memory* (New York: Oxford University Press, 1994), 244, 246.

6. David H. Donald, *Lincoln* (New York: Simon & Schuster, 1995), 680.

7. Kathryn Kane, *Visions of War: Hollywood Combat Films of World War II* (Ann Arbor: UMI, 1982), 101–149.

8. Philip French, "Ryan's Slaughter" (13 September 1998), http://film.guardian.co.uk/News_Story/Critic_Review/Observer/0,4267.36480.00html

9. Robert D. Richardson Jr., *Emerson: The Mind on Fire* (Berkeley: University of California Press, 1995), 275.

10. Brooks Atkinson, ed., *The Complete Essays and Other Writings of Ralph Waldo Emerson* (New York: Modern Library, 1950), 150.

11. Clay Blair, *The Forgotten War: American in Korea, 1950–1953* (New York: Free Press, 1987).

Thomas Doherty

The New War Movies as Moral Rearmament: *Black Hawk Down* and *We Were Soldiers*

As Plato sort of said: "Only the dead have seen the end of war movies." The latest cycle of star-spangled and combat-ready motion pictures—*Behind Enemy Lines* (John Moore, 2001), *Collateral Damage* (Andrew Davis, 2002), *Hart's War* (Gregory Hoblit, 2002), *Black Hawk Down* (Ridley Scott, 2001), and *We Were Soldiers* (Randall Wallace, 2002)—was born of Y2K-ruminations and CGI revolutions: part historical retrospection, spurred by the fin-de-siècle glance back at World War II, the twentieth century's most dramatic and film-friendly event; part technological innovation, a product of the digital magic that made cost-effective the cyberspace creation of antique ordnance and battalions of lifelike troops. The greatest generation meets computer generation: no industrial light and magic, no *Pearl Harbor* (Michael Bay, 2001)—and, of course, the good war was never the only war to look good on film.

Nor is it, at present, the war uppermost in mind. To watch the current cluster of combat films is to be caught in a spectatorial time warp. Decades from today, undergraduates hazy about the historical dateline will likely read these films not as emanations from the penumbra of Y2K but as bursts of patriotism ignited by 9/11, expressions of a renascent nation ready to kick ass. "The artist is the antenna of the race," boasted the poet Ezra Pound, whose own antenna for the political wave of the future was bent. Somehow, though, Hollywood's aerial picked up on the zeitgeist shockwave undetected by Washington's agents.

All of the war-minded films embrace a set of suddenly au courant values—a respect for public servants in uniform, a sympathy for military codes of conduct, and a celebration of the virtues forged in the crucible of combat. As recently as the cynical, antimilitary-minded *Three Kings* (David O. Russell, 1999), a Hollywood depiction of the Gulf War could portray George Bush the Elder as a more sinister offstage presence than Saddam Hussein. Now (and, one suspects, for the duration) the nitwits, psychos, and conspirators that served so long in Hollywood's military ranks have been supplanted by a duty-honor-country cadre recruited from chapel hour at the Citadel. Rudyard Kipling's rueful rhyme about

Cineaste 27:3 (Summer 2002). © 2002 by Cineaste Publishers, Inc. Reprinted with permission of the editors of *Cineaste*.

In Colonel Hal Moore (Mel Gibson) we see "a celebration of the virtues forged in the crucible of combat." We Were Soldiers. Courtesy: Photofest

peacetime civilian attitudes toward the everyman British soldier Tommy Atkins seems apt: "It's Tommy this, an' Tommy that / an 'Chuck him, out, the brute!' / But it's 'Savior of 'is country' when the guns 'begin to shoot."

In critical prestige, literary heft, and box-office success, *Black Hawk Down* and *We Were Soldiers* rank as the elite guard. Whatever their copyright dates, the two can't help but be viewed through the smoke of that other twin pair. Significantly, each springs from a companion book that bestows instant credibility. Despite the difference in battlefields (Somalia, Vietnam) and tonal register (Ernest Hemingway, Ernie Pyle), *Black Hawk Down: A Story of Modern War*, written in 1999 by journalist Mark Bowden, and *We Were Soldiers Once . . . and Young*, written in 1992 by Lieutenant General Harold G. Moore (Ret.) and reporter Joseph L. Galloway, have both already become certified military classics, required reading among the officer corps and the armchair infantry of The History Channel. The stature of the books and their huge core audience assured compliance with the Hollywood rule of thumb for screen versions of literary works: you can do anything you want to a book no one has read (a Booker Prize-winner) and anything you want to a book everyone has read but no one cares about (a John Grisham potboiler), but you must remain true to a book everyone has read and everyone cares about.

Both *Black Hawk Down* and *We Were Soldiers* telescope the action and edit down the cast of characters (*We Were Soldiers* deletes the entire second half of the book chronicling the second bloody clash in the Ia Drang valley, the disastrous ambush at Landing Zone Albany), but, by the standards of the average John Forbes Nash biopic, the screen versions are quite faithful to their literary sources and, more to the point, the raw human inspirations. The end credits of each film unscroll an honor roll of the names of the men killed in action; in *We Were Soldiers*, the motion picture screen reverently dissolves into a panel from the Vietnam Memorial.

Like Bowden's gripping narrative, Ridley Scott's *Black Hawk Down* is the tale of a debacle redeemed. On 3 October 1993, a milk-run mission to kidnap henchmen of warlord Mohamed Farrah Aidid in Mogadishu, Somalia, met disaster. When the smoke cleared, nineteen Army Rangers had been slain and more than seventy were wounded. Bloodied and bowed, the United States cut and ran from the field of fire so quickly the humvees left skid marks in the sand. Already, in retrospect, that failure of American nerve is being configured as a green light for 9/11. In the paperback edition of the book, published in 2000, the scrupulously even-handed Bowden ventures a single comment. "The lesson our retreat taught the world's terrorists and despots is that killing a few Americans, even at the cost of more than five hundred of your own fighters, is enough to spook Uncle Sam," he declares. "Routing Aidid would have, in the long run, saved American lives."

In generic if not geopolitical terms, *Black Hawk Down* exemplifies a popular subset of the combat film, the extraction film. Its genesis and basic template is a schematic expression of the martial impotence felt during the Iranian hostage crisis: trapped by hostile, usually Arab-coded depredators, Americans must be rescued by the tactical brilliance and dauntless courage of elite military forces, fulfilling in fantasy a scenario that ended in catastrophe when rescue helicopters crashed in the sands of Desert One in 1980. All the more anguish, then, when the expert extractors in the Delta Forces and the Army Special Rangers not only fail to extricate primitive warlords but then also require emergency extraction themselves. On the soundtrack, Jimi Hendrix's "Voodoo Child" kicks in as the helicopters take off for downtown Mogadishu. This is not a good omen.

No less troubling for the dream work of psychic escapism, the site of the mission is not Arabia but Africa, the most guilt-ridden and crime-soaked landscape in the American imagination. (*Black Hawk Down* is one of the very few Hollywood combat films since *Sahara* [Zoltan Korda, 1943] to set foot in this particular heart of darkness.) On the motion picture screen, the racial politics of the battle surface with visceral and visible force. Though not quite as faceless as the luckless natives in the old Tarzan films, the profusely slaughtered Somalis might as well be crocodile meat. Viewed from on high via real-time video transmission, the African hordes circling around the Americans and lurking around every corner evoke nothing so much as the swarming aliens in the series originated by Ridley Scott and reinvented as sci-fi combat by James Cameron.

Discomforting though it may be, the black and white face-off is the story as it happened, mainly white (include Hispanic here) GIs besieged and attacked by what seems to be the entire population of Mogadishu, men, women, and children descending in a furious mass. Unlike the book, the film provides little explanation as to why a city should erupt in spontaneous rebellion against good-hearted Americans who want only to deliver food and medicine to a starving people. But rebel they do: a civilian militia dependent on a tom-tom network of cell phones, outfitted in shirtsleeves and trousers, and armed with AK-47s, RPGs, and the local narcotic *khat,* fights tenaciously against the high-tech, well-protected Rangers and Delta boys, encased in body armor, night-vision goggles, and headsets.

No wonder the cyborg-like American warriors seem only slightly more individualized than the native cannon fodder. The brisk character delineation and hoary ethnic stereotypes of the World War II combat film at least made the soldiers easy to tell apart. These guys really are an Army of One. Teenpic heartthrob Josh Hartnett, the ostensible point of audience identification, is a cipher as the idealistic and soon to be battle-scarred Sergeant Eversmann. As Specialist Grimes, the coffee-making clerk typist suddenly promoted to frontline Ranger duty, Ewan McGregor wrestles with an American accent, dodges grenades, and slinks into the background. Even an excruciating scene of a soldier who bleeds to death in increments is painful to watch, not because of the man dying, but due to the forensic verisimilitude of the makeshift surgery. The cigar chomping Sam Shepard as Major General Garrison, a well-meaning soldier-diplomat out of his depth, and the William Bendix-like Tom Sizemore as Lieutenant Colonel McKnight, a no-nonsense convoy task force leader ("Everybody's shot," he points out, unimpressed, when a soldier balks at a duty because of his wounds), come closest to imprinting a personality. Combat action figures all, they are overwhelmed by the clash of combat and the choreography of carnage.

As a rush of pure cinematic spectacle, *Black Hawk Down* is undeniably breathtaking. Helicopters spiral to earth like wounded eagles and shell casings cascade through the air in a scorching metallic downpour. Blood spurts, flesh flies, and men crumple in slow-mo. Always entranced by uniforms, vehicles, and sleek weaponry, Scott fixes a caressing, fetishistic gaze on the fashion accessories of modern military. The made-in-the-USA haute couture surely enlivens the dreary knock-offs designed by the locals. Dusty, sun-baked, and crisp, the cinematography renders Africa as an ungodly, blighted landscape, not so much Third World as Ninth Circle of Hell World.

Befitting the high-velocity and high-impact violence, the editing of the film flows with televisual speed and fluidity, never hitting the pause button to allow viewers with slower eye movements the chance to catch up. Often, MTV-esthetic and AVID-based editing make for a cuisinart of film grammar, but the battle scenes in *Black Hawk Down* are almost classical in composition. Despite the fog of war and the multiple planes of action—Army Special Ranger teams stranded and stunned, two downed Black Hawks, two convoys meandering helplessly through byzantine streets in a hostile city, and helicopters soaring overhead unleashing a merciless fusillade of cover fire—the extraction mission, the tactical improvisations, and the spatial layout are as clear as the coordinates on a grid map. Back at the command center, viewing the action via real-time video, General Garrison and the spectator share a privileged point of view that is safe from danger but seething with frustration. In Scott's *Gladiator* (2000), the presumably more primitive battlefield action between the Romans and Huns was a cinematic muddle. In *Black Hawk Down*, ironically, the chaos of modern combat inspired precision guidance.

If *Black Hawk Down* is kinetic *Aliens*-style combat (James Cameron, 1986), Randall Wallace's *We Were Soldiers* is *They Were Expendable* (John Ford, 1945) with swearing and squibs. Unabashedly Fordian in its elegiac embrace of military ritual, Roman Catholicism, and victory in defeat, it is Hollywood's first major Vietnam War film to portray American soldiers more concerned with killing the enemy than killing each other. Unlike *The Green Berets* (John Wayne and Ray Kellogg, 1968), which attempted it, *We Were Soldiers* makes Vietnam safe for the World War II combat film.

Set in 1965, before drugs, before fragging, before Jimi Hendrix, the film harks back to a truly bygone America still flush with the new frontierism of a slain president, willing to pay any price and bear any burden. The steep price paid in the Ia Drang valley would be only a down payment, but the sheer scale of the American body count racked up during the campaign (305 American KIAs) remains shocking. It is hard to imagine that in the age of twenty-four-hour cable news networks so grievous a death toll—more men were lost in a single company in the first twenty-four hours at Landing Zone X-Ray than in the entire Somalia debacle, more men were lost in Ia Drang than in the entire Gulf War—would be endured so stoically, that the lifeblood of America will ever again be spilled so casually and cruelly as it was in November 1965, and I don't mean by the North Vietnamese Army.

True to its roots, the film is star-dependent and character-driven in a very old-fashioned way. Lugging his *Braveheart/The Patriot* persona as ballast (Mel Gibson, 1995; Roland Emmerich, 2000), Mel Gibson anchors the film, filling John Wayne's boots, helmet, and silhouette with quiet authority. Likewise, the rank and file are as rock-solid and familiar as the stock company from another kind of cavalry film—scene-stealing Sam Elliott as the gruff noncom lifer Sergeant Major Plumley, Greg Kinnear as the hotshot helicopter pilot "Snakeshit" Crandall, Chris Klein as the doomed lieutenant Jack Geoghegan, and Madeleine Stowe, in a bad wig and Jagger-sized collagen lips, as the steadfast military wife, Julie Moore. The fact that the screen types are real war types imported whole from the book only confirms the power of generic convention over life no less than cinema.

Where *Black Hawk Down* is all frantic testosterone, *We Were Soldiers* is a family affair, not just a band of brothers but a community of men, women, and children. Colonel Moore and his troops may be mean fighting machines but they are also husbands and fathers, women-centered and God-fearing. "Daddy—what is a war?" bleats Moore's cute-as-a-button little girl on the eve of his deployment, and Daddy can only struggle to explain that there are bad people in the world. Still, the unrushed, confident quality of the opening act is impressive. Not itching to split from the home front and begin firing off mortar rounds, director Wallace actually pauses to stage a Fordian dance sequence.

Against the claustrophobia of close-quarter urban infighting in *Black Hawk Down, We Were Soldiers* luxuriates in the spacious terrain of the Ia Drang valley as an occasion for wide-open vistas of fiery destruction. In huge tidal gushes, clouds of napalm streak across the Panavision screen, satisfyingly incinerating the enemy—until canisters hit too close to American lines and horribly burn one of *our* guys. The biggest jolt in the film, however, comes during a quiet moment of close contact at night. In pitch black, a grunt whispers that he can smell the enemy, very close. A flare lights up the screen and a squad of NVA suddenly looms above him.

Back on the home front, Army wives wait for the regrettable information from the Secretary of the Army, which, unbelievable but true, is delivered by Yellow Cab drivers hired by Western Union. Here too, though, the military is absolved from insensitivity. "No chaplains, no counselors," gasps an appalled housewife. "The army was caught by surprise," replies Mrs. Moore, who thereafter takes the task upon herself.

If the respectful attention paid to the feminized home front conforms to World War II conventions, the fraternal portrait of the enemy defies expectation. The North Vietnamese forces are neither demonized nor glamorized, but, something rarer, humanized. A remarkable dual dedication to American *and* North Vietnamese soldiers begins the film, whereupon a prelude set in 1954 depicts an unheeded foreshadowing, a massacre of French troops in the Ia Drang valley. Throughout *We Were Soldiers,* the first-person plural in the title includes the NVA, who are portrayed as worthy and honorable opponents, fighting on their native soil against alien invaders. An American officer sneers at "cave men in black pajamas," but the bookish and battle-hardened Colonel Moore, wary of overconfidence and a student of military history, knows better. Prior to deployment, he is informed that his regiment has been rechristened with the nomenclature of the First Battalion, Seventh Cavalry, "Custer's regiment." This is a worse omen than Jimi Hendrix music.

On the frontier of the new Indian country, Moore's best weapon is the non-equestrian variety of cavalry. In modern military adventures (and soon modern cinema) the helicopter emerges as the ur-vehicle for American forces at war, the perfect vessel for the mobile deployment of infantry and swooping, vertiginous camera movements. On the soundtrack, too, the distinctive, percussive whoop-whoop-whoop of the overhead rotors rumbles as the ominous overture of the Vietnam combat film, the musical cue to let loose the dogs of war.

During the battle at Landing Zone X-Ray, the high flying mobility of the Air Cav is crosscut with the underground-dwelling foot soldiers of the North Vietnamese Army. The parallel editing between the two unites, not separates, Colonel

Moore from his ideological but not spiritual opposite, North Vietnamese Lieutenant Colonel Nguyen Huu An (Don Duong). No sooner does Colonel An order his men to attack the American flank than Colonel Moore intuits the tactic and prepares to counterattack.

Besides the helicopter shots and widescreen aspect ratio, *Black Hawk Down* and *We Were Soldiers* are also linked by an unironic fidelity to a blood oath ridiculed in *Full Metal Jacket* (Stanley Kubrick, 1987): never leave your dead on the field of battle. The Army Rangers protect the tomb that is the first Black Hawk down as sacred ground and Colonel Moore promises to bring all "his boys" back home, alive or dead. To protect from violation and retrieve the corpse of a fallen comrade at the risk of life is noble, not foolish. "Leave no man behind" is the above-the-title tagline for *Black Hawk Down*.

The pagan oaths and blood rituals in both films preach the gospel of the oldest war story, older than Hollywood, older than Homer: that war is not hell but a place called heaven, far nobler than the candy-ass home front, a celestial arena for true glory and mystical brotherhood. Speaking to his battalion before shipping out to Vietnam, Colonel Moore expounds on the bond grafting together men in combat, regardless of race, color, or creed. "We're going to what home was always supposed to be," he declares, savoring the prospect.

Being so locked and loaded onto the target of military brotherhood, neither picture brings into focus the Big Picture. Better not inquire too deeply into why American soldiers must be helicoptered into the killing fields of a sun-drenched African desert or a Southeast Asian jungle. Whether inflicted on or by Americans, death and destruction rain down on the just and unjust as an extrapolitical force of nature, an immutable fact of military life. "It's about the man next to you and that's all it is," says a soldier at the end of *Black Hawk Down*, a sentiment echoed nearly verbatim in the coda to *We Were Soldiers* when reporter Galloway (Barry Pepper) intones in voice-over that the men of Landing Zone X-Ray fought "not for their country or their flag—they fought for each other."

In the Somalia of *Black Hawk Down* and Vietnam of *We Were Soldiers*, American soldiers are creatures of Alfred Lord Tennyson, not Wilfred Owen: theirs not to reason why, theirs but to do or die. Only in Moore and Galloway's book, in a poignant moment passed over in the movie, does a soldier consider the morality of riding headlong into the cannons at the whim of his superior. In 1965, in a televised address, President Lyndon Johnson orders an escalation of forces in Vietnam, but refuses to declare a state of emergency to extend the service of soldiers in uniform. Colonel Moore is thus deprived of his most experienced men on the eve of deployment overseas. LBJ's desire to deliver guns and butter, to conduct a discretionary war without undue inconvenience, became emblematic of the compromises and deceptions that defined the American tragedy in Vietnam. According to Moore and Galloway, the next morning General Harold K. Johnson, Chief of Staff of the U.S. Army, rides to the White House intending to resign in protest. He thinks better of it, "a decision that haunted Johnny Johnson all the rest of his life." Well it might.

No second thoughts about motives and mission will haunt Hollywood when the raw material of 9/11 is shaped into motion picture scenarios. For most Americans, the fog of war that blankets the high grass of the Ia Drang valley or the corrugated shacks of downtown Mogadishu dissipates in the ruins of Lower Manhattan. A moral clarity heretofore the exclusive province of World War II will likely guide the sensibility of the cycle of the future while the built-in elements of high drama will provide a plethora of pretested plotlines. Just as December 7th loomed in wartime cinema as a ticking bomb timed to detonate at the end of the first act to shatter the blithe frolics of peacetime and jump-start the action, September 11th will serve its television movies of the week and motion picture blockbusters as another red-letter date for audiences who know what the characters do not: a happy couple arranging to meet cute at the base of the towers on a perfect Tuesday morning, cell phone calls connected and missed, and—this will happen—a trip right inside the passenger cabin of Flight 93. You get the picture.

But not for a while. Almost certainly, the first true wave of post-9/11 films will be one step removed, wrapped in disguise, erased from the skyline, revealing themselves as "about" 9/11 only decades later. For the time being, the date is a blunt trauma too close to the bone for a small-screen Movie of the Week or the big-screen CGI-fest. Better to read the memory onto films made before the act than to contemplate its shadow straight on.

Selected Bibliography

Adair, Gilbert. *Hollywood's Vietnam: From The Green Berets to Full Metal Jacket*. London: Heinemann, 1989.

Adams, Michael C. C. *The Best War Ever: America and World War II*. Baltimore: Johns Hopkins University Press, 1994.

Anderegg, Michael, ed. *Inventing Vietnam: The War in Film and Television*. Philadelphia: Temple University Press, 1991.

Arlen, Michael. *The Living-Room War*. New York: Viking, 1969.

Auster, Albert, and Leonard Quart. *How the War Was Remembered: Hollywood and Vietnam*. New York: Praeger, 1988.

Beidler, Philip D. *The Good War's Greatest Hits: World War II and American Remembering*. Athens: University of Georgia Press, 1998.

Bérubé, Allan. *Coming Out Under Fire: The History of Gay Men and Women in World War II*. New York: Plume, 1991.

Birdwell, Michael. *Celluloid Soldiers: Warner Bros.'s Campaign Against Nazism*. New York: New York University Press, 1999.

Broyles, William, Jr. *Brothers in Arms: A Journey from War to Peace*. Austin: University of Texas Press, 1986.

Castonguay, James. "The Spanish-American War in United States Media Culture." http://chnm.gmu.edu/aq/. *Hypertext Scholarship in American Studies*.

Chambers, John Whiteclay, II, and David Culbert, eds. *World War II, Film, and History*. New York: Oxford University Press, 1996.

Cripps, Thomas. *Making Movies Black: The Hollywood Message Movie from World War II to the Civil Rights Era*. New York: Oxford University Press, 1993.

——. *Slow Fade to Black: The Negro in American Film*. New York: Oxford University Press, 1977.

Cullen, Jim. *The Civil War in Popular Culture: A Reusable Past*. Washington: Smithsonian Institution Press, 1995.

DeBauche, Leslie Midkiff. *Reel Patriotism: The Movies and World War I*. Madison: University of Wisconsin Press, 1997.

Desser, David, and Gaylyn Studlar, eds. *Reflections in a Male Eye: John Huston and the American Experience*. Washington: Smithsonian Institution Press, 1993.

Devine, Jeremy M. *Vietnam at 24 Frames a Second*. Austin: University of Texas Press, 1999.

Dick, Bernard. *The Star-Spangled Screen: The American World War II Film*. Lexington: University of Kentucky Press, 1997.

Dittmar, Linda, and Gene Michaud, eds. *From Hanoi to Hollywood: The Vietnam War in American Film*. New Brunswick: Rutgers University Press, 1990.

Doherty, Thomas. *Projections of War*. Rev. ed. New York: Columbia University Press, 1999.

Easthope, Antony. *What a Man's Gotta Do: The Masculine Myth in Popular Culture*. New York: Routledge, 1992.

Engelhardt, Tom. *The End of Victory Culture: Cold War America and the Disillusioning* of a *Generation*. Amherst: University of Massachusetts Press, 1995.

Fussell, Paul. *The Great War and Modern Memory*. New York: Oxford University Press, 1975.

———. *Wartime: Understanding and Behavior in the Second World War*. New York: Oxford University Press, 1989.

———. *The Boy's Crusade: The American Infantry in Northwestern Europe, 1944–1945*. New York: Modern Library, 2003.

Fyne, Robert. *The Hollywood Propaganda of World War II*. Lanham, Md.: Scarecrow, 1997.

Gilman, Owen W., Jr., and Lorrie Smith, eds. *American Rediscovered: Critical Essays on Literature* and *Film of the Vietnam War*. New York: Garland, 1990.

Glancy, H. Mark. *When Hollywood Loved Britain: The Hollywood "British" Film 1939–45*. Manchester: Manchester University Press, 1999.

Goldstein, Joshua. *War and Gender: How Gender Shapes the War System and Vice Versa*. Cambridge: Cambridge University Press, 2001.

Gray, J. Glenn. *The Warriors: Reflections on Men in Battle* [1959]. Lincoln: University of Nebraska Press, 1998.

Holmes, Richard. *Acts of War: The Behavior of Men in Battle*. New York: Free Press, 1986.

Hynes, Samuel Lynn. *The Soldier's Tale: Bearing Witness to Modern War*. New York: A. Lane, 1997.

Isenberg, Michael T. *War on Film: The American Cinema and World War I, 1941–41*. East Brunswick, N.J.: Fairleigh Dickinson University Press, 1981.

Jeffords, Susan. *The Remasculinization of America: Gender and the Vietnam War*. New Brunswick: Rutgers University Press, 1989.

Jeffords, Susan, and Lauren Rabinovitz, eds. *Seeing Through the Media: The Persian Gulf War*. New Brunswick: Rutgers University Press, 1994.

Kinney, Katherine. *Friendly Fire: American Images of the Vietnam War*. New York: Oxford University Press, 2000.

Koppes, Clayton R., and Gregory Black. *Hollywood Goes to War: How Politics, Profits and Propaganda Shaped World War II Movies*. Berkeley: University of California Press, 1990.

Lentz, Robert J. *Korean War Filmography: 91 English Language Features Through 2000*. Jefferson, N.C.: McFarland, 2003.

Modleski, Tania. *Feminism without Women: Culture and Criticism in a "Postfeminist" Age*. New York: Routledge, 1991.

Musser, Charles. *Edison Motion Pictures, 1890–1900, An Annotated Filmography*. N.P.: Smithsonian Institution Press, 1997.

———. *The Emergence of Cinema: The American Screen to 1907*. New York: Charles Scribner's Sons, 1990.

Neale, Steve. *Genre and Hollywood*. London: BFI, 2000.

Paris, Michael, ed. *The First World War and Popular Cinema*. New Brunswick, N.J.: Rutgers University Press, 2000.

Polan, Dana. *Power and Paranoia: History, Narrative, and the American Cinema, 1940–1950*. New York: Columbia University Press, 1986.

Rogin, Michael. *Ronald Reagan, the Movie and Other Episodes in American Demonology*. Berkeley: University of California Press, 1987.

Rollins, Peter C., and John O'Connor, eds. *Hollywood's World War I: Motion Picture Images*. Bowling Green: Bowling Green State University Popular Press, 1997.

Rowe, John Carlos, and Rick Berg, eds. *The Vietnam War and American Culture*. New York: Columbia University Press, 1991.

Sandweiss, Martha A. *Print The Legend: Photography and The American West*. New Haven: Yale University Press, 2002.

Schatz, Thomas. "World War II and the Hollywood 'War Film.'" In *Refiguring American Film Genres*, ed. Nick Browne. Berkeley: University of California Press, 1998.

Silverman, Kaja. "Historical Trauma and Male Subjectivity." In *Male Subjectivity at the Margins*, 52–121. New York: Routledge, 1992.

Suid, Lawrence. *Guts and Glory: The Making of the American Military Image in Film*. Rev. and exp. ed. Lexington: University of Kentucky Press, 2002.

Terkel, Studs. *The "Good War": An Oral History of World War Two*. New York: Pantheon, 1984.

Theweleit, Klaus. *Male Fantasies*. Vol. I, *Women Floods Bodies History*. Trans. Stephen Conway. Minneapolis: University of Minnesota Press, 1987.

————. *Male Fantasies*. Vol. II, *Male Bodies: Psychoanalyzing the White Terror*. Trans. Erica Carter and Chris Turner. Minneapolis: University of Minnesota Press, 1989.

Virilio, Paul. *War and Cinema: The Logistics of Perception*. Trans. Patrick Camiller. London: Verso, 1989.

Wetta, Frank J. *Celluloid Wars: A Guide to Film and the American Experience of War*. New York: Greenwood, 1992.

Woll, Allen L. *The Hollywood Musical Goes to War*. Chicago: Nelson-Hall, 1983.

Wood, Robin. *Hollywood from Vietnam to Reagan*. New York: Columbia University Press, 1986.

Contributors

ALBERT AUSTER is an associate professor (clinical) in the Department of Communication and Media Studies at Fordham University. He is co-author with Leonard Quart of *American Film and Society* (1984; 3d ed., rev. 2002) and *How the War Was Remembered: Hollywood and Vietnam* (1988). He is currently at work on a study of *thirtysomething*, co-authored with Quart, to be published by Wayne State University Press.

JEANINE BASINGER is the Corwin-Fuller Professor of Film Studies, director of the Film Program, and co-curator of the Cinema Archives at Wesleyan University. In addition to *The World War II Combat Film: Anatomy of a Genre* (1986; rev. ed. 2003), she has written numerous articles and books, the most recent being *Silent Stars* (2000). She is currently at work on *Stardom: Old and New*, to be published by Knopf in 2005.

ROBERT BURGOYNE is professor of English at Wayne State University. In addition to *Film Nation*, he has published *Bertolucci's 1900: A Narrative and Historical Analysis* (1991), and, with Robert Stam and Sandy Flitterman-Lewis, *New Vocabularies in Film Semiotics: Structuralism, Poststructuralism, and Beyond* (1992). His research interests include public memory and national identity in film, digital imagery, and the representation of the historical past.

GUERRIC DEBONA is a Benedictine monk of Saint Meinrad Archabbey and teaches homiletics and communication at Saint Meinrad School of Theology. He is currently writing on the relationship between American film culture and religion.

THOMAS DOHERTY chairs the Film Studies Program at Brandeis University. In addition to *Projections of War* (1993; rev. ed. 1999), he has published *Teenagers and Teenpics: the Juvenilization of American Movies in the 1950s* (1988); *Pre-Code Hollywood: Sex, Immorality, and Insurrection in American Cinema, 1930–1934* (1999); and *Cold War, Cool Medium: Television, McCarthyism, and American Culture* (2003).

ROBERT EBERWEIN is Distinguished Professor of English and co-director of the Concentration in Film Aesthetics and History at Oakland University. His most recent book is *Sex Ed: Film, Video and the Framework of Desire* (1999). He is completing a study of masculinity and the war film.

SUSAN JEFFORDS is a professor of English and Women's Studies at the University of Washington, where she is currently serving as Vice Provost for Academic Affairs. In addition to *Hard Bodies: Hollywood Masculinity in the Reagan Era* (1994), she has published *The Remasculinization of America: Gender and the Vietnam War* (1989) and, with Lauren Rabinovitz, co-edited *Seeing Through the Media: The Persian Gulf War* (1994).

ANDREW KELLY is a film historian, though he earns his money through working on cultural development in Bristol and the West of England. He is a visiting professor at the University of the West of England. His books include *Cinema and the Great War* (1997) and *In Short: Short Film-making in the Digital Age* (2002). His next book is a biography of Lewis Milestone.

TANIA MODLESKI is the Florence R. Scott Professor of English and professor of English, comparative literature, and gender studies at the University of Southern California. She has published several books in addition to *Old Wives' Tale and Other Women's Stories* (1998), including *Loving With a Vengeance: Mass Produced Fantasies for Women* (1982) and *Feminism without Women: Culture and Criticism in a "Postfeminist" Age* (1991).

DANA POLAN is professor of critical studies at University of Southern California's School of Cinema-TV. He is the author of five books, including, most recently, *Pulp Fiction* (2000) and *Jane Campion* (2001). He is currently completing a historical study entitled *The Beginnings of the American Study of Film*.

MICHAEL ROGIN held a Chancellor's Professorship at the University of California, Berkeley, where he taught in the Political Science Department from 1963 until his death in 2001. He published several books in addition to *Blackface, White Noise: Jewish Immigrants in the Hollywood Melting Pot* (1996) and *Ronald Reagan, the Movie and Other Episodes in Political Demonology* (1987).

YVONNE TASKER teaches film and television studies at the University of East Anglia, United Kingdom. She is the author of books on popular cinema, including *Spectacular Bodies* (1993) and *Working Girls* (1998) and is currently working on a study exploring the representation of military women in cinema and television since World War II.

MIMI WHITE is a professor in the Department of Radio/Television/Film at Northwestern University. In addition to many articles on film and television, her publications include *Tele-Advising: Therapeutic Discourse in American Television* (1992), and, with James Schwoch and Susan Reilly, *Media Knowledge: Popular Culture, Pedagogy, and Critical Citizenship* (1992).

BRIAN J. WOODMAN is a doctoral student in the Department of Theatre and Film at the University of Kansas, Lawrence. His research interests include race representation and popular culture of the 1960s.

Index

Page numbers in italics indicate images.